THE
BIG GOODBYE

ALSO BY SAM WASSON

IMPROV NATION: How We Made A Great American Art

FOSSE

PAUL ON MAZURSKY

FIFTH AVENUE, 5 A.M.: Audrey Hepburn, Breakfast at Tiffany's,
and the Dawn of the Modern Woman

A SPLURCH IN THE KISSER: The Movies of Blake Edwards

photos tk

THE BIG GOODBYE

CHINATOWN
and the Last Years
of Hollywood

SAM WASSON

FLATIRON
BOOKS
NEW YORK

THE BIG GOODBYE. Copyright © 2020 by Sam Wasson. All rights reserved. Printed in the United States of America. For information, address Flatiron Books, 120 Broadway, New York, NY 10271.

WWW.FLATIRONBOOKS.COM

Library of Congress Cataloging-in-Publication Data 2019

ISBN 978-1-250-30182-6 (HARDCOVER)

ISBN 978-1-250-30183-3 (EBOOK)

Our books may be purchased in bulk for promotional, educational, or business use. Please contact your local bookseller or the Macmillan Corporate and Premium Sales Department at 1-800-221-7945, extension 5442, or by email at MacmillanSpecialMarkets@macmillan.com.

First Edition: February 2020

10 9 8 7 6 5 4 3 2 1

For
Lynne Littman and Brandon Millan

Contents

Contents

We still have dreams, but we know now that most of them will come to nothing. And we also most fortunately know that it really doesn't matter.

—Raymond Chandler, letter to Charles Morton, October 9, 1950

THE
BIG GOODBYE

Prologue

Jack Nicholson, a boy, could never forget sitting at the bar with John J. Nicholson, Jack's namesake and maybe even his father, a soft little dapper Irishman in glasses. He kept neatly combed what was left of his red hair and had long ago separated from Jack's mother, their high school romance gone the way of any available drink. They told Jack that John had once been a great ballplayer and that he decorated store windows, all five Steinbachs in Asbury Park, though the only place Jack ever saw this man was in the bar, day-drinking apricot brandy and Hennessy, shot after shot, quietly waiting for the mercy to kick in. Jack's mother, Ethel May, told him he only started drinking when Prohibition ended, but somehow Jack got the notion that she drove him to it.

Robert Evans, a boy, in the family apartment at 110 Riverside Drive, on Manhattan's Upper West Side, could never forget watching his father, Archie, a dentist, dutifully committed to work and family, sit down at the Steinway in the living room after a ten-hour day of pulling teeth up in Harlem and come alive. His father could be at Carnegie Hall, the boy thought; he could be Gershwin or Rachmaninoff (who lived in the building) but he was, instead, a friendless husband, a father of three, caught in the cycle of earn-and-provide for his children, his wife, his mother, and his three sisters. But living in him was the Blue Danube. "That wouldn't be me," Evans promised himself. "I'll live."

Robert Towne, a boy, left San Pedro. His father, Lou, moved his family from the little port town, bright and silent, and left, for good, Mrs. Walker's hamburger stand and the proud fleets of tuna boats pushing out to sea. More than just the gardenias and jasmine winds and great tidal waves of pink bougainvillea cascading to the dust, he could never forget that time before the war when one story spoke for everyone—the boy, his parents, Mrs. Walker and her customers, the people of San Pedro, America, sitting together at those sun-cooked redwood tables, cooling themselves with fresh-squeezed orange juice, all breathing the same salt air.

There was the day, many raids later—a hot, sunny day—when Roman Polanski, found the streets of Kraków deserted. It was the silence that day that he could never forget, the two SS guards calmly patrolling the barbed-wire fence. This was a new feeling, a new kind of alone. In terror, he ran to his grandmother's apartment in search of his father. The room was empty of everything save the remnants of a recent chaos, and he fled. Outside on the street a stranger said: "If you know what's good for you, get lost."

When these four boys grew up, they made a movie together called *Chinatown*.

Robert Towne once said that Chinatown is a state of mind. Not just a place on the map of Los Angeles, but a condition of total awareness almost indistinguishable from blindness. Dreaming you're in paradise, and waking up in the dark—that's Chinatown. Thinking you've got it figured out and realizing you're dead—that's Chinatown. This is a book about Chinatowns: Roman Polanski's, Robert Towne's, Robert Evans's, Jack Nicholson's, the ones they made and the ones they inherited, their guilt and their innocence, what they did right, what they did wrong—and what they could do nothing to stop.

PART ONE

Justice

1

Sharon Tate looked like California.

Studying her from across the restaurant table, Roman Polanski could see it was impossible. She was laughably wrong for the part. He needed a burnished, preferably Jewish look, the kind of wintry shtetl waif Chagall might have painted onto a black sky. Polanski had named his character "Sarah Shagal"—*Shagal*—for that reason— and, with Roman, there was always a reason. He had deliberately set *The Fearless Vampire Killers* against the heavy, fragrant bygones of the Eastern Europe of his childhood, his home before the Nazis, before the Polish Stalinists. But this girl was as Eastern European as a surfboard; casting her, he would desolate, again, all that they had desolated before.

There was no reason, therefore, to continue the meal. In fact—as Roman had explained, quite clearly, to Sharon Tate's manager, Marty Ransohoff—there really was no reason to have this dinner in the first place. But Ransohoff, in addition to managing Tate, was producing *Vampire Killers*, and had insisted on the meeting. Forget her inexperience, he implored Roman. She's a sweet girl and she's very pretty and she's going to be a big, big star. Trust me. I've seen thousands of girls, and Sharon's different. She's the one. Trust me. "Ransohoff is a perfect example of a hypocrite," Polanski would come to understand. "He's a philistine who dresses himself up as an artist." Why hadn't Roman recognized the type earlier? He had never worked with a Hollywood producer, but he was no naïf. He knew the stories; they were all the same: Well, the producers always said, we love the rushes, we love the dailies. What you're doing is great, but can you do it cheaper and faster? "Creative" dinners like these were precisely the sort of feigned artistic roundelays, so agonizingly familiar to Hollywood code and conduct, that made him want to throw down his napkin and run screaming, back to *Repulsion*, back to *Knife in the Water*—films he made his way, the European way, according to his reasons.

But Roman did not throw down his napkin. Instead he let the girl know—in little ways, silences, mostly—that he did not want to be there.

When Roman reported back to Ransohoff the next day, Ransohoff insisted on a second dinner. Find something for her, Roman, he said.

They had another dinner, this one worse than the first. Polanski could see she was trying to impress him, an Oscar-nominated director, talking, babbling, laughing too much. But he was not impressed.

Still, after dinner, walking through London's Eaton Square, he tried to embrace her. She recoiled and ran home.

This, Polanski recognized, was his old behavior. He knew that his attraction to Sharon, or any woman, stirred in him feelings of terrible sorrow as ancient as long-lost wars. For years now, the certainty of loss had corrupted his every longing, and his resultant sadness summoned up the worst in him; for it was better, life had showed him, to be sorry than safe. So he would make himself superior. He would be arrogant, callous, abrupt; with women, and there were many women, he would lie and cheat and hurt. Over the course of those first two dinners, he would reduce Sharon to the size of her own waning self-esteem, and then, in the days and nights to follow, he would admonish himself for doing it. It was a pattern. He knew that. And he knew the reasons. He didn't like it, but it made sense.

At their third dinner Polanski apologized. This time he seemed to take a dedicated interest. Where did she come from? Texas. Who were her parents? Dolores and Paul Tate, an officer of the U.S. Army. They moved around a lot, she said, depending on where he was stationed. By the time she was sixteen, in fact, she had lived in Houston, Dallas, El Paso, San Francisco, and Richland, Washington. In Italy, in high school, she learned Italian. Moving as often as they did, Sharon didn't make many friends, but the friends she made were *real* friends. At home, the oldest of three sisters, Sharon found herself assuming parental responsibilities, helping with the cooking—she loved to cook—and tried to shoulder her father's absences and her mother's loneliness. "What Sharon was," her sister Debra Ann said, "was extremely dutiful."

Duty was her pattern. She was a smiler, an actress.

Sharon signed with Ransohoff at nineteen. Dutifully she faced Hollywood with professional dedication, taking courses in singing, dancing, and acting, the latter with Jeff Corey in the fall of 1963. "An incredibly beautiful girl," Corey reflected, "but a fragmented personality." Self-disclosure was a problem, so Corey one day put a stick in her hand, and demanded, "Hit me, do something, show emotion!" Beauty was not enough. And she knew she wouldn't be beautiful forever.

She was twenty-three.

She was seeing someone, Jay Sebring, a hairstylist to the stars. They'd been together about three years, almost since as she had arrived in Los Angeles. He was there in London now, waiting for her to finish this film, *Eye of the Devil*. He had the most beautiful, the sweetest, home in Benedict Canyon on Easton Drive. It was Jean Harlow's old house, the one where her husband, producer Paul Bern, shot himself (unless he was murdered) two months after they were married. But it really was the sweetest house, the kind you would discover if you got lost wandering a forest in a fairy tale, like the cottage where Snow White found the Seven Dwarfs. It actually looked like that. To think that someone would be shot, or shoot himself, in a place like that—it didn't make sense.

Sharon and Roman, party people, could agree that they loved London. The city still bounced to the beat of the Beatles—their sound, their look, the cheeky enthusiasm that remade stuffy old London into the mod capital of the world—and in flooded an international miscellany of the young and creative, decked out in long beads, billowy shirtsleeves, and miniskirts, to enjoy a little of the goofy good time they saw in *A Hard Day's Night*. They were musicians, photographers, Warren Beatty, Twiggy, Vidal Sassoon, the debonair production designer Richard Sylbert, fledgling producers like Robert Evans—dispatched by Gulf & Western's chairman, Charles Bluhdorn, to shake the postwar dust off Paramount's London office. They all crossed paths at the Ad Lib Club, one of swinging London's hot spots. Most of them liked a little grass, only a little. But—as Polanski told Sharon—he couldn't stand the dropouts at the margins of the city, the bleary-eyed, perpetually drugged grass smokers with their pedantry and fogged reasoning.

Sharon smoked grass a little.

Had she ever tried LSD?

Yes. A few times. With Jay.

Roman had done it once or twice. The first time, driving past Harrods, the steering wheel changed shape in his hands, and he and his date got lost on their way to his flat. Once they arrived, the woman marveled at how beautifully green the red stairs were, and in the bedroom, Roman, blinded, draped a shade against the searing glare of night. His hair turned pink and green, and when he tried to vomit out came a dribble of rainbow circles. Even tripping, he knew why. Observing his own brain—ordinarily as rigorous as a geometric proof—betray its own logic, Polanski fought back, commanding himself to stay rational. He turned to his date and saw that her eyes and mouth were swastikas.

Where was Sharon staying?

Eaton Place.

Around the corner from him. Would she like to try some acid tonight? They could split a tab. It would be an easy trip.

At Roman's Eaton Place flat they lay down together and split the sugar cube in two. Sharon, biting her fingernails, accepted her half and confessed to feeling guilty for being there. She did love Jay. But not like he loved her. Jay was completely in love with her. But—this confused her—she also knew he had other women; they literally lined the block around his salon. But, she tried to reason with herself, free love was natural and therefore good, and since she had come to London, she had heard so many sophisticates, people like Roman Polanski, denigrate middle-class American hang-ups like fidelity, that she had almost come to agree with them herself, at least for tonight.

Roman lit candles as the acid covered them and they talked on for hours, and nearing sunrise, it was obvious to what remained of Roman's thinking mind that they were going to go to bed together. She started screaming.

Terrified, he dropped to her side. "Please don't," he reassured her. "Please."

But she wouldn't stop. She was weeping uncontrollably.

"Please, no, don't. Please," he begged. "Everything's all right."

He would stare at Sharon, unbelieving. It was impossible, someone so perfect, and yet, there she was. Wasn't she?

"She was just fantastic," Polanski would say. "She was a fucking angel." Her hair of yellow chaparral, the changing color of her eyes, the unqualified kindness of her face. Did people like this exist? In a world of chaos, was it naive to trust, as a child would, the apparent goodness of things, the feeling of safety he had known and lost before?

If the horrible could happen once, it could happen again. Simply knowing it happened, he was doomed—his mind was doomed—by the possibility of recurrence. Despite even the facts, "could" forever opens the aqueduct of nightmares that eyes don't see. But no mind, even when the sun is shining, sees everything with its eyes. A broken mind sees instead the black chasm of "could," waiting, smug as gravity, to ravage every newborn thought. Again it sees only what it saw before.

But there she was, Sharon. They were together, in their hotel room, on location in the Italian Dolomites: Roman, writer, director, and star of *Fearless Vampire Killers*; Sharon playing his love interest, Sarah Shagal.

Outside their window there was snow.

She would ask him about his first marriage, to Barbara Lass, a Polish actress, "but I really hate talking about it for some reason," he would say. "Not because it's so painful to talk about but because it's so futile."

Would he ever lose the loss, or was the best one could hope for to exchange one loss for another? Or could Sharon, like a dam, hold off the flood of losses forever?

The hemorrhaging: When would it go away? It did not begin with Barbara. When Roman was three, his father, Ryszard, for reasons he would quickly regret, forfeited his painter's life in Paris, and moved the family back to Kraków. It was the summer of 1936. An old feeling: Though Roman was too young to understand why, he could feel a certain tension in his mother and father when they spoke the names Hitler and Göring. Uncomprehending, he would listen to the grownups discuss the trenches being dug in Planty Park, why the shopwindows were crisscrossed with construction tape, and the anti-Semitic slogans in the local papers. What did they mean? In 1939 Ryszard decided to send Roman, his mother, and his half sister to Warsaw. "They thought Warsaw would be safer," Roman reflected. "[Because] Warsaw was far east within the Polish territory."

They thought wrong. In Warsaw the piercing air-raid sirens rushed the Polanski family, without Ryszard, along with screaming babies and hysterical strangers, down into a muggy cellar piled with make-shift gas masks. Roman would spend many nights there, in silence, squeezing his mother's arm in the dark. Why was this happening? The boy didn't understand what they had done wrong. As the raids increased—they would hide in the shelter sometimes three times a night—the Polanskis ran short of money and food. "Our emergency plan had been a complete miscalculation," Polanski would write. "Instead of staying put in Kraków, which had seen no fighting at all, we had headed straight for the very epicenter of the war."

In October 1939 the Germans occupied Warsaw.

Without their father, Polanski and his elder sister, Annette, clung to their mother. When she went out to scavenge, Roman clung to Annette. He was a small boy, even for his age, and she could nearly hold his whole body in her arms. "Let's sleep," she would say. "Time passes quicker that way." Listening for his mother's approaching footsteps, Roman waited where he had last seen her, sometimes for hours, for the door to open.

She was elegant. Even as a boy, he knew that. Deliberate in her presentation, Bula Polanski dressed in fox stoles and livened her face with the discreetly aristocratic touches of her Russian forebears, carefully drawing lines over tended eyebrows and, in accordance with the fashion of the day, painting her upper lip just so, like a cherub's. She was as neat as the house she had kept before the war, and just as welcoming, ready to conduct conversation through all rivers of thought. Roman's mother was half Jewish but decidedly agnostic, practical above all, and demonstrated, in her wartime resourcefulness, the resilience and audacity Roman would come to inherit. People told him, and he could almost see, that she was a survivor; and never more so than when—after hours of feeling what it was never to see her again—the door opened.

In time, Ryszard came from Kraków, haggard and unshaven.

Roman took him to see an abandoned dog, shivering in the bombed-out skeleton of a nearby building, whimpering for help. Ryszard shrugged at the animal: "What can we do?"

Soon after the Polanskis relocated back to Kraków, to Podgórze Square, Annette drew Roman to their apartment window and pointed across the street. The Germans were building, red brick after brick, a wall. Then came more bricks, bricks against windows, against the main entrance to their apartment, bricks to build the wall higher and longer—bricks, Roman realized, not to keep something out, but to close them in. He knew then he was in danger. "But at the same time," he said, "I didn't know anything else, so I just accepted it." And accepting the routines of ghetto life, he anticipated its only just outcome: It would be just a matter of time before the Germans realized they had made a giant error; neither he, nor his family, nor the other Jewish families, had done anything wrong. All this would end well, the way it should.

"Children don't have any point of reference," Polanski would explain. "They're optimistic by nature."

Inside the ghetto Roman met Pawel, an orphaned "smart kid," as Polanski described him "with an extraordinary capacity for absorbing and marshaling facts." They shared an obsessive, surgical interest in the workings of things: how to build, from abandoned parts, simple motors; how to apply the principles of aerodynamics to toy planes. "I'd always had a craving for practical information of all kinds," Polanski would says, "and Pawel could supply answers to everything." What was electricity? What was gasoline and how did it make cars go? Coming to consciousness in an increasingly incoherent world, Polanski clung to Pawel, and together, attached at the brain, they set out—the streets echoing with gunfire and old women screaming in Yiddish—looking for scraps of metal and mechanical discards. As Roman's parents began to fight, regularly now—"My own worst fear at this time," Roman recalled, "was that my parents might split up"—he and Pawel engineered themselves to make order. They were building. The world was made of truths, Roman discovered, like a wall made of bricks. If one looked closely, if one asked why, one could discover, buried in the heap, explanations for everything. It came down to science. That was the highest truth. Truth was power. "Of course, science gives hope," Polanski said. But the ghetto population reduced—"Germans would raid families," Polanski said, "and they wouldn't take all of them. They would just take one"—leaving the boys more rubble to sift through, more deserted bits to choose from. "[Pawel] was my first friendship in my life," Polanski said.

Roman and his mother would practice. She, who worked as a cleaning woman outside the ghetto, would take him to the home of Mr. and Mrs. Wilks, where Roman was told he was to flee—through an opening they'd found in the wall—in case, for whatever reason, he could not find his parents. "That's what [war] means to me: not bombs and tanks, that's just the backdrop. War is separation." He was told if this separation ever happened he was then to wait at the Wilkses' until either his mother or father appeared to bring him home.

The raids continued. At the sound Ryszard would turn off all the lights and they would stand still, trying not to hear. But once, Polanski said, "We heard noises coming from upstairs, screams and shouts and shots. And my father stepped out on the landing discreetly to see what was happening, and at that time they were dragging a woman by her hair down screaming. These were the first—some kind of memories from me—of violence."

He saw a murder. It was a woman, shot only steps from his feet. The blood, he noted rather clinically, burst from her back, but it didn't gush, it gurgled, like water from a garden fountain.

One day Pawel disappeared.

"I remember," Polanski said, "as a child, I was never really scared of any ghosts, but I was very much scared of people—of a thief in the house, for example—or robber getting in—something of this kind."

Pawel: Roman's heart. It was the first loss that didn't go away.

He befriended a younger boy, a neighbor named Stefan. Stefan told Roman that he wanted to be a racecar driver and that his parents were gone. "He had a photo of him with his mother standing in a field of rye," Polanski said. "And he was always showing me this photo. Of him with his mother."

Then the day came. His parents woke him early one morning with suspicions of another raid. Just as they had practiced, Roman's mother, known to the guards, rushed the boy clear of the ghetto wall to the Wilkses', but it was his father who, later that same day, collected Roman from his hideout. On the street Ryszard hugged and held his son with unsettling intensity, squeezing him, kissing him too much; on Podgórze Bridge, returning to the ghetto, he was weeping uncontrollably: "They took your mother. . . ."

There was nothing he could do.

He loved Sharon.

He loved Sharon's Los Angeles once he came to be with her there, the bare feet and early nights; he loved the funny science-fictional house—like being on the moon, she said—she rented from a friend. "I have never made love more often," he recalled, "or with greater emotional intensity, than I did with Sharon during those few days together." He loved the city's free embrace of sensuous ideals, the wide red carpet into the Beverly Hills Hotel, the world-within-a-world tranquility of its spacious estates and, at every turn, unbroken vistas. "Here in L.A.," he reflected, "there were no skyscrapers; it was countrified living with all the desirable advantages of a city." Having spent much of his childhood in the ghetto and, after his father was taken from him too, in hiding at the Wilkses' cottage, he was predisposed to love the safety and seclusion of Los Angeles's vast and variegated topography and big open spaces. He loved to drive. He loved cars. He put the top down and drove. He loved to go fast. Polanski *was* speed. He cherished the freedom—in every respect anathema to his film-school days in gray, angular Communist Poland—of Disneyland, which he had visited for the first time, in 1963, with Federico Fellini and his wife, Giulietta Masina. "For all of us," Polanski remembered of their afternoon, "it was like discovering the America of our childhood dreams."

At Disneyland he remembered Kraków: He was a boy, salvaging mangled *Snow White* trims from ghetto trashcans. Fascinated by the very filmstrip, the sprockets, the emulsion, the literal medium and science of film, he remembered quite vividly the moment, before the war, when a grammar school teacher carried a tantalizing little gadget into class, "an epidiascope," he recalled, "used for projecting illustrations onto a screen in the school hall. I wasn't at all interested in the words or even the pictures it projected, only in the method of projection." He wanted to understand. What was this contraption? How did it work? He carefully examined its lens, its mirror; he flicked fingers into the beam and grinned at the flickers on the wall. The physics; it made sense. "As a matter of fact," he said, "my dream was to have a projector and you see, there was a boy in the ghetto who had a projector—it was a 35 mil projector, but a very little one with a handle and it looked like a—peddler grinding machine—and very primitive. It was for kids." Polanski made his own.

There was another memory from before the war: the time Roman saw his first movie, the Jeanette MacDonald and Nelson Eddy musical *Sweethearts*, of which he understood nothing, but he didn't have to; from that point on the complete enterprise of moviegoing obsessed him, the light, the dark, the muffled click-click-*whir* of the projector, everything movie down to the dusty smell of the half-empty Kraków theaters and the squeaks of the folding seats. "I read whatever I could on filmmaking," Polanski said. How were these things made? Who made them? Carol Reed's *Odd Man Out* Polanski saw at age sixteen: "The whole atmosphere, strangely enough, resembles very much my childhood city of Kraków," he said, "with the change of seasons that can happen in one day. That atmosphere seduced me, and then I thought of the acting, of the photography. And then I realized much later that there was something deeper in the story [that attracted me]; it was the story of a guy who is a fugitive."

Entrapment: He understood that. "I always liked the movies that happen within some kind of cocoon rather than on the fields," he said. "As an adolescent I preferred a film like Olivier's *Hamlet*, which had tremendous influence on me, to *The Charge of the Light Brigade*. I like the *lieu clos*, as we say in French. I like to feel the wall behind me." Futility, he learned, forced character out of hiding: "Let's imagine that all of a sudden this house collapses and we find ourselves trapped here for two or three months," he said. "Our true nature would be unleashed as we fight over who's going to eat the flowers over there."

At film school in Lodz after the war, he met the future master of Polish cinema, Andrzej Wajda. In 1954 Polanski appeared in Wajda's seminal *A Generation*. "Roman was an insatiable presence on the set back then," Wajda recalled. "Voraciously interested in everything technical—lighting, film stock, makeup, camera optics—with no interest whatever, on the other hand, in the sorts of thematic concerns that obsessed the rest of us, like politics, Poland's place in the world, and, especially, our recent national past. He saw everything in front of him and nothing behind, his eyes firmly fixed on a future he already seemed to be hurtling toward, at maximum speed. And for him that future was out there, in the world, and particularly Hollywood, which he equated with the world standard in cinema. Even then. And that was absolutely unique among us."

He was not ashamed, as many of his film-school contemporaries were, of swimming in the warm gush of thrillers, musicals, Westerns, *The Adventures of Robin Hood*, *The Maltese Falcon*, *Snow White* ("It's so naïvely beautiful. What is it, corny or something? But I just love this movie. . . ."), popular genres that were to Polanski "what cinema"—what Hollywood—"is all about." These were not dreams;

Roman didn't understand his dreams. These were hopes, as real as the people who made them, sent to Poland from a magical but non-imaginary place on an actual map fantastically far from Soviet rule. "*Go West*," Roman said "very quickly became a necessity for me."

He had come to Hollywood, to Sharon's Los Angeles, to show Ransohoff his rough cut of *The Fearless Vampire Killers*, a film Polanski made "to recreate, in a sense, the joy of childhood," of his earliest genre-love. Ransohoff detested it.

"Listen, sweetie," the producer told Sharon at La Scala restaurant in Beverly Hills "I'm going to have to cut some stuff out of *The Vampire Killers*. Your spanking scene has got to go."

"Oh, don't do *that*. Why would you do that?"

"Because it doesn't move the story. The story has got to move. Bang, bang, bang. No American audience is going to sit while Polanski indulges himself."

"But Europeans make movies differently than Americans," she protested. "*Blow-Up* moved slowly. But wasn't it a great film!"

"I'll tell you something, baby. I didn't like it. If I'd have seen it before the reviews, I'd have said it'd never make it. It's not my kind of picture. I want to be told a story without all that hocus-pocus symbolism going on."

It had always been Ransohoff's contention that while Polanski understood European audiences, Ransohoff understood *his*. "I know the American public better than you do," he had warned Polanski, "and I'd like to reserve the right to change the American cut of the film." Polanski had signed, concluding that Ransohoff, in his unpretentious baggy pants and sweatshirts, was trustworthy, a vagrant connoisseur, and, based on Ransohoff's investment in Polanski's previous films, even artistically inclined. But he had misinterpreted the facts. "What's funny is that I should have foreseen the problem," Polanski complained to *Variety*. "When Ransohoff bought my previous film, *Cul-de-sac*, for the U.S., he cut 15 minutes from it and did some redubbing." There was nothing Roman could do: Ransohoff took control. He slashed twenty minutes from *Vampire Killers*, re-dubbed actors to make them sound American, drastically curtailed the score, and added an inane cartoon prologue utterly out of tone with the rest of the picture. When Polanski saw what Ransohoff had destroyed—of his script, his film, his own performance and Sharon's—he nearly vomited. The film, storywise, was now a shambles; it didn't make any sense.

The dissolution of Polanski's relationship with Ransohoff's Filmways left him, in 1967, professionally adrift. His problem, as ever, was one of timing: Had Polanski come to Hollywood two decades earlier, at the height of the studio era, when he had been foraging for scraps of *Snow White* in Kraków, he would have encountered a power struc-ture more amenable to artistry and exploration. "The studio pio-neers might have been tyrannical," Polanski said, "but at least they understood the business they'd built. They also took risks."

Beginning in the fifties, the incremental dissolution of the Hol-lywood studio system—formerly the world's wellspring of motion pictures—curtailed production of domestic film product. Antitrust legislation (*United States vs. Paramount Pictures*, 1948) had di-vested Hollywood of its monopolies, slashed its assets, decreased its profit margins, and the dominoes fell: Long-term contracts, in-house resources, and production efficiency declined drastically. The machine slowed. The number of motion pictures Hollywood produced each year reduced steadily, and the rise of television made matters worse. There was suddenly less money to make fewer films for smaller audiences. "The movie business," Richard Zanuck announced in 1966, "has become a weekend business." Fewer films meant fewer hopes. Knuckles whitened. Poststudio Hollywood could no longer afford to risk as it once had; thus did Polanski, in the midsixties, sense correctly that a certain caliber of creativity was dying.

Big business smelled blood in the water. Kinney National Company swallowed Warner Bros., Transamerica merged with United Artists, Gulf + Western engulfed Paramount. "Not since the start of the talkies nearly four decades ago," wrote the *New York Times* reporter Peter Bart, "has the movie industry gone through a total overhaul like this—new policies, new faces, new corporate control." Hollywood was in a semipanic: on the one hand, relieved to be rescued; on the other, dubious of its rescuers. What did these mega-corporate CEOs know about running movie studios? What did Charles Bluhdorn, the obstreperous, impulsive chairman of Gulf + Western, who started a coffee-import house at the age of twenty-three, and later parlayed an investment in the Michigan Bumper Company into a great fortune, know about filmmaking? Did he even like movies?

It was the old Los Angeles story, gold, bandits, fool's gold, fools. "The greatest talents from all fields—as much artistic or scientific or literary—have passed through Los Angeles," Polanski would say. "At the same time it's a place where there aren't any new developments— either intellectual or cultural." It was a kind of dreamer's physics: For every California promise, there was an L.A. disappointment. The sun set over the ocean; night emptied the streets; the Beverly Drive estates that once delighted also isolated. The moon rose. It got quiet. Where'd everyone go? "It's like an immense suburb," Polanski complained, "where you rarely, if ever, see other people. There's no communication—people live as gentleman farmers, and this might explain why some people there are no longer actually creating anything."

At least in the studio days, when contracted film artists had an actual home on a lot, a sense of community workplace—the commissaries, the soundstages, the writers' offices—facilitated an atmosphere of social and creative synergy, mitigating the city sprawl. As the studios cleared and the streetcars disappeared and Los Angeles grew too big for its local roads alone, new freeways—the 101 in 1960, the 405 in 1961—strained the small-town ambience that once characterized driving-optional neighborhoods like Beverly Hills and Santa Monica. This was Polanski's city of no communication, Joan Didion's car megalopolis: By the middle of the 1960s it gave native Angelenos good reason to ask themselves: Do I still live in Los Angeles? Just as Roman Polanski asked himself—for his dreams depended on it—Is Hollywood still Hollywood?

Grieving the destruction of his film and a future that once seemed assured, Polanski told Sharon he was leaving town for a short skiing vacation in Vermont—when a call came from Paramount's new, and incredibly young (thirty-six), head of production, Robert J. Evans. Evans's phone voice was as snug and sultry as bourbon and a fireplace, and he maneuvered it into and around Polanski's ear with the ease of the ace radio actor he had been in New York a few lifetimes ago. "You're a genius," the voice gushed; it sounded like movie talk, but Evans meant it. He had seen and loved Roman's work, and—news travels fast—he offered Roman condolences for Ransohoff's slashings—whatever Ransohoff liked, Evans proudly hated—and invited him to come in for a meeting at Paramount. The voice said he had Polanski in mind to direct *Downhill Racer*, a skiing picture (Evans had done his homework) starring Robert Redford. Polanski replied: I'll ski myself first.

Returning from Vermont, Polanski met Robert Evans in his office at Paramount and took a quick look around. Evans, Polanski understood immediately, was, despite his love for imperial Hollywood, not the typical Hollywood executive, let alone head of production. Foremost, Evans was great looking. He looked relaxed, satiated, sexy, like someone who was still enjoying the movie business, or what was left of it. In fact, he looked so good it almost worked against him. His black velvet hair and pressed collars belied how impossibly hard he worked, and wrongly assured many, at first glance, that they had been right to dismiss him as a pretty playboy loafer riding high and lucky on the expense account of a lifetime. After all, there was reason for suspicion: Evans's appointment didn't quite make sense. With virtually no producer's credentials, Robert Evans had been hand selected, by CEO Charlie Bluhdorn to run what many still argued was once the greatest movie studio in the world. The job came with a superabundance of power, money, glamour, prestige, the whole enviable avalanche of the American dream, which is what shone so clemently on Robert Evans's beautiful face—he had had his dream and eaten it too—and why so many in Hollywood were quick-with both good reason and jealousy—to ask, This guy? Why him?

As soon as Polanski walked into Evans's office, he began an investigation of Evans's bookshelves, his ashtrays, his professional bric-a-brac, sizing up the producer (and liking what he saw), all the while entertaining him with hilarious anecdotes about Ransohoff and about his ski adventures that had Evans laughing throughout.

When they settled down to really talk, Evans leveled with him: "*Downhill Racer* was just a pretext to get you here. Would you read this?"

He pushed a bound galley—a copy of pre-published manuscript— across the desk.

Rosemary's Baby, a novel by Ira Levin. Roman flipped a couple of pages. "This isn't about skiing."

"Read it. If you don't like it, your next ski trip is on me."

That night, back at the Beverly Hills Hotel, Polanski read the book in one sitting. The plotting amazed him; the pages turned; this story of a young woman impregnated by the devil sped along like a perfect thriller. The only thing that rankled him about the book was the presence of the devil himself. Polanski did not believe in God, and, therefore, he did not believe in Satan. (Reality was sinister enough.) Going supernatural, Polanski felt, Levin had compromised the potential for actual terror. In his adaptation, Polanski would change that. "I thought that I can get around it by creating a film in which the idea of the devil could be conceived as Rosemary's folly. We never see anything supernatural in it and everything that occurred that has any kind of supernatural look occurs in a dream . . . it could have been all question of her paranoia, of her suspicions during the pregnancy and postpartum craze."

The next morning Polanski called Evans and told him he loved the book.

In April 1967, Sharon, then filming *Valley of the Dolls*, rented them a mansion at the southernmost beginnings of the Pacific Coast Highway, on the Santa Monica beach. The place, they were told, had once been the home of Cary Grant, and to Polanski's eyes, it even resembled a lavish old studio movie with its laughably large closets and centerpiece stairway that recalled Norma Desmond's last luscious descent. Sharon and Roman, antique lovers both, reveled in the anachronisms. By day, hunting for the mansion's secrets lent an air of mischief to their idyll, and, come twilight, when playtime ended, the view of the darkening ocean hushed and humbled them to bed. Was this really life? When the moon rose spectacularly over the water, or when anything at all looked beautiful, Roman's eyes saw Sharon's, and he felt the slow, too-tender joy of knowing this was it, these were the happiest moments he had ever lived. He was terrified. "This cannot possibly last," he told himself. "It's impossible to last."

But happiness kept coming. They couldn't stop it. It poured out of Los Angeles in great green waves of sage and sycamore. It raced up with them to visit Sharon's friends on top of Topanga Canyon. Roman couldn't stop it from filling their home, their dinner parties, their candle-lighting, their kissing. On top of Topanga, they flew up together on an old tire swing, "and I shall never forget," Polanski recalled, "the thrill of soaring higher and higher through the branches, over the cliff, glimpsing the extraordinary view, hearing the wind whistle around us."

Sharon introduced him to her America, junk food, pop music, drive-ins, Big Sur. The sheer size of the country moved Polanski, "the wide open spaces," he said, "and the natural beauty." He loved the vitality of Americans, their appetite for success. A free people, they were allowed hope. "When I came to the States," he said, "I was struck by the fact that the American Dream existed. It all seems when I first got there, it was all about the middle class. It seemed like everybody was well-off. I don't remember seeing, during those times, any homeless people. It was just a paradise, unthinkable."

Young Americans particularly impressed Polanski. Their level of discourse, their plans for change, the revolution in their voices. "They seem to be much more intelligent than previous generations," he said. Demonstrations of democracy—so unimaginable in his boyhood—were astonishing. "It was Utopia," he said. "Society was moving forward on the hopes of young people." He went to a Be-In. He ambled the meadow of painted faces and picnicking couples, their denim and tie-dye and goddess gowns, their blithe collapse, their drums and flowers. "This is fantastic!" he exclaimed.

"There are no young people in Hollywood," Polanski had grumbled in 1964. By 1967, that had changed. *Bonnie and Clyde*, which opened that year, was a watershed; it ushered into Hollywood an era of hot blood, fresh sex and violence, and introduced a vision of America—less romantic, more realistic—that would change the game and the players, pervading the movie industry, and thus, the city of Los Angeles. "The change has come with startling speed," wrote Peter Bart. "Hollywood, a town traditionally dominated by old men, has been but taken over by 'young turks.' The big deal and the big news are being made by men 40 and under." Even the executives were getting younger. There was Robert Evans, of course, at Paramount; Richard Zanuck, 31, at Fox; David Picker, 35, at United Artists. Something was indeed happening. In an aging industry, the sudden omnipresence of youth was in itself hopeful "Most top executives here believe that Hollywood now has its greatest opportunity in a generation to emerge again as the world's filmmaking capital," Bart wrote. "It has a new infusion of venture capital,"—this from the corporations buying up studios—"money for experimenting. It also has an intangible asset: movies suddenly seem to be in again. Young people seem to be caught up by movies, not TV—witness the vast Bogart cult and the emergence of about 4,000 film societies on college campuses." Bogdanovich, Coppola, Altman, Friedkin, Polanski, the generation that had grown up with the movies was now, at long last, preparing to make them.

They hung out together. Roman and Sharon and the rest of young, hip Hollywood partied at the Daisy, Beverly Hills' uptown answer to the friskier Whisky a Go Go. But unlike the Whisky, the Daisy was a private nightclub, the first of its kind in a generation, and founded by Jack Hanson, owner of the posh boutique Jax, jammed with the young and famous who bought tight pants at his store. ("There are three important men in America today," Nancy Sinatra said. "Hugh Hefner, my father and Jack Hanson.") A year and a half after he opened the place (pool table, Du-par's pies, dance floor), Hanson wisely declared membership closed, and the most alluring hangout in the city became, officially, the most exclusive. Hitchcock and company still had their chili at Chasen's, and the older business set preferred the Playboy Club; but here, in the middle of Beverly Hills, still the center of after-hours Hollywood ("Few stars have ever been east of Doheny Drive unless they are going to the studio," the *L.A. Times* reported, and "south of Wilshire Blvd. only to go to the airport"), grooved the players of the next wave, Roman and Sharon and their friends Warren Beatty, Mike Nichols and Richard Sylbert. "It sounds absurd to call the scene innocent," Dominick Dunne recalled, "but it was." The Daisy was good, happy fun, and, after hosting a fund-raiser for the Student Nonviolent Coordinating Committee, "underscored an interesting change in Hollywood mores," Peter Bart reported in the *New York Times*, "namely, that it is becoming stylish in the movie colony to be a liberal thinker," barely possible in the previous generation when moguls kept their stars' public images on a tight leash. But since the end of the Hollywood blacklist shamed those who stayed silent, Bart observed, it was no longer considered gauche in Hollywood to talk politics; it was gauche not to. "We were all enchanted," wrote Eve Babitz, "under a spell of peace and love and LSD that we thought had changed the world. In those days, people might drop by for one joint, get hung up on some transformational conversation, and wind up staying for the whole day or three weeks and then leaving for different skies, other adventures."

Hollywood's golden days were gone, but from his Daisy gang, Polanski cultivated his own kind of studio. He hired Sylbert, whose early work on Elia Kazan's *Baby Doll* he loved, to do the production design for *Rosemary's Baby*. Sylbert turned Roman on to his sister-in-law, the costume designer Anthea Sylbert, and Mike Nichols's editor, Sam O'Steen, then cutting *The Graduate* (also Sylbert's) at Paramount, and Roman snapped them up. "That was the beginning of this group," Polanski said. "They all had a good time working together," said Susanna Moore, then Sylbert's girlfriend, "because they were all friends. That intimacy made a difference in the work. Oftentimes on movies intimacy is a bit feigned but in this case it was real, between people who saw each other for dinner sometimes every night. Nobody was really threatened, jealous, secretive or private. The atmosphere was one of a workshop. Their work was a collaboration."

Richard Sylbert, the oldest and tallest of the group, was still not even forty, but by far the most experienced. In his safari jacket—cribbed from Clark Gable—spotted neckerchief, pressed khakis, and loafers, he conveyed the crisp New England aplomb of an English professor who just got laid, and filling his Dunhill pipe, pulling up to Cyrano's in his little Mustang in herringbone and tweed, he promised the smart good taste he was well respected for. Sylbert was, like his sister-in-law Anthea, a real New Yorker in L.A. She wore her dark hair, dark skirts, and black turtlenecks stringently straight. Mike Nichols called her "the Ant," but only jokingly; she was a pistol, utterly unafraid to speak truth, no matter how ugly, to anyone, no matter how powerful. "The hardest thing to find in Hollywood is the truth," Nichols had said. "The Ant will give you the truth. Even if you don't want to hear it." Polanski, relying on the reasonable good sense of her imagination, loved her for it. "If I think they're not doing their jobs right," the Ant said, "I'll tell anyone on set." Both she and brother-in-law Richard were verbal, sophisticated, electrified—so alike, in fact, they were often confused, per their surname, as siblings—"and they were smart enough," Susanna Moore said, "to realize how integrated their individual work could be, and how that could benefit the film." What they shared, artistically, perfectly suited them to Roman Polanski: a dogged commitment to realism, and absolute precision. "That's how we do it," Anthea Sylbert said. "We do it right. And if we don't do it right, let's do another take. But we don't arrive on the stage not having thought that we had got it right to begin with."

Theirs was not an ethic of wholesale design; on *Who's Afraid of Virginia Woolf?*, which won him his first Oscar, Sylbert had personally selected each book on George and Martha's shelves Here realism and precision went hand in hand: The book titles elevated the characters from generic types to actual, specific individuals. As designers, the Sylberts were psychologists. Anthea aimed not for beauty or for chic—as Edith Head and costumers of an earlier generation so often did—but to amplify character. In her work there were no accidents. "By nature, I am a very analytical person," Anthea said, but she could have been speaking for both of them. "Nothing that I do in my life is arbitrary. It's all thought out. Even making breakfast. Everything's lined up. Then I cook." The object was to convey, visually, as much as possible, as quickly as possible. To do that, she said, "you have to marry reality to drama. What will make the audience instinctively know this character as who they are? That was always the motivation." The Sylberts synchronized their visual intellects. "I would always get a photo of the location," Anthea said, "to know what the background was colorwise." They united under a kind of aesthetic thesis statement, an overall dramatic notion, generally formulated by Richard, that they would tie to the look of the film.

Thus was *Rosemary's Baby*—or any film by the Sylberts—given a *visual* story, in this case, in conjunction with Polanski. They decided: (1) The film was to look *real*, not like a horror movie, in other words, contrary to convention, pleasantly colorful. Per Ruth Gordon's outrageous outfits, "Roman's instruction," Anthea said, "was you don't suspect people who are loud." (2) "Roman insisted *Rosemary* be kept the year the pope came to New York, so it was a period film but only two or three years before. [The film] was set the year that every three weeks you had to shorten your skirt. It didn't happen all at once, the miniskirt, it happened in increments. So all during the movie, as her pregnancy goes on, her skirts get shorter and shorter. That was the period. All young women, especially in New York, follow the trends, especially if your husband is an actor. That's who Rosemary was."

Mia Farrow was cast as Rosemary. For the part of her husband, Polanski auditioned a young actor who had appeared in a couple of Roger Corman films. Polanski liked him, but his roguish air was deemed wrong for the character, and Jack Nicholson was dismissed. The part went to actor/filmmaker, John Cassavetes.

Production of *Rosemary's Baby* began in the summer of 1967.

Polanski's perfectionism suffused the set. Filming took time; not because he didn't know what he wanted, but because he did. As much as his meticulousness, it was Polanski's expertise with every office in the production, his total hands-on investment in the mechanics of things, that slowed the process down to the pace of careful consideration. Everything—behind and in front of the camera lens—he put under the microscope of his own eyes. "Roman understood more about the camera than any director of photography than I worked with," recalled first assistant director Howard Koch Jr." "He understood the grip and the electric. He understood all of it. He could do—and did—everything on the set." He manned the camera, he acted for the actors. What some called controlling, Anthea Sylbert called direction. "Roman, like all great filmmakers, was a dictator," she said, "a benevolent dictator." He did not curb his creativity to meet the pressures of the schedule. His allegiance, in the end, was to the work. "[Cinematographer] Billy Fraker would take an hour and a half to light the hallway of the Dakota," Koch said, "and Roman would tear it out and say, 'This is how it should be done! I want this here and I want that there!'" And so "the movie went on and on," Koch said, "and the studio was all over him to hurry up—a fifty-five-day schedule went into something like eighty days."

Robert Evans, responsible for protecting Paramount's investment, was summoned to location in New York a week into production. The call had come from Bill Castle, producer: He wanted Polanski off the movie. Evans balked; he had seen the dailies. They were fantastic.

"Listen," Evans said to Polanski, away from the crew. "You better pick up the pace. The first ten days, you're ten days late."

"I can't work this way."

"*Start* working this way."

Evans's ass was on the line too. The year 1966 had been a terrible one for Paramount, and '67, so far, wasn't looking any better. Of course Evans couldn't be blamed for the box-office duds—*Is Paris Burning?*, *This Property Is Condemned*, *El Dorado*—he had inherited from the previous regime, but for Blake Edwards and Otto Preminger, two top directors currently working on new projects for Evans (*Darling Lili*, *Skidoo*), he had no excuse. Their dailies stunk—and in Edwards's case, stunk very expensively. Was Evans doing something wrong? Just as baffling was the possibility that he was doing something right: The success of 1966's biggest hit for Paramount, *Alfie*, which Evans had helped along in London, utterly defied conventional good sense; the movie (a) starred a newcomer, Michael Caine, and (b) cost almost nothing. Yet it soared. Why? To Paramount's old guard, who held fast to their prestige formula of stars and spectacle—two assets they figured TV couldn't offer—

Alfie looked like a fluke; but to Evans it looked interesting. In the same spirit—fresh talent, new stories, reasonable budgets—he had green-lighted the audacious political satire *The President's Analyst*. But it tanked. Why? Was it really because, as Evans argued, the FBI wanted it buried? Or had Evans buried it to save himself?

To show the New York money he was in control of their asset and show Polanski he supported *him*, Evans would appear—infrequently but meaningfully—on set to demonstrably endorse his director before the entire cast and crew. "He stuck his neck out for me," Polanski said, "and showed himself to have quite a courage." Assuaged, Polanski continued to make *Rosemary's Baby* at his pace, and Evans guarded him, at his own peril, every step of the way, careful throughout to keep his distance from the production, out of respect to Polanski, and keep close, out of respect to Paramount. So it was that both sides were kept in balance and that Polanski could explore, without compromise and to his satisfaction, the Hollywood—more than industry, it was a *way* of working—of his boyhood dreams. "Hollywood was just the name of the place," he said, "but it happens that this Hollywood is giving me the tools to do what I want to do." On *Rosemary's Baby*, at Paramount, he learned "how to drive this machine," of "the best technicians in the world." They allowed him, for the first time in his career, to rise to the peak of his imaginings. Richard Sylbert showed him how a set could be built to maximize camera placement. Sam O'Steen taught him more than he ever knew about editing. Evans, signing the checks, gave him—them—the time. "Hollywood is the best place!" Polanski told a journalist after he completed *Rosemary*. "It's like asking Michelangelo, 'Would you like to live in Carrara?'"

Roman and Sharon opened their home to new friends, collaborators, Sharon's ex-boyfriend Jay Sebring, Polish writers and filmmakers, and Sharon's family. No one was denied. "Sharon couldn't turn any friendship down," Polanski said. "Every time I came home from the studio there was Sharon, the dogs and friends." Having spent the bulk of her life traveling, first as an army brat and later as an actress, Sharon savored home life, and Roman in it. She doted on him. She cut his hair, packed his bags (placing tissue paper between the layers), cooked dinners for all to enjoy, on the beach, under the Malibu moon. They sang aloud to "Baby, It's Cold Outside" and "Suzanne," their music presiding over "the radiance of those California evenings," as Polanski recalled them. They were golden, their friends were golden, and with so much gold to go around, all were happy at each other's shine. Even apart, Polanski, the Sylberts, Beatty, Evans, and Nichols seemed to work together. "I never knew life could be a luxury," Polanski said. "It had always been hotel rooms and struggle," he added, "and now I loved this life, I loved the place, I love the people, I loved the work." Polanski paid his maid more than two hundred dollars a week—probably what a Polish laborer earned in six months. "We wanted to settle for good in Los Angeles," he said. "We had big plans. It seemed to be a kind of peculiar, happy dream."

It was a dream that seemed to belong to California, its natural landscapes of purity and spiritual rebirth. "In California," wrote British journalist Michael Davie, "the European traveler cannot fail to be struck by the absence of the political, social, and religious arrangements that the rest of America derived from Europe. Institutions that have grown up elsewhere in the United States have here scarcely taken hold, because the population has grown so fast." But whereas San Francisco, a tuxedo town, retained a social structure that recalled Europe and the East, it was Los Angeles, to borrow a line from Walt Whitman, that offered "the new society at last, proportionate to Nature." Los Angeles was young. It was promise. With their long hair and shaggy beards, the youth of L.A. looked like runaways—and indeed some were, come south from Haight-Ashbury or West from the old East to the new Sunset Strip for a taste of the counterculture they manufactured here. Old-timers remembering the street outside of the old Ciro's, Mocambo, and Crescendo (rechristened the Trip) crowd with Rolls-Royces and Aston Martins, now watched the motorcycles rev by the Whisky a Go Go, one after the next. "You had Paris in the 20s, Hollywood in the 60s," said record producer Kim Fowley. "And you wanted to get there because those places had hope. If you could get the bus ticket to get to paradise, even if you were a waiter, at least you were there." L.A.'s music scene, Fowley added, was so hungry for talent that "anybody who had charisma or a line of bullshit could walk into any record label and get a deal—maybe just one record, but that's how it worked." Hence the gold, the shine on bearded faces. The music industry, a terminal oasis of quality in an increasingly debauched society, drew the nation's itinerant dreamers, some enlightened, some lost, to the desert campgrounds, beaches, and secluded canyons above Sunset, where—removed from the rhythms of urban life—they could live differently and remake America as one new community, one new family, at a time. To their parents—the squares and nine-to-fivers back East—these "families" looked more than a little like cults, but what is a family if not its own love cult sharing its own dream?

Since the good life had always been L.A.'s message to the world, the city was ready-made for flower children; it was the perfect convergence of place and time. "People felt free," Polanski said. No one in L.A., it was said, locked their doors. "[Polanski] and Sharon Tate," said filmmaker Paul Mazursky, "were like a king and queen. He was a genius and she was this stunningly gorgeous hippie. They were John and Yoko in Hollywood. They were making art and making love. They were what L.A. at that time was all about."

Still, there was the old twinge, memories. There was Polanski's father, weeping on Podgórze Bridge: "Your mother. . . ." There was, later, the night his father woke him before dawn with news of another raid. As ever, Polanski slipped through his hole in the barbed wire and made for his hiding place in the Wilks family home. But that day, their door was locked. He ran back to rejoin his father, and as he approached the bridge, he saw two rows of ghetto prisoners being marched away by armed guards. Among them was Polanski's father. The boy ran to him, flailing desperately for his attention. The father would not acknowledge his son so the boy flailed harder. "Shove off," his father whispered—*get away before they see you*-as he was marched away. There was nothing Roman could do. He only stood there, watching his father recede, dwindle in the distance, and disappear.

Roman didn't see his father again till the war was over.

Soon thereafter, he learned what had happened to his mother: She was killed at Auschwitz.

The old twinge, Pawel, Sharon: "I've always been very afraid of any ties." Polanski said, "I felt that any type of family tie, anything that means nest, ends in tragedy."

Sharon held his fear. She understood. "Being around me," he said, "she still made me feel absolutely free, and she made it clear that she was not going to engulf me." There was the old discussion, never totally resolved, about the value and nature of fidelity, of modern men and women, Polanski's untethered definition of love, and how Sharon, a "puritanical" American, might come around to his "European" view of sex. Polanski was persuasive, a flash dancer with words and philosophical rationalizations. But she held on, or tried to. "Sharon wasn't a dummy," their friend Victor Lownes said, "but she wasn't an intellectual giant either. She was sweet and kind almost to a fault, loved everybody . . . and she didn't argue with Roman. He was rather dictatorial with her, but that suited her anyway." Polanski's thinking was clear: He said she was hung up on fidelity.

Finally Sharon relented. She told Polanski she didn't want to change him, she loved him, she loved all of him, and cultivated a "sophisticated" pose to cradle her discomfort. "It's that European attitude, you know, where it's natural and normal for the man to have the drive to want to go out and see another girl," she said, "even after he's married." But it hurt, Sharon cried to Elke Sommer, her costar on

The Wrecking Crew. "She was unhappy," Sommer said. "But she saw no way out. She didn't know what to do." She wanted to have a child.

Polanski proposed a few days shy of Sharon's twenty-fifth birthday. On January 20, 1968, they were married, she in a taffeta mini-dress, he in a green Edwardian jacket. "Just about the only really happy married couple I knew in Hollywood," Robert Evans said, "were Roman Polanski and Sharon Tate." It was true. There was no more room for happiness. Polanski had married, it seemed to him, more than the love of his life, but the love *in* his life, the glory of Hollywood, their circle of friends, the euphoric spirit of an entire age and country. "They were the happiest years of my life," Polanski said, "just as they were for anyone who was lucky enough to have been caught up in it all."

In June *Rosemary's Baby* opened to tremendous box office. The victory belonged to Polanski and Evans; apart, they had had successes, but together, in *Rosemary's Baby,* they had a Hollywood triumph, their first. It was a victory sweetened by the relative risks of the production—soap-opera source material; Mia Farrow, in her first starring role; a director running over budget—granting them hard-won assurance that *Rosemary's Baby* was no fluke but the fruit of their vision, mutual trust, talent, and tenacity. *They* had done it.

Hot off a hit, Polanski left the elephantine William Morris Agency for Ziegler-Ross, joining their small but high-end roster of Hollywood's literary beau monde, a client list that included writers Robert Towne, Joan Didion, Irving and Harriet Ravetch, and William Goldman, for whom Evarts Ziegler negotiated a four-hundred-thousand-dollar fee—an enormous salary for a screenwriter—for his script *Butch Cassidy and the Sundance Kid.* Ziegler himself—an elegant, Princeton-educated WASP—was renowned for his superlative good taste (Z-R represented the estates of Fitzgerald, Faulkner, and Steinbeck); he drove a white Cadillac with red leather seats and enjoyed his two-martini lunch at the Polo Lounge every day; his office, calm, unostentatious, peopled with readers and intellectuals, was more like a New York publishing house than an L.A. agency, and centrally located at 9255 Sunset Boulevard, between Beverly Hills and West Hollywood, perfectly positioned between the old and the new. "It was a comfortable place to be because these were sophisticated New York guys," said Marcia Nasatir, who joined the agency in 1969. "The tone was that we all knew the queen; we were like British upper-class people."

In late-sixties Hollywood the Ziegler-Ross Agency may have been atypically refined, but it did not corner the market on intimacy. Before the age of CAA, which would excel at servicing not the discreet needs of its clients but the omnivorous bottom line of the corporation, boutique talent agencies like Ziegler-Ross proliferated in the movie business, fostering personal relationships and personal projects, many of them tough sells, like Z-R's *They Shoot Horses, Don't They?* a pitch-black night-of-the-locust drama that eventually won Oscar nominations for director Sydney Pollack and writer James Poe, clients both.

Polanski's agent at Ziegler was Bill Tennant. "Everyone on his list seemed to be 'happening,'" wrote Peter Bart, "and Tennant seemed the fulcrum." With its six or seven agents hand selected for their intelligence, Ziegler-Ross, between phone calls, nurtured a salon environment wholly unthinkable at William Morris or MCA. "Clients would just come by the office," said Nasatir. "Hollywood was like a small town then."

Sharon got pregnant. "Bob," she cooed to Robert Evans, "the baby's kicking!"

"How does it feel?"

"It's the best feeling in the world."

"I'll tell Roman."

"While you're at it, tell him he'd better be home for his birthday. Remember, it's the eighteenth."

"He'll be here, baby."

Polanski was in London with Richard Sylbert preparing their next film, *Day of the Dolphin*, for Sharon and Jack Nicholson, who had only months earlier made a big noise in *Easy Rider*. Enveloped in love, friends, and film, Polanski tried to accept his incredible good fortune. "I know that on one hand success gives you some kind of satisfaction but it doesn't give you the bliss," he reflected. "On the other hand I know that love gives you the happiness but I know that it ends." In his mind there was always the ghetto, and the still present starved and depleted position utterly hostile to new life. "To get a woman pregnant was a catastrophe [during the war] at [that] time," he said, "and that's how I grew up." But a stronger part of Polanski intervened, reminding him that it was safe now, that everyone around him, in America, was having children, "that I can have a child and we can have a normal life."

Sharon and Polanski worked up "an astronomical phone bill," he said, discussing the pregnancy, the baby books she was reading, how she wanted a natural childbirth, how Polanski, when he came back to Los Angeles, would be going with her to Lamaze class. She stopped smoking grass, she said, quit wine, and was drinking whole milk. He wanted a girl; she was convinced it would be a boy. They agreed the baby would be born in the United States.

"When are you coming home?"

"Soon," he would say. "Soon."

Grocery shopping on Cañon Drive in Beverly Hills, Sharon ran into Julie Payne, new girlfriend of the screenwriter Robert Towne. They hadn't seen each other for a few years, since they were neighbors up Benedict Canyon on Yoakum Drive. Roman was coming back in a few days, Sharon told Julie, and they were house shopping.

Payne, a native Angeleno and first-rate house person, had friends who were selling their place up Benedict, not far from Yoakum. It had a fantastic screening setup, an outdoor projector that threw light over the pool against a large wall. Roman would love that. "I know a house that's going on the market," Payne told Sharon. "It's a Byrd house"—so called because of the architect Robert Byrd—"It's perfect. You could see it next week?"

"Great!"

"Come up for dinner soon?"

Sharon would come for dinner ("She weighed herself in the bathroom," Payne said, "bra and panties and eight months pregnant") but would pass on the Byrd streets for a high-up and spacious Benedict Canyon property very close to Towne's home on Hutton Drive. The day she met realtor Elaine Young "Sharon wore no makeup and was wearing jeans and she was the most beautiful woman I have ever seen. She was so excited and fell in love with the house." It was her dream house, she confessed to Young, as they ambled the grounds, the garden, the astonishing city view below. Roman, Sharon knew, would flip for the view; he loved the burnt rainbow of Los Angeles at dusk, its million lights twinkling like stars on earth. Even Paris, city of his birth, couldn't argue with Los Angeles's great ocean of night light, visible, in its tranquil entirety, from the yawning cliffsedge lawn of 10050 Cielo Drive.

Sharon took the house and, as was her custom, opened its doors to everyone. "It was the crowd from the Daisy," Warren Beatty said. All were welcome to stay the night, or even the week.

"When are you coming home?"

"Soon," Roman would say. "Soon."

She went to visit him in London. There was a strangeness.

Though her pregnancy only increased his devotion, Polanski found himself unable to make love to Sharon, an equivocation she took for withdrawal, the sure sign, she thought, of infidelity. Of course, she knew Roman had had other women. That had been their agreement. Ashamed of his shortcomings, Polanski assured Sharon she was as beautiful as ever, and he loved her only more for carrying their child. But she worried the change foretold inevitable changes ahead. She knew there was a threshold in every long love where romance cedes to reality, and certain passions, once abundant, begin to appear for the last time. A day would come. The garden gate would lock behind them, and suddenly they would be different forever. Or were they already?

On the day she was to return to America, aboard the *QE2*, Polanski drove her to the dock at Southampton, and they climbed aboard the ship hand in hand, exploring its nooks and cabins like excited children, the way they had their house on the Santa Monica beach, haunted all the while by the coming good-bye. Sharon couldn't bear it.

"Okay, go now," she said.

He held and kissed her and thought, for reasons he couldn't explain, that he would never see her again.

They continued to speak on the phone every day.

Polanski, caught up in script problems, further postponed his return to Los Angeles, and Sharon grew impatient: He was missing it, the crucial final stretch of the pregnancy. Suddenly the baby was due in two weeks. Couldn't he finish the script at home in Los Angeles? Would he at least be home for his birthday? Bitterness edged into her voice and they were strange again. The double intrusion of a Southern California heat wave and ill-timed houseguests, Roman's friend Wojciech Frykowski and his girlfriend, Abigail Folger, only increased her irritation. When was he coming home? She couldn't ask them to leave, she said, they were her friends. . . .

"That's it," Polanski told her. "I'm coming. I'll finish the script over there. I'll leave tomorrow."

But it didn't work out that way; it couldn't. Polanski still needed a U.S. visa, and the consulate was closed on Saturdays.

That day, Saturday, August 9, 1969, they spoke again.

She told him she and Wojciech and Abigail had found a kitten in the hills and were feeding it with an eyedropper. They were keeping it in the bathtub.

"I'm coming Monday," Polanski said, "whether I'm through with the script or not."

That night Polanski and his friends Andy Braunsberg and Michael Brown were discussing the script. A whiz with story and a first-rate screenwriter, Polanski was pacing the room in thought, gesticulating his ideas into a potential scene when the phone rang. Braunsberg reached for it.

"Hello?" Braunsberg could hear something was wrong. "What is it?" Suddenly overcome, he passed the phone to Polanski.

"What is it?" Polanski lowered himself into a chair.

"Roman." It was Bill Tennant, his agent. "There was a disaster in the house."

"Which house?"

"Your house."

Had the hillside collapsed?

Roman held the phone to his ear. "Sharon is dead," Tennant said. "And Wojtek and Jay and Abigail."

"No . . . ," he said. "No, no, no. . . ."

A landslide. It was a landslide. They had been crushed.

"How?"

"I don't know," returned Tennant. "I don't know, . . ."

When they cleared the rubble, Sharon would be rescued.

"This is insane . . . ," Polanski pleaded. "This is insane. . . ." He kept saying it.

Finally Tennant said, "Roman, they were murdered."

"Shove off," his father had said. "Shove off." The phone slipped from Polanski's hand. He was crying, banging his head against the wall. He did not understand. They had just spoken. He heard the words, but he did not understand because the words were not true. They had just spoken. She found a cat.

Joan Didion and her brother-in-law, Dominick Dunne, were poolside, sitting out the Southern California heat wave at Dunne's soon-to-be-ex wife's when the call came—from Natalie Wood. She was petrified. Sharon Tate and Jay Sebring and their friends had been murdered, *viciously* murdered, at the house on Cielo Drive. Details were scant but more calls came: the reports were grotesque, confusing and contradictory, but soon the facts emerged: One body was found outside the Cielo Drive house, stabbed dozens of times; another, a woman, was stabbed to death in her nightgown; in the living room Sharon's pregnant body, caked in blood, was found in the fetal position, a nylon rope tied twice around her neck and thrown over a rafter. The other end of the rope was tied to a man's neck a few feet away; a bloody towel covered his face. Another body—that of a young man—was found shot to death in a car. There were no motives, no suspects.

The bizarre depravity of the crime scene, the number of victims, the pedigrees of the dead—a movie star, a celebrity stylist, an heiress—would make the Cielo Drive slayings, next to the Kennedy assassination, the most publicized murder case in history. The apparent meaninglessness of the massacre was intolerable to logical minds; no one, not least the detectives, knew what to think about the little they knew. To fill in the gaps, crackpot theories, perpetuated by a grasping press, ruled all conversation. These were sex crimes, gossip said; these were drug crimes; these were Hollywood killings; the killers were Klansmen, satanists; Polanski, conveniently out of town, was the evil mastermind; it was a ritual slaying, a *Rosemary's Baby* murder. Polanski even *looked* evil. Didn't he? Well, he certainly *knew* evil. Only a man capable of such a sinister film—a film Robert Windeler in the *New York Times* wrote was "conceived by the devil himself"—could commit such an inconceivably psychopathic act. And Polanski had survived the Nazis. That *had* to mean something. Didn't it? He was such a party animal, too; he *must* know those sorts of people, the type who stalk the Whisky a Go Go at two in the morning looking for a ride or a toke or a girl. Personal grudges on the grand scale—against hippies, against liberals and conservatives, against the young, against the rich and beautiful, against Hollywood, against the 1960s—legitimized all hypotheses. "The murders seemed the consequence of everything all of us had done," wrote Dore Schary's daughter, Hollywood scion Jill Robinson: "We had gone too far, done all of the things our parents warned against—and more." The whole of Los Angeles was implicated.

The following evening, August 10, 1969, Leno and Rosemary LaBianca were found murdered, stabbed to death, in their home in Los Feliz. The word "War" was carved into his stomach. She had been gagged with a lamp cord and stabbed forty-one times. On the walls, "Death to pigs" and "Rise" were written in blood. "Helter Skelter," in blood, dripped down the refrigerator door.

Los Angeles panicked. "Everybody was thinking, 'we're next,'" Andy Braunsberg said. "We were all running around with guns in our purses," said Michelle Phillips of The Mamas and the Papas, a friend of Roman and Sharon's. "We all suspected each other." The police, with no leads, suspected everyone. They even targeted Phillips's husband John, whose "outward calm," Polanski would write, "concealed a capacity for deep, burning anger." They came to her house, asking, "Would your husband have any reason to have any animosity toward anyone in that house?" Marcia Nasatir's phone at Ziegler-Ross rang around the clock with phony well-wishers digging for dirt. "I kept saying to these people, 'She was a *mother*,'" Nasatir said. "'She was eight months *pregnant*.'" Dominick Dunne sent his children to his mother-in-law's in San Diego. Sharon's sister, Debra Ann, said, "Everybody was off frantically trying to make some kind of sense of this horrific tale that was forced upon us. But there was no sense to be found."

Joan Didion, though horrified, was not surprised. No one, she would think, was *that* surprised. After all, this was Los Angeles: "This mystical flirtation with the idea of 'sin'—this sense that it was possible to go 'too far,' and that many people were doing it—was very much with us in Los Angeles in 1968 and 1969. A demented and seductive vortical tension was building in the community. The jitters were setting in." She kept a record of license plate numbers in her dressing-room drawer.

Hotels wouldn't take Polanski. As soon as he landed, Robert Evans moved him into a dressing room at Paramount. A guard held watch. A doctor kept him sedated. Most of his meals, he ate with Evans.

Friends surrounded him. Sylbert, Beatty, Evans. Work, work, everyone said. That's the best medicine. Work.

"I'm sure everybody tells you to work," Stanley Kubrick said to Polanski by phone.

"That's right."

"I know you can't work."

He met with a psychiatrist. It would take Polanski at least four years, he was told, to recover.

He went to the wake Warren Beatty held at the top of the Beverly Wilshire Hotel.

He went to Sharon's funeral. He watched her coffin, dazed.

He made a decision. He would stay in L.A. If he found the murderer himself, Polanski reasoned, it would ease his grief.

He was brought in for questioning. Barely lucid, he murmured: "The whole crime seems so illogical to me. I'm looking for something which doesn't fit your habitual standard in which you are used to working as the police. I would look for something much more far out and that's what I'm going to do. I'm devoted now to this and I'm going to do it. Maybe it was somebody who hated me. It's difficult for me to imagine that somebody hated me to this point."

He offered a reward for any information leading to the arrest of the killers.

He went to Cielo Drive, determined to find something, anything, that made sense. His mind was fogged in grief, but he would force himself to think.

As he approached the house, he noticed a rail broken off the fence. The dead boy in the car—maybe he broke it trying to get away.

He walked through his front yard, past the wishing well, the flowerbeds, a bloodied blue bedsheet left under a pine tree.

He walked to the swimming pool, covered in brown leaves. Sharon's inflatable swimming tube.

He walked to the front porch. "PIG" in brown blood on the door.

Living room. On the floor, two smears of blood where Sharon and Jay were found. Beside them, a candle stub, a bedroom slipper, a book on natural childbirth.

Master bedroom. Two big pillows across the bed. She always kept them that way, to hold on to when he was gone.

Blood on the door leading to the pool. She was awakened by the screams, he reasoned, got up, and went to the living room, where she was attacked before running back to the door to the pool. They must have dragged her back. . . .

He spoke slowly. "There is something here. I can feel it. Something the police missed. I must find the thread."

Outside again, he found a broken lantern in a flowerbed. He recognized it. The lantern. It meant something. What did it mean? It should be hanging on a nail on the front door. It must have fallen off. Or was it taken off?

He looked up to the door, to the nail. He looked hard. Then he picked up the lantern and stared at it for some time, waiting for it to answer. Then he dropped it back into the flowers. It wasn't a clue.

In the master bedroom, he wept.

The next day, August 18, was his birthday. Newspapers and magazines, even the most reputable, ran lies: Sadomasochistic drug orgies, "a scene," *Time* said, "as grisly as anything depicted in Polanski's film explorations of the dark and melancholy corners of the human character."

The day after, he appeared before the press at the Beverly Wilshire Hotel. "Excuse me," Polanski sobbed. "This is difficult for me. The last two months of my life were the happiest. I turned thirty-six yesterday and my birthday present was this treatment of me by the press. It isn't true, these things they say. These were selfish newsmen who said horrible things about my wife. You all know she was one of the most beautiful women in the world, but what few of you don't know is how good she was. She couldn't refuse any friendship."

He moved into Dick Sylbert's rickety beach house overlooking the water on Old Malibu Road, secluded, but not far from the Malibu Colony, its gaggle of concerned and suspicious neighbors. Polanski stayed under Sylbert's care for six months.

As he had with the Wilkses, he hid.

What little energy he could muster, he devoted to the case. The police, who kept in constant contact with him, maintained that the killer or killers were out for personal revenge, and advised Polanski to keep a sharp eye on anyone he knew, or had ever known. "We sat around," Sylbert said, "thinking anybody could have done it 'cause we had no idea . . . So it was, 'Hey, I wonder which one of our friends did it?'" On the theory that Polanski's friends would be more vulnerable with Polanski than the police, he was advised to go under cover as himself, to act as "some kind of amateur sleuth." Polanski, a gifted actor, assumed the part without hesitation.

It couldn't be Sylbert. Sylbert was innocent. He was with Polanski in London.

One clue—a pair of horn-rimmed glasses found by the police at the scene—persisted, unaccounted for. With caution, lest his intentions be discovered, Polanski charged himself with matching the prescription of the glasses in question to those of his friends. He wouldn't let on, even to Sylbert, his reasons for examining their dinner guests' frames, or engaging pals in conversation about their eyesight; it was too dangerous.

Sylbert unwittingly provided a lineup. "The house was always full of interesting people," said Susanna Moore. "Warren, Anthea, Joan Didion, and [Didion's husband] John Dunne, who had just moved up the road." The devastation Polanski showed Sylbert he hid, in public, behind bravado. At dinners he entertained arduously. He soliloquied. He sprayed the air with outsize moods and gestures, one minute laughing, too hard, the next bursting with unchecked rage. He pounded the table, drunkenly slapped backs, rudely and brilliantly forced his voice into conversation. "Roman," Moore said, "was not what you would call, by most standards, mature. He was so egocentric and so needy and so restless. He was manic, jumpy, talkative, dominating. Like an imp. He was often funny, but he would go on too long, and it would get boring. He would interrupt. He needed to be the center of attention. His clowning was a sign of insecurity and vulnerability. He was devastated by Sharon's murder."

"I think I was probably a better human being before [the murders]," he said. "It's difficult to define, but I think I was more gentle with people before."

He had sex. He partied.

Because he seemed to be singled out by fate, the public suspected and feared him, and because, in the midst of death, he tried to enjoy life, they hated him. There was a way, they said, to suffer, to grieve properly. This wasn't it. Where was his heart?

The girls were young, too young, but he didn't see any problem. He didn't hide it. "I like young women," he would say to the press.

He didn't think. He ran.

"Shove off."

"What happened to me diminished my contact, my rapport with people," he said. "It reduced me."

Alone with Sylbert, he cried.

The randomness of the tragedy reinforced Polanski's belief in the chaotic absurd, that "our destinies are the result of apparently meaningless coincidences." "After all," he said, "even sitting here at some stage may be dangerous." There was no reason for the murders, for his mother's murder, for his unborn son's murder, no reason why he, Roman Polanski, should be the recipient of so much misfortune. It would be frankly immoral to draw lessons from it, for to organize it was, in some way, to justify it. "Unfortunately," he said, "there is no lesson to be taken. There is just nothing. It's absolutely senseless, stupid, cruel and insane. I'm not sure it's even worth talking about. Sharon and the others are dead. I can't restore what was." Meaning was for art. That's what art *was for*. The rest was . . . *what*?

By night he ran amok; by day he fixated on the horn-rimmed glasses. Bruce Lee, formerly Polanski's martial arts instructor, and now his friend, had casually mentioned he had lost his glasses. Could it be? Laying a trap, Polanski suggested they stop by the optician's for a new pair. But there he discovered Lee's prescription didn't match that of the glasses found at the crime scene. Lee was innocent, mercifully. But what now? Who? Plunged back into chaos, Polanski reevaluated his methodology. He realized leading suspects to the optician was a clumsy and impractical tactic, and over time, would arouse the suspicions of the shop people. Instead, he bought himself a pocket-size Vigor lens measure gauge and carried it with him everywhere. Now, in case he should encounter anyone else who had lost their glasses, he would examine them himself, stealthily and undercover.

He bought a pin mike, a transmitter, a tape-recorder, and bugs. He would place them in his friends' homes.

Paranoia was a kind of obsessive perfectionism; the microscope went under the microscope. There was the possibility that the killer, after the murders, would have left bloodstains—surely cleaned, but still detectible—in his or her car. Polanski's attention to detail: Equipped with testing chemicals and Q-tips, he sneaked into friends' garages, swabbing inside their Chevrolets and Porsches, but quickly, before he could be found out. He went to work on John Phillips's Jaguar, finding nothing of relevance—nothing, that is, save for a machete stashed in the trunk, but there was nothing linking such a weapon to the murders. Onward, he applied his Q-tips to Phillips's Rolls-Royce convertible, swabbing the brakes, seats, and steering wheel. He found Phillips's diary. Inspecting the handwriting, he noted a resemblance to the blood lettering of "PIG" written on the front door. Or was he imagining the resemblance? Would discovering it was his friend who had murdered his wife ease his suffering? He pinched the diary and photocopied a sample he sent off to a handwriting expert in New York, but the results came back negative. Was that a relief?

Had he missed something?

The mystery of loss, the unceasing consequence analysis of history. Did what happened have to happen? Rational deduction was leading him nowhere, so Polanski pressed his mind to think irrationally. He tried to think sideways. To think backwards. Would they kill him next? What-ifs lured him through endless nightmare scenarios, conspiracy theories, false hopes, and he lost, slowly, incrementally, bits of his mind. "All of a sudden," he said, "you realize that the remote light at the end of the tunnel is the train going in the opposite direction." He melted. "Shove off."

His mother, her lacquered hair and cherry lips, the songs she used to sing to him. She was pregnant when they came for her.

PART TWO

Eucalyptus

photos tk

1

Julie Payne always had stories. She soaked up words, books, facts from newspapers, pictures in magazines. She soaked up memories. When prompted, complete family histories, the contents of civic archives, nuanced accountings of entire events, the provenance of this or that vintage fabric or lampshade, rose from her mind's reservoirs in rich and instantaneous detail. Where others saw trivia, she saw pieces. Everything begins somewhere; Julie Payne asked why. Was there a beginning before it began? She understood context, that every context had a context, and that no truth—if such a concept even existed—could ever be grasped in isolation.

Mother was actress Anne Shirley, who had, after retiring from movies at twenty-six, retired to her bedroom for good. Stepfather was Shirley's third husband, screenwriter Charlie Lederer. Mother and daughter had moved into Lederer's home on Bedford Drive in 1950, where Julie, at ten years old, was sent up to the attic playrooms.

"These are yours," her mother said, indicating, Julie thought, the toys left on the attic floor.

Julie played. "I was a dreamer," she said. "I had to be." In the attic, she played with wooden blocks and a large renaissance style Punch and Judy Show, "The Christoper Welles Puppet Theater" painted over the proscenium, a hand-me-down from uncle Orson to his friend Charlie.

Downstairs, the grownup house was unadulterated Beverly Hills

Tudor, wrapped in smooth oak wainscoting, rose print linen drapes around diamond shaped windows, cherry red carpeting, ceiling friezes, and closed doors. Charlie's closed office door was right off the foyer, by the closed front door. As a girl, Julie was told to tiptoe by so as not to disturb him. She obeyed. "We all did," she said. "It was the fifties."

When she was young, she tiptoed past, but as she got older, she tiptoed up—and pressed an ear to the door.

"Marion . . . My poor . . . darling Marion . . ."

These were pieces of a story, she realized. Marion was Marion Davies, Charlie's beloved aunt, the perfect love of a powerful man named William Randolph Hearst. Julie knew better than to ask questions, so she would find more pieces herself. She found pictures of a blue-eyed angel—paintings and scrapbook photographs of Marion—"a real fairy princess come to life," she would say, "and from what I overheard I made up stories about her and her king who lived in a castle on a hill and who protected her."

Julie's father, actor John Payne, she saw on weekends. ,

Charlie, when he was writing, popped prescription methedrine and Demerol paid for with a chocolate Bentley convertible he gifted to his doctor. As Marion deteriorated, dying of a cancerous tumor on her jawbone, his addiction worsened. Julie, still too young to understand the wherefores of either condition, would remember Marion's last appearance on Bedford Drive and the mask she used to cover the lower part of her face.

"Why is Miss Davies wearing a mask?" Julie asked her mother.

She did not answer.

"No one in my family told the truth," Payne would explain. "Not about death."

Isolation made her a detective.

There were books. She could look in books. She started with fairy tales and the stories sent to her from her godmother, Phyllis Cerf, Mrs. Random House (Bennett Cerf, the publisher, was her husband)

and head of its children's department. Then came *The Yearling, Black Beauty*, Laura Ingalls Wilder. Then, a girl of ten at her stepfather's prodigious bookcase, she discovered the weird, Heinlein, Saki. Her pastoral period ended. Suddenly she grew up. She read of murders terrible and mundane, men who murdered their children, children who murdered their mothers, women who murdered their men. While the rest of Beverly Hills went to bed early, Julie stayed up with *Los Angeles Murders*, and read of Madalynne Obenchain, who, with one lover, murdered five others, of Winnie Ruth Judd, who locked her bodies in luggage, and of Dotty Wallburger—her favorite—who hid her boyfriend in an attic for eleven years. "Reading this book," she said, "left me with some of these murders in my mind all my life." She was still too young to know that murders were her metaphors, salacious replays of the wrongs that had already been done her. But by who? When?

The present was the crime. The past was the clue.

Julie tried to understand. Her girlfriends on Crescent and Roxbury and Beverly Drive lived differently; they had dinner with their families. She had been there; she had seen it; they all sat at the table together. The mothers and fathers went to their children's school plays. Julie's mother never went to one of her plays. The pieces, how did they go together?

"Why don't we live like other people do?" Julie asked her mother.

"Oh," her mother said to her needlepoint, "everyone's house is like this."

"My friends don't live like this."

"You think *we're* crazy?" She pointed to the house across the street, where Lana Turner's daughter murdered Johnny Stompanato. "Do you?"

Julie ate dinner alone.

When Julie noticed, in her own eye, a blemish, a dark spot in the iris, she turned to her mother.

"That?" her mother scoffed. "That's just a beauty mark."

There were more maids than there were people living in the house. There was one maid for ironing alone.

There were no family photos on the shelves. Her mother kept scrapbooks, but she filled them only with pictures of her famous friends—Frank Sinatra, Lauren Bacall, Bogie, Judy Garland. "I never left Beverly Hills," Payne said. "I thought the poor people lived south of Santa Monica Boulevard." Weekdays she rode her bike to school ("People didn't drive kids in those days"). On Saturdays she went to the movies. At the Beverly Hills Hotel she was enrolled in cotillion with Maureen Reagan and Lynne Wasserman, daughter of Lew. Her mother, "a delicate person," wouldn't take Julie shopping, so she enlisted her friends' mothers to go with her. It was clear to Julie that they disdained Hollywood.

"What do your parents . . . *do*?" they would ask knowingly.

"Movies."

"Movies?"—a snicker—"Julie, movies aren't a *business*."

In those days, when movie people and their product were valued as morally and fiscally dubious, Los Angeles was two towns, one for the normal people, one for Hollywood. In Beverly Hills, far west of business life downtown, Hollywood tried to set itself apart from the older-money holdouts of Hancock Park and Pasadena, but the city kept growing west, toward the ocean, and a certain degree of overlap west of Doheny, though irksome, was unavoidable. The camps sidestepped each other around Beverly Hills. Movie people ate at Chasen's and Romanoff's; normals ate everywhere else.

After school, Payne bicycled home to mix drinks for Charlie and friends like Billy Wilder (martini) and powerful entertainment lawyer Greg Bautzer (Wild Turkey on the rocks). They came to the English Tudor house at 727 Bedford Drive every day at four to play cards, gin or bridge, and they didn't play for money; they played for time (Bautzer bet with legal counsel, Wilder with script notes). When Charlie's great friend and collaborator, Ben Hecht, joined the game, Charlie won two additional endings to his script for *Mutiny on the Bounty*, one from Ben and one from Billy.

The game ended around eight, and Charlie, likely the highest-paid script doctor in Hollywood, and Ben Hecht, Hollywood's most respected screenwriter, would sit around the oak-paneled living room drinking, dreaming up perfect murders.

"The Oval Office. A body in the Oval Office."

"In *Congress*."

"*Hanging* in Congress."

"A woman's body."

Their most perfect: in *Kiss of Death*, pushing an old woman down the stairs.

Hecht and Lederer had written *His Girl Friday* together. Between the two of them they had more than two hundred writing credits, and countless uncredited rewrites. But in a town famous for its disaffected writers, both homegrown and Eastern imported, Hecht and Lederer were peaches and cream about their business. Sure, there were the usual agonies—the philistines, the studio politics. But look around: They lived like kings in paradise. "They never had this 'poor-little-me-screenwriter' attitude," Payne said. "Their attitude was, first there was the word, and if you don't come to us, then you're not going to have anything."

She grew up, fell into acting, and appeared here and there in movies. She dated glamorously, married and divorced actor Skip Ward, and opened Haystack, a needlepoint shop in Beverly Hills, with Lynne Wasserman. By 1969 Payne was a fixture at the Daisy, where she ran into Warren Beatty and his friend Robert Towne, roundly regarded the most promising young screenwriter in Hollywood. "I knew him from around town," she said. He had written for Roger Corman and here and there for television, but the film that made his reputation was a rewrite of a script by Robert Benton and David Newman on which he received the mysterious and tantalizing credit

"Special Consultant." The film was *Bonnie and Clyde*. Though few at that time were sure what, exactly, Towne's contribution to the script had been, and none of his previous credits were distinguished enough to color him brilliant, *Bonnie and Clyde* was such a watershed moment that, Towne's name, overnight, shot to the top of everyone's list. He was, insiders whispered, *Bonnie and Clyde*'s secret weapon, a miraculous Mr. Fixit. What he fixed or how almost didn't matter; the mystery only advanced Towne's professional standing. He was in demand.

In March 1969, when Towne and Payne danced at the Daisy, he was tall and handsome, with tempting brown eyes and a beard, and spoke slowly, thoughtfully, forever leaning into his deep leather chair, or seeming to, like a rabbi toying with a parable. He took the time to think: Thoughts left his mouth fully formed. Discoursing on subjects Sophoclean or cinematic, cigar smoke drawing curlicues around his eyes, he was perhaps the only screenwriter in history ever to look relaxed, not to mention successful, respected. More than that, Towne looked brisk and healthy, like the native Californian (swimmer, tennis player) he was. He liked the sun. He wrote at night. In fronds of moonlight, when the day ended and the stories set in, Towne was given to pangs of gentle disenchantment, the soft underside, common to artists, of a life lived in the mind. He was a romantic.

Towne and Payne lived in Towne's rumpled house atop a tiny hill at the end of Hutton Drive in the mountains above Benedict Canyon. The property, with its thirty thousand square feet of live oak, dead oak, foxtails, and weeds, had been completely neglected for the year and a half Towne was away writing *Villa Rides* in England and Spain, and the interior of the house wasn't much better. "It looked like Miss Havisham's," Payne said. But the terrain still smelled of virgin L.A., and, Southern Californians both, they lived in harmony with the dirt roads and coyote calls and fell in love with the sanctuary of birds and brush that surfaced from their piece of earth, and in love with each other. Julie Payne said: "I understood the care and feeding of screenwriters."

He was working on a script, *Shampoo*, with Warren Beatty.

Several months after Payne moved in, Towne, complaining of allergies, went to bed for a month. "My head," he would groan. "My eyes." The symptoms and allergies kept changing, Payne came to see, and so did the doctors and the prescriptions. But Towne made progress, slowly—always slowly—on his work. When he worked, he largely kept to a routine, beginning with breakfast at nine. He would write—in a small second bedroom with three windows and a door to the open hillside—till lunchtime, play tennis for an hour at the Beverly Hills Hotel just down the street or the Beverly Hills Tennis Club, then he would return to the office on Hutton Drive and work until dinner and sometimes after.

They were good days, green and gold. Days of love and good work. Days of dreams.

Los Angeles, 1969.

Payne and Towne were having dinner with Buck Henry the night after the murders. The mystery altogether possessed the two writers. Into the night they pontificated on likely suspects, possible motives, rearranging the jigsaw of fact and rumor to no results the way Julie remembered Charlie and Ben Hecht doing, but this time not for a script. When Julie woke up on the couch, Towne and Henry were still at a loss. The whole city was.

"Nobody knew what was happening," she said. "We were terrified. Nothing like this had ever happened in Beverly Hills before." Flailing and desperate for leads, the police started calling Payne every week. They knew—maybe, she thought, Warren told them—that she had had dinner with Sharon. "They were so out of it," Payne said, totally unprepared to handle a murder investigation of this magnitude. She had already learned the LAPD couldn't be counted on. In July a colleague of Payne's was raped in Laurel Canyon. Payne reported the name of the rapist to the Sheriff's Department. The police did nothing. *Plus ça change*: after the murders the police didn't know where to begin. They hardly knew what questions to ask. To Payne and they confessed they didn't know how to get in touch with anyone in Hollywood. "They're with the guilds!" Payne admonished them on the phone. "Just call the *guilds!*"

Beatty, Towne's buddy since *Bonnie and Clyde*, was spinning, "completely turned inside out," Payne said, "trying to figure out what the hell was going on, trying to help Roman any way he could." Ever the friend, Beatty threw Polanski a birthday party upstairs at the Aware Inn, and sat Payne and Towne with Polanski and Bill Tennant and his wife. Two police officers sat beside Polanski. "Roman was trying so hard to talk," Payne remembered, "but he was in some kind of trauma." Bill Tennant, who had identified the bodies, got drunk and sobbed through the party.

The night after the murders Towne and Payne fled the house in Benedict Canyon for her former place, the Villa d'Este, a cluster of courtyard apartments in West Hollywood, where they would hide, they decided, until the case was solved. They were terrified.

"Before Sharon Tate's murder," wrote author Jeff Guinn, "Beverly Hills sporting goods stores sold only a few handguns a day. In the two days since her death, one store sold two hundred. Guard dogs were previously for sale for $200; now the price jumped to $1,500." Murder, of course, was not new to Los Angeles, but the apparent randomness of the slaughters defied explanation and halted the serene illusion of invulnerability. Overworked locksmiths couldn't handle the incoming calls. Reckless youth stayed home. Hitchhiking, once a secure means of transport, and, in the context of the era, a gesture of peace and good faith, ended abruptly. After the murders Sharmagne Leland-St. John, a friend of Roman and Sharon's, would think twice before accepting an invitation, before going out alone, or leaving the house at all. "We lost trust," she said. "We lost our naïveté. We grew up. We saw there was evil out there and there were evil people."

"It was the ending," Towne would say. "There were so many, but that was the end of the Sixties. The door closed, the curtain dropped, and nothing and no one was ever the same."

Towne would meet with Warren Beatty at the Aware Inn, at 8828 Sunset, a hippie stronghold in a darkening city, to discuss *Shampoo*. The Aware Inn, arguably the first gourmet organic restaurant in the country, introduced fresh, naturally sweetened juices, and dandelion root coffee to a city religiously committed to the exotic salad. The food and shaggy ambience of both it and its sister restaurant the Source were hip enough to keep older executives away, but younger ones would use the come-as-you-are vibe as a pretext to pull up a chair next to Beatty and Towne—a maneuver not native to the stratified Naugahyde establishments of Beverly Hills. "It was that kind of town, that kind of business then," said Paul Mazursky. "We didn't speak on the phone as much as we saw each other at parties and at places like the Source. It made everything more fun and friendly and fast. 'You wanna make this movie?' 'Let's do it.'"

Beatty considered setting *Shampoo*, his lissome ode to sex and politics in late-sixties Los Angeles, against the backdrop of the murders. "The original version of *Shampoo* was strongly influenced by the killings," he would explain. "The story was stretched out over a period of months, got into drug running, and was headed towards an apocalyptic ending." Towne's ideas, in Beatty's view, were slow and unformed. He said, "Robert had written a script that was very good in atmosphere, and in dialogue, but very weak in story, and each day the story would go in whatever direction the wind was blowing. He would just never finish." The producer Gerald Ayres regarded Towne's freeze as kind of stage fright. "Bob would love to work for money on rewrites on which he got no credit," he said, "and would do it quickly. Over three weeks, he'd have a whole new script ready. But something that had his name on it would become all involved in the neurosis of completion and failure, and take forever."

At the Aware Inn, Beatty gave Towne a deadline of December 31: "If you don't do it," Beatty warned, "let's forget it."

Towne stalled on *Shampoo*.

Nostalgia, in the wake of the murders, redolent of a greener, guileless city, paled Towne's vision. Thick with memory, he discovered, in a pile of *West* magazines Julie had collected, "Raymond Chandler's L.A.," a photo essay alive with his own childhood. There, in ringing color, was the green Plymouth convertible. There was J. W. Robinson's department store. The lazy gush of banana leaves. An imperious, piercingly white Pasadena mansion, with its porte-cochère, towering over the palms like Shangri-La. Their colors threw Towne into the past. "The best time to see Raymond Chandler's Los Angeles," he read in *West*, "is in the grey mists of the early morning, or better still, in the very late afternoon, when streets are in shadow broken only by golden yellow sunshine; times when your eye can be tricked into ignoring the long lines of franchise eateries and gas stations, each with its own plastic sign in one or another primary color; times when you don't notice the cheapjack apartment buildings glittering their anodized metal geegaws at you; times when your eye can pick up the Los Angeles which existed prior to 1942." Towne had been eight in 1942. "That is not an arbitrary choice of years," the essay continued, "for after 1942 the swarm of defense workers, the maddened construction of factories, homes, apartments, the industrial and automotive smog, all irrevocably altered the physical face of Los Angeles."

Change.

It was a city, inclined to growth, inclined to loss. "So great is the rate of change," wrote Richard G. Lillard in *Eden in Jeopardy*, "and so rapid is the increase in land values, that the life of many structures is from fifteen to thirty years, and it is a rare landmark building that can survive the crane." "Planned or unplanned," Lillard wrote, "the Southern California cities gave way to the motor vehicle. Men tore down buildings to make way for parking lots or service stations. Men chopped down trees lining streets, broke up curbs, scraped up lawns, and widened streets to the front steps of houses." Elsewhere the freeways were developed to tie cities together, but in Los Angeles, freeways were developed to solve congestion inside the city itself, ironically creating more congestion: More roads led to more traffic, more traffic to more roads, "which smash," Michael Davies wrote, "the city to pieces."

Towne could remember another Los Angeles. He was born in San Pedro, a sandy port town twenty miles south of downtown L.A. The 1930s, the 1940s: he remembered more sky, fewer impediments to the sun. The trees were not so tall in those days, and the stucco fronts of Pedro reflected light onto the brick buildings of the waterfront. Los Angeles, in Towne's memory, was then a haven of pastel and desert moods softly dusted in hues of Spanish rust, "a light wash of colors," he observed, "that had the delicacy of a gouache." Even the sunsets whispered their pinks and golds. "Only the bougainvillea blinded you," Towne recalled. "I remember the first time I saw some—an ecstasy of San Diego reds, tumbling along and over a white wall, across a trellis, then smothering a garage with its crimson wildness."

Towne had never read Raymond Chandler before—his old roommate, Edward Taylor, was the big mystery reader—it was the loss that got him. Chandler's detective novels preserved prewar L.A. in a hardboiled poetry equal parts disgusted and in love, for while

Chandler detested urban corruption, the dreaming half of his heart starved for goodness. Poised midway, the city held his uncertainty; Philip Marlowe, his detective, bore its losses. "I used to like this town," Marlowe confessed in *The Little Sister* in 1949. "A long time ago. There were trees along Wilshire Boulevard. Beverly Hills was a country town. Westwood was bare hill and lots offering at eleven hundred dollars and no takers. Hollywood was a bunch of frame houses on the interurban line. Los Angeles was just a big dry sunny place with ugly homes and no style, but goodhearted and peaceful. It had the climate they just yap about now. People used to sleep out on porches. Little groups who thought they were intellectual used to call it the Athens of America. It wasn't that, but it wasn't a neon-lighted slum either."

"In reading these words and looking at these pictures," Towne said, "I realized that I had in common with Chandler that I loved L.A. and missed the L.A. that I loved. It was gone, basically, but so much of it was left; the ruins of it, the residue, were left. They were so pervasive that you could still shoot them and create the L.A. that had been lost."

A city was its crimes, Towne read in *West*. In New York money was the motive. In Los Angeles, where people lived far from their neighbors and loneliness dried the landscape, criminals were sicker, their crimes more personal and perverse. "One thinks of a woman incinerating her husband so that she may live with her lover," Towne read, "of a man gnawing at himself until he is certain that his wife must be seeing someone else, and then methodically beating her half to death; of, in general, individuals so trapped within themselves that they can only contemplate slaughtering whoever is closest to them." Who had killed Sharon Tate?

"I want a gun," Julie Payne declared.

"No, no," he said. "We need a dog, a guard dog."

They drove out to a steel factory in the valley to see a pack of Komondors, "wolf-killers," Payne said.

"Take this one," the breeder advised, pointing to the most ferocious-looking of the lot.

"No," Towne said. "I want this one."

Towne brought her home, and Payne named her Scylla, but it was soon apparent she was a lady, not a killer. On the recommendation of screenwriter Carol Eastman, Towne and Payne got a German shepherd, but she proved to be as docile as the Komondor. A breeder pointed them to Tony Silas, an undercover vice cop, owner of a new litter of Komondors. Silas, at his home in Chatsworth, offered up one of the pack. Towne fell in love with it. He named him Hira. As soon as Hira came home, he ran into Towne's office and under his desk ("Hira was a born writer's dog," Payne observed) bringing Hutton Drive's dog count up to three—too many. One went to Towne's mother, and the count fell back down to two, but Scylla went into heat and "[neighbor] Quincy Jones's dogs were barreling under my gate," Payne said, "and the next thing I knew Scylla's pregnant." Seven puppies later, Mike Nichols called. "Puppies?" he asked. "Killer puppies? I'm coming right over" (He picked one, named it Louis, and took it home.)

In due time, Tony Silas paid a visit to Hutton Drive and instantly understood why Payne wanted that gun. Their house, up on a hill at the end of a curled driveway, was, like the house atop Cielo Drive, distressingly isolated. Should anything happen, there would be no escaping.

"Get her the gun," Silas told Towne. "If anybody came up this driveway," Silas continued, "*forget it*. Women shoot to kill."

Towne got the message. "Where do you work?" he asked the vice cop.

"Right now we're working in Chinatown."

"What do you do there?"

"Nothing."

"What do you mean, nothing?"

"Well, that's pretty much what we're told to do in Chinatown, is nothing. Because with the different tongs, the language and everything else, we can't tell whether we're helping somebody commit a crime or prevent one. So, we just . . . we do nothing."

Forget it. Towne went down to Kerr's Sporting Goods on Wilshire and bought Julie a .38 police special, blue steel. She kept it on a closet shelf in the bedroom.

In March 1970, Towne was summoned to Eugene, Oregon, where Jack Nicholson was filming *Drive, He Said*, his directorial debut. Nicholson was running behind schedule ("I work from eight to eleven. After eleven I chase around"), and the crew was threatening to quit; stretched thin, he called up Towne, his pal of fifteen years, to play a small part in the movie.

They had met in Jeff Corey's acting class. Towne was twenty-three, a graduate of Pomona with an interest in writing; Nicholson was twenty, an actor, writer, director—an everything and anything, a PA if he had to be—angling for a break in Hollywood. "We had similar ambitions," Towne said. "The good-looking girls in our acting class would not go out with us because they were going out with guys who were older who could take them to the Crescendo or the Mocambo. So we shared dreams and hope for the future. In that sense I was never much closer to anyone than Jack."

After a week or so in Oregon, it seemed that Nicholson's first-time screenwriter, Jeremy Larner, needed a little extra help with the adaptation of his novel, so, at eleven dollars a night, a separate room of the Eugene Hotel was added to the budget, Towne and Payne unpacked their things, and Towne, for free, agreed to a little doctoring of *Drive, He Said*.

For Towne there was no great glory in this work, no screen credit, and certainly very little money, but Jack Nicholson was his great friend, and "I do favors for friends.". In these matters trust was key. Out of respect for the patient, script doctoring was often confidential, and the intimate nature of the job—of diagnosing, and hopefully healing, a wounded script—made for tender collaborating. "To do it and make it work," Towne said, "you've got to really like the director. " In this case Towne more than liked the director; he loved him.

In the old days—L.A. in the fifties—Towne and Nicholson palled around at Pupi's, a Viennese pastry shop on the Sunset Strip. "Jack always had his buddies," said one roommate, Dale Wilbourne. "The ladies I met that he was with were always in competition with his pals." He gave all his friends nicknames: Towne was "Beaner." Carol Eastman, a slow writer, was "Speed." Bob Raphelson was "Curly." Harry Dean Stanton, who to Jack resembled one of the Rice Krispies trio, was "Snap." Jack himself was "the Weaver" for the way he discoursed in long, rambling sentences—"I like the stream-of-consciousness approach"—crammed with philosophical ponderings and Big Ideas on Life and Art and Love. That's what acting, he would say, is all about. Acting *is* everything. "[Jeff] Corey taught that good actors were meant to absorb life," Nicholson said, "and that's what I was trying to do. This was the era of the Beat Generation and West Coast jazz and staying up all night on Venice Beach. That was as important as getting jobs, or so it seemed at the time." They needed money, but they didn't really want it. Rather, lit with the visions of youth, they craved excellence, purity. Film. "Nicholson doesn't do television!" the out-of-work actor proclaimed about himself one Pupi's night.

His friends laughed. Because they knew he meant it. "Cinema's what it's about for me," Nicholson would say, and he was not messing around: "Ray's *The Music Room*, Olmi's *Il Posto, Bitter Rice, Umberto D., Seven Samurai, Rififi* at the Beverly Canon. . . . Through all these permutations and youthful poetry," he said, "I came to believe that the film actor was the great *literateur* of his time." He believed what Nietzsche believed, that nothing not written in blood is worth reading, and *his* work, his *films*, would be written not just in his blood, but the blood of his friends.

Corey, a respected character actor before he was blacklisted in 1951, turned his bungalow on Cheremoya Avenue into a kind of Actor's Studio West. Nicholson, Towne, Robert Blake, Richard Chamberlain, Sally Kellerman, Barrie Chase, and Carol Eastman filed in around 1957. "A lot of the kids were dislocated," Corey said, "and they came to Hollywood, as Jack did, living Lord knows where, in what sort of closet on some miscellaneous street in a temporary neighborhood. And our house was a refuge." With no money, little prospects, and nothing to lose, Corey's students made Cheremoya into their world apart. Corey, their acknowledged father figure, was bright, patient, and supportive, and the injustice dealt him by the House Un-American Activities Committee swelled their allegiance, adding an urgency, a sense of cause, to their enclave. They would stand behind Corey and one another, working together, sleeping together, playing and yearning together. They would do it all together and they were almost *there*: Hollywood—this dream they shared—was only down the street.

Watching Nicholson, a natural, Towne learned "that what an actor says is not nearly as important as what's behind what he says, the subtext." Towne literally studied Nicholson. Amazed by his staggering ability to draw out the shortest line of dialogue, to make a long meal of crumbs, he realized that Nicholson's innate mastery of suspense, of making the audience wait and wait for him to reach the end of a line, added drama to the most commonplace speech, and Nicholson's monotone, rather than bore the listener, inflected the mundane with an ironic tilt. With a great actor like his friend Jack, Towne realized a writer didn't have to force depth and emotion into his dialogue. In fact movie dialogue itself, "in a certain sense, is insignificant," Towne concluded. "I think that's important when it comes to all forms of dramatic writing, but probably even more important for screenwriting, because the overwhelming size of the picture conveys so much information that it's almost impossible for dialogue to add anything to it."

If Jack was improvising a seduction, he'd talk about anything but seduction. He'd interrupt the mood with an emotional outburst. He'd play *against*. The sheer surprise of his changes—as funny as they were uncomfortable, as intense as they were human—added the sense of unpredictable real life to the scene. He was alive. *That* was character. "I learned to write as much by watching Jack as anything else," Towne said.

Those outbursts—"Jack's capacity for indignation," Towne said—revealed a very real side of Nicholson. One night at Pupi's, Mrs. Pupi got mad at Jack for hanging out so late without ordering more than a cup of coffee. At her reprimand, Towne watched Jack's smile fade. His face fell. He turned slowly to Mrs. Pupi, took up his napkin holder, and threw it down on her pastry tray.

"One more word out of you," Jack drawled, "and I'll kick your pastry tray in."

Towne loved it. For all his bravado, Jack's outraged Don't-Fuck-With-Me contained a little secret—a dose of futility. Anyone could relate to that.

"Kid, you're going to be a movie star," Towne offered one day.

Jack grinned.

"And I'm going to write scripts for you."

It happened. In 1969 Nicholson appeared in *Easy Rider* and he became, if not quite a leading man, a name co-star. His touch of rebellious everyman howled out the national ethos, the distress of an entire population waking up from a happy dream. The end of the sixties, the beginning of Vietnam, of blatant and widespread corruption, the end, in short, of the just American promise, had a surrogate in Nicholson's impotent outrage, the way his characters, standing for the oppressed good, could do nothing but rail—absurdly, pitifully, triumphantly—against the organized bad. He went on to star in *Five*

Easy Pieces for his friend Bob Rafelson, and *Carnal Knowledge* for his friend Mike Nichols, and after writing and directing *Drive, He Said*, would star in *The Last Detail*, written by Towne and directed by Hal Ashby, good friends both. Success, his oldest allies discovered, did not sway Nicholson's loyalty; if anything, success enhanced it. Nicholson shared. He opened his home to all in his circle, gave them work, looked after their interests. They were his family, but better; family was fate; friends chose one another. In gratitude the Weaver kept his chosen safe.

Safe in their hotel room in Oregon, Towne and Payne settled in for the evening.

"I want to write a movie for Jack," Towne told her. That is, he wanted to write a leading-man part for Nicholson, his first. Jack had had his share of big roles in small movies and small roles in big movies, but he never played a big part, the romantic lead, in a big Hollywood movie. Towne would change that.

"What kind of movie?"

"A detective movie. Maybe Jane Fonda for the blonde."

"What's it about?"

"Los Angeles. In the thirties. Before the war." He was still thinking about Raymond Chandler, about the Los Angeles they had both lost.

"What happens?"

"I don't know. That's all I know."

"I'll go to the library," she said. "Let me see what I can find."

Payne went to the Eugene library the next day and pulled off the shelf *Southern California: An Island on the Land*, by Carey McWilliams. She had never heard of it, and flipped to the table of contents, "The Folklore of Climatology," "The Cultural Landscape," "'I'm A Stranger Here Myself,'" "The Politics of Utopia," "The Island of Hollywood," and drove the book back to Towne. What he found inside enchanted him: "It is this combination of mountain ranges, ocean breezes, and semi-desert terrain that makes the 'climate,' and the climate in turn makes the land." . . . "As a region, Southern California lacks nearly everything: good soils, natural harbors . . . forest and mineral resources; rivers, streams, and lakes; adaptable flora and fauna; and a sustaining hinterland." . . . "Virtually everything in the region has been imported: plants, flowers, shrubs, trees, people, water, electrical energy, and, to some extent, even the soils.". . . . "San Francisco is a consciously historical city, mindful of its traditions, enamored of its past; a city of parks and monuments and statues. One can look in vain for a statue in Los Angeles." . . . "Other American cities have gone through a boom phase and then entered upon a period of normal growth. But Los Angeles has always been a boom town, chronically unable to consolidate its gains or to integrate its new population." Los Angeles, it keeps changing. "In the past the region has been variously titled, usually with eloquence or contempt, with devotion or repugnance. Not a neutral land, it has long aroused emotional reactions ranging from intense admiration to profound disgust." . . . Why?

It began at the turn of the century, as a fresh-start frontier, the way to freedom. "This was the old rural American dream in full romantic maturity," wrote Richard G. Lillard. New industries were founded, work and land were plentiful, and Los Angeles was, as advertised, a functional paradise. But it grew too fast. "Los Angeles, it should be understood, is not a mere city," wrote Los Angeles historian Morrow Mayo. "On the contrary, it is, and has been since 1888, a *commodity*; something to be advertised and sold to the people of the United States like automobiles, cigarettes, and mouthwash." Other cities experienced booms, whose migrants settled gradually and came from neighboring regions, but Los Angeles, the most advertised city in the world, experienced constant booms, drawing migrants from all corners of the country, and at such an incredible rate that each boom, to accommodate the influx, inflicted destructive erasures on self and city. If the city ever knew what it was, it kept forgetting.

Into the thirties the automobile furnished Los Angeles with "the largest internal migration in the history of the American people," Towne read in McWilliams, and the city, once again, changed. Los Angeles had always been home to America's largest nonindigenous population, and perhaps for that reason, it could be argued, was America's most American city, but the combined impact of alienated migrants and the Great Depression initiated a peculiar strain of isolation and anxiety that cast a dark cloud over the city once promised to be Eden on earth.

Short on work, dislodged from their families, their communities, their traditions, Angelenos of the thirties were uncommonly lonely. Exiles all, they were, in addition, geographically isolated from one another by a sprawling metropolis built nonsensically on a scramble of unnumbered streets and boulevards. (Was Wilshire north or south of Olympic?) And where other American cities grew outward from an urban center, Los Angeles, growing too fast, too far, lost its hub. There is no meeting place in Los Angeles, no commons. "Quadrangular, reticulated cities (Los Angeles, for instance) are said to produce a profound uneasiness," wrote philosopher-critic Roland Barthes. "They offend our synthetic sentiment of the City, which requires that any urban place have a center to go to, return to, return from." Downtown L.A.? It was the ocean sound in a sea shell. In 1938 the average apartment tenancy in Los Angeles was six weeks long.

"I like a conservative atmosphere, a sense of past," Raymond Chandler protested against the changing city one year later. Attempts by migrant communities, or the city itself, to construct a past were vulnerable to kitsch, self-consciousness, and fraudulence, characteristically erroneously ascribed to Hollywood's influence. The incongruity of Los Angeles's physical selves impedes whatever exists of a native past. What is inherent to the city? Does it even matter? When one is always in one's car, after all, one isn't really in one's city. One isn't with people. No wonder Los Angeles, into the forties, had the largest number of dog and cat hospitals in America, and the nation's most prestigious animal graveyard, the Hollywood Pet Cemetery. It was loneliness.

"The succession of booms has bred in the people of Los Angeles a rather easy code of commercial ethic," McWilliams wrote. "To put it bluntly, the booms have periodically corrupted the civic virtue of the body politic." Thus was Los Angeles, contrary to its pretty face, vulnerable to corruption: It grew too fast. Either the cops couldn't keep up with the growing vice industry, or they were in on the action. In the twenties Los Angeles was the national leader in embezzlement, bank robbery, narcotic addiction, and bizarre murders. In the thirties Los Angeles led not just in the number of bankruptcies but also in total net losses due to bankruptcy. Into the forties the divorce and suicide rates of Los Angeles were more than double the national average. It was a good place to be Philip Marlowe.

As the Great Depression began to eclipse the city sun, and the latent criminality of a country emerging from Prohibition started to manifest, detective fiction took hold of Los Angeles. Along with the postwar introduction of European artists and intellectuals into Hollywood, many of them critical of their new setting, which felt to them like a decadent Weimar-by-the-Sea, writers of L.A. detective fiction "radically reworked the metaphorical figure of the city," according to Mike Davis, into a pessimistic antimyth of American free enterprise that the German exile Theodor Adorno, adept at recognizing totalitarianism, would decry as "the absolute power of capitalism," and the French, when they saw its likeness on screen, would call *noir*. But the fiction—distinctly Southern Californian— preceded the film. On the heels of Dashiell Hammett's *The Maltese Falcon*, set in a San Francisco that could be Any City, USA, came the stories and novels of Chandler; James M. Cain's *The Postman Always Rings Twice* (1934), *Double Indemnity* (1936), and *Mildred Pierce* (1941); Horace McCoy's *They Shoot Horses, Don't They?* (1935); and Nathanael West's *The Day of the Locust* (1939). Their nightmare *was* the city. As David Wyatt observed, these were tales characterized by speed of a particularly Angeleno strain. It was the boom sound, the race of get-rich-quick, of get-'em-before-they-get-you. "[The novel of speed] tends to be short," Wyatt wrote, "and to be marked by striking economies of style. It leaves little room for the direct expression of emotion, preferring fascinating surfaces to mere depth. . . . And it is a kind of novel that seems to arise from, and to be especially suited to, the place called Los Angeles," where haste is always a question of life or death, and contemplation, or any consideration of the past, is intolerable.

These authors, each compromised by his tenure writing for Hollywood, its own microcosm of the capitalist antimyth, used hardboiled fiction as an emotional exhaust valve. It was desperately needed. Since Hollywood had only started talking in 1927, this first wave of screenwriters had been early and unprepared to discover what their scions would almost take for granted,—that their kind, in the words of Lester Cole, were "the niggers of the studio system." "Like every writer, or almost every writer who goes to Hollywood," Chandler wrote, "I was convinced in the beginning that there must be some discoverable method of working in pictures which would not be completely stultifying to whatever creative talent one might happen to possess. But like others before me I discovered that this was a dream." Be they dreamers or detectives, the original heroes and antiheroes of L.A. crime were palpably screenwriters in disguise, losers of varying degrees of honor as far from their big score or big bust as screenwriters, divested of their creative ownership, were from their dream, *their* writing. For, as Chandler wrote near the end of his Hollywood career: "I am a writer and there comes a time when that which I write has to belong to me. . . . It doesn't have to be great writing, it doesn't even have to be terribly good. It just has to be mine." (The Screenwriters Guild was formed in 1933, in tandem with the hard-boiled takeover.) Chandler's portrait of the archetypal screenwriter—a figure of "brief enthusiasms [that] are destroyed before they can flower," who "wears his second best suit, artistically speaking, and doesn't take things too much to heart," who has a touch of cynicism "but only a touch," who is "scrupulously honest about his work, but should not expect scrupulous honesty in return," who, when he's ready to quit, says "goodbye with a smile, because for all he knows he may want to go back"—could easily describe his alter ego, Philip Marlowe. Why don't they quit if they're so miserable? Just like a screenwriter, "Marlowe knows everything," Chandler wrote in *The High Window*, "except how to make a decent living." Yes.

A Southern Californian. A screenwriter. Towne's patrimony was crime.

Memories. The lost sensations McWilliams described agreed with the orange blossom still in his nose; the chill he remembered when October chiseled the sun; the *whoosh* of muddy tires in the February dump of rain; the prickled scent of Santa Ana pepper trees and hay; the ocean air racing Santa Monica Boulevard as far east as Westwood—erased, all of them, by smog and time. "Along with Chandler," Towne said, "[McWilliams] made me feel that he'd not only walked down the same streets and into the same arroyo—he smelled the eucalyptus, heard the humming of high tension wires, saw the same bleeding Madras landscapes—and so a sense of deja vu was underlined by a sense of jamais vu: No writers had ever spoken as strongly to me about my home."

The chapter "Water! Water! Water!" particularly seized Towne's attention. It told the nefarious history of water in Southern California. While the Los Angeles Basin is home to nearly half the residents of California, it contains—according to McWilliams's statistics—only .06% of the state's natural water flow. There is not a single Southern California river, natural lake, or creek with a steady, year-round supply of water, he writes. In fact, the entire region is no more than a semi-arid desert masquerading as a paradise. Without the water imported from Owens Valley, the Colorado River and other sources, life as it exists in Southern California would be unsustainable.

In 1905 and again in 1910, as the city's population increased and water worries escalated, a group of Los Angeles's most prominent and wealthiest residents acquired a hundred thousand acres of the San Fernando Valley, and approached the Water Board of the City of Los Angeles with a proposition: The city should build a 238-mile aqueduct from the Owens River to Los Angeles, "and," McWilliams wrote, "thereby hangs a tale."

"The Owens Valley Tragedy", he continued, was a scheme kept secret from both the citizens of Los Angeles and the members of the city council. The first maneuvers took place two years before the first land purchase, in 1903, when J. B. Lippincott, chief engineer of the U.S. Reclamation Service in California notified the residents of the Owens Valley of an extensive reclamation project, persuading many residents, mostly farmers and low-wage laborers, to forgo their priority claims on water they desperately needed. But it was a trick. Once a sufficient amount of their land had been purchased, Lippincott announced that the "reclamation project" was off and promptly resigned. In short order the City of Los Angeles, seeming to come to the rescue, submitted to the citizens a bond issue of twenty-five million dollars to build the Owens Valley aqueduct—and to force the passage of the bond, to create scarcity, they secretly dumped thousands of inches of water into the sewer, manufacturing the effects of drought. The citizens of Los Angeles, naturally, approved the bond issue to build the aqueduct. They needed the water.

But rather than supply the City of Los Angeles with the water it had paid twenty-five million dollars for, the masterminds brought the aqueduct only as far as the north end of the San Fernando Valley, a hundred thousand acres of which they had clandestinely bought up a year earlier. The newly irrigated land, which they had purchased for a song, netted them an estimated profit of one hundred million dollars. They got rich, but the citizens of Los Angeles were robbed, Owens Valley land workers lost their livelihoods, hundreds of acres were decimated, and the "the rape of Owens Valley," as McWilliams put it, persisted unvanquished. The bad guys won.

Reading on, Towne was overcome with indignation. This was living injustice, corruption on a massive scale. "When a crime can no longer contain or content itself with the past," Towne said, "and insists on visiting the future it's no longer a crime—it becomes a sin, and very difficult to punish." A crime that happened, that *is* happening, right in front of our eyes.

In Los Angeles, developers were carving up the earth around Hutton Drive. To make room for a new, middle-class neighborhood, hundreds of acres of mountains and wildlife were being bulldozed by seventy-foot Caterpillar D9s, blown apart by dynamite, and, it was evident to Payne and Towne, outmoded laws and nefarious loopholes—all to wrest a small section of private road from canyon residents. The developers had assured the residents of Hutton Drive they would cut a new road from Mulholland and keep off their driveway, but giant trucks and tractors kept rolling in, destroying, in succession, twelve mailboxes and any semblance of canyon peace. The noise was incessant and rubble was everywhere. "They're dynamiting," Payne said, "and patios are falling down, there's dirt in the air, you can't turn on your air conditioning, you can't breathe. There are actually divorces."

Payne, undaunted, started to investigate. She discovered that their city councilman, who was supposed to protect their interests, was developing a golf course one canyon over. "We started snooping around," Payne said. "It turns out if you wanted to dynamite, you just go file the paperwork at the fire department." The Benedict Canyon Association scraped together the money to file a California Supreme

Court lawsuit against the development, and while they waited for their court date, seventeen different federations of canyons, drawing together in Benedict's defense, were called in to forcibly block the developers out of the private road. Hundreds of cars parked at the bottom of Payne and Towne's driveway, walling in a mammoth D9 and in retaliation, a D9 dumped on Payne's car as she was driving up the hill and she slid dangerously.

"That drove me down to City Hall," Towne said, "to see just exactly how City Hall worked." There, at a meeting, he saw "how crooked and corrupt things were." He watched as a prominent committee member, after mulling the improbable terms of the development, declared, incredibly, "This project is so bad, it will never get made. So I'm going to approve it." Towne was dumbstruck. "The destruction of the city had been affecting me even then," he said. "[The] city was so naturally beautiful, seeing it indiscriminately chewed up. . . . I mean, Los Angeles, more than most cities, seems to me to have always been a place where people never thought they would come to live but had to strike it rich and get out of there. It was a place to be mined, whether for gold or oil, or fame and Hollywood. You make your bundle and get out regardless of the collateral damage that's done to the city."

My God, he thought. My home. "Everybody's out to make a buck," he realized. "They're hustling. They're going to mine it until it runs dry."

But there was nothing they could do. The noise, the devastation, the unceasing invasion raged on.

Towne, meanwhile, kept writing as best he could. *Shampoo*, the script he was still cowriting with Warren Beatty, was hitting red lights at every studio, but his adaptation of the novel *The Last Detail*—about a group of sailors escorting a maligned convict to prison—was proceeding at a healthy clip. In the script, he decided, his sailors would swear like actual sailors. The draft he turned into

Columbia had as many as forty "motherfuckers," Towne explained, "because it was actually an expression of their impotence. All one [could] do in the face of the injustice in there was swear."

Columbia wouldn't have it.

In a letter disseminated to the principals, executive Peter Guber presented the studio's demands in no uncertain terms:

1. In the fight on the train, excise "fucking asshole" and "you fucking move."
2. After the fight, Buddusky says, "He's a fucking mess."
3. In front of the café, Buddusky says, "Fuck the crowd," and Mule says, "We'll miss the fucking train."
4. Inside the bar scene, take out the third "mother fucker."
5. Etc.

In light of the violence of *Bonnie and Clyde*, the drugs in *Easy Rider*, the sex in *Carnal Knowledge*, in light of "this newfound freedom we suddenly had," Towne said, it was flat-out regressive to stall a project in 1971 for profanity. The toppling of the Production Code, Hollywood's cobwebbed bureau of self-censorship, had yielded an extraordinary wave of freer filmmaking that may have raised conservative eyebrows, but, as its strong box office indicated, was at long last luring Americans away from their televisions. For the first time since its inception, Hollywood was a young business again. But Columbia's David Begelman—at fifty, the oldest studio head in power—apparently hadn't gotten the message.

"Bob," asked Begelman, "Would twenty 'motherfuckers' be more dramatic than forty 'motherfuckers'?"

"Yes, David, but the swearing is not used for dramatic emphasis. It's used to underline the impotence of these men who will do nothing but swear even though they know they're doing something unjust by taking this poor, neurotic little kid to jail for eight years for stealing forty bucks."

Columbia held its stance. "[It] was," Towne said, "a sort of Mexican standoff." Jack Nicholson, who by now had considerable leverage, stood by Towne and his script. *The Last Detail* would be made their way or not at all.

Outside Towne's home-office window the Caterpillar D9s chewed up more earth. "We lived that way," Payne said, "for four years" while they waited for the movie to be made.

Towne needed money.

To self-finance the writing of the detective movie he envisioned for Nicholson, he took a quick job with Francis Ford Coppola, a friend from their Roger Corman days. On the phone a panicked Coppola told Towne he was about to lose Brando and still didn't like the scene he had written, late in *The Godfather,* where Don Corleone and Michael speak father to son, master and apprentice. As written, the scene was too explicit. The emotion, Coppola said, needed to be underneath the words, not in them. Towne dropped everything and flew to New York. where he looked at the rushes and conferred with Pacino and Brando for ideas. "Just once," Brando told him, "I want Vito not to be inarticulate. He's talking to his son; he's telling the truth; he'd know what he has to say." Towne raced back to the hotel, ate some deli, and wrote from ten that night till four-thirty the next morning, Coppola picked him up at seven, and they hurried to the set. Pages in hand, Brando read his new dialogue aloud: "I refused to be a fool, dancing on the string held by all those big shots. I don't apologize—that's my life—but I thought that, that when it was your time, that you would be the one to hold the string." The "string" Towne got from the jacket of Mario Puzo's novel. Coppola liked it, they rehearsed it, they shot it. Towne flew home, the rescuer. He said: "It's like the relief pitcher in baseball coming into the game with the bases loaded."

Coppola wanted him to stay on and keep working, but Towne,

after three weeks, wanted to get back to Los Angeles, to his detective movie, and left.

Apprised of Towne's last-minute save on *The Godfather*, a Paramount picture, Robert Evans invited the conquering hero to Woodland, his stately, storied home in Beverly Hills, for dinner. More coveted than an invitation to a Woodland screening (comfortable for about a dozen), itself far more selective than an invitation to a Woodland party (whose guest list could number into the hundreds), an invitation to dinner was not only Evans's most exclusive social proposition (Woodland's intimate dining-room table sat only eight), but coming as it did in the first part of the evening, before the time-honored screening and before the party, a dinner invitation implied a long visit, an offer to come early to Woodland and stay late. It was, for Towne, a sign of great promise. It meant Evans was very interested in his work.

"Do you want to come?" Towne asked Payne.

"No, no," she said. "You go alone."

That night at Woodland, Towne would tease Evans with his idea for an original screenplay. Playing hard to get, he would dangle a couple choice details, let Evans inhale a few bouquets. Enough to sting his imagination—then withdraw.

"What is it?" Evans asked. "I want to see it."

It was not for sale, Towne said.

It was his.

It was *him*.

Wanting to maintain control of his unwritten detective movie, Towne wouldn't sell, but that left him with a problem: He still needed money. So he took a rewrite job on *The New Centurions*, an LAPD drama, and worked feverishly, believing in it throughout. "It should have been a great movie," he said. It wasn't.

He had his name removed from the picture. Forfeiting the recognition and residuals that came with screen credit, Towne revealed a measure of integrity that wouldn't fill the bank account but reaffirmed Payne's devotion. She respected him. "Robert was not working for money," she said. It was a relief. Having grown up in Hollywood, Payne had seen her share of disconsolate compromise, especially in screenwriters—their ideals, careers and even marriages corrupted by misguided ambition and its ancillaries self-denial, artistic failure, addiction. Her stepfather, the screenwriter Charles Lederer, was then caving to methedrine and Demerol, nodding off in his yellow chair in his book-piled office on Bedford Drive, his mind lost to the empty vials at his toes. "Twelve bloody babies . . . ," he droned to Payne and Towne, clawing at his arms. There were big bugs under his skin, he insisted between weeping jags, crying out for his aunt, Marion Davies, William Randolph Hearst's famous mistress, ten years in her grave. Grief and memory collided in chemicals, and all that he lost Lederer gurgled back in broken haikus that Payne, fluent in the family psychosis, pieced together for Towne: "Twelve bloody babies," she explained to him, "means the twelve months of the year."

Too many screenwriters ended this way, in waste. True to himself, Towne wouldn't; he wouldn't take a job he didn't believe in.

Payne earned a little from her shop in Beverly Hills, and while Towne fought Columbia for *Last Detail* from his home office on Hutton Drive, she did what she could to make their place more habitable, laying new bedroom floor, enclosing the patio in greenhouse glass, and clearing brush "where they had taken out the oak trees, which was illegal because they were California oaks, to make room for new property." She made dinner. She cleaned up. Inside his office, where Towne sat frozen under an art deco lamp, no keys typing, she installed stained-glass picture windows to brighten the gloom. "There I was," he said, "thirty-seven, thirty-eight years-old and feeling like a failure with nothing produced, other than having a position as sort of a subterranean character who'd done some uncredited work on *Bonnie & Clyde* and *The Godfather*." When the sun crested and the hot air blew down from Mulholland, the windows turned green and purple pinwheels across his blank pages.

It was the beginning of summer. A Santa Ana had been blowing for three days. Now it settled.

Towne would take Hira for a walk.

He took the dog into the Santa Monica Mountains above Will Rogers Park. He hiked the fire trails up through the Spanish broom and yellow star thistle, the periwinkle and bay laurel. Soaring over the Pacific, he paused in the sun. Visibility was perfect. He breathed in the mentholated tang of eucalyptus. There was a breeze. It brought with it billows of sage, scrub oak, pine, pepper trees, mustard, and foxtails. And breathing in, he was a ten-year-old boy again, on the bluffs of Rolling Hills, just outside San Pedro, overlooking Portuguese Bend, investigating the origins of life in cliffside tide pools, reeling from the boom-crash of the waves.

He breathed again and it disappeared. *Forget it.*

This feeling, such a twisty admixture of euphoria and demise, where did it come from? Maybe it was being a child, living closer to the ground, source of aroma, that had preserved those smells so completely. Maybe it was the city then, before cars and smog and freeways stained the air gray. Maybe it was just Robert Towne, the romance he fused with irrevocable loss. "Memories swell [like a bee sting]," he wrote. "When we first feel them in our skin there's that breathcatching moment before knowing whether we'll feel grief or joy."

Adventure took him over. In search of what remained of the city that made him, he set off, right then, for the harbor town where he was born, San Pedro. "You know, I can't honestly say that I ever thought, at its best, Los Angeles was a great city," he said. "I'm not even sure it *is* a city." L.A. was impossible to fathom and vital to comprehend. "I always start out saying, 'I'm just going to show how this place has turned to shit.' And then I can't stop myself. My eye keeps going to the things that were beautiful, the things that I remembered as a kid."

Instead of the freeways, he took Western south to Pedro. The wholesale houses he remembered had ceded to strip malls, shopping centers, parking lots. He missed the agrarian patchwork of animal farms, oil derricks, escaped cows, and roadside burger joints.

Largely untouched by development, San Pedro was as he remembered it. The brick buildings of Beacon Street, Whispering Joe's and Shanghai Red's, the tattoo parlors, the ferry to Terminal Island. He stood listening at the waterfront where, as a boy, he'd watched the tuna fisherman set off to sea and, as a young man one summer, set off with them. He watched his childhood home on Sixth Street, and revisited his earliest memory, sitting in the backyard by the paint-splattered Philco radio, listening to Seabiscuit win yet another race. And then there was his father, Lou, also a race fan, a local shopkeeper—before he made it big in real estate and moved the family to Brentwood—listening to Joe Hernandez call the seventh at Santa Anita.

They lived across the street from the Warner Brothers' Theater, "which dictated my future profession," Towne said. He remembered back to 1941, the day he saw *Sergeant York*. He remembered his shock when Gary Cooper, a conscientious objector caught between God and country, finally decides to fight. He remembered the conversation of electrified Americans leaving the theater and the crystal clarity of their convictions. "At the time this movie came out," he said, "most of the audience that saw this movie believed in

God and they believed in country, in one permutation or another." He remembered feeling part of a community—a group of people with shared values—and that sense of moral unity—"the notion that some things are not for buying and selling"—that seemed to have left America after World War II. Or was it after the Kennedy assassination? Or the murder of Sharon Tate?

"I have no regrets," he would write, "about having missed that semi-fabled epoch when men were men, women women, and writers rogues, but I increasingly feel—I suspect we all do—that the history of life on earth is not one of evolution so much as devolution. With each succeeding generation we get weaker and smaller; the Titans are always in the past."

Remembering the reactions to *Sergeant York*, he found himself longing not just for the shared American feeling of right and wrong, but for the way of making movies that came from such crisply dramatic distinctions. "It's a lot more efficient," he reflected, "and a lot easier to tell a story when everybody has shared values." Those days, those values, the belief that an individual's actions actually counted for something, those kinds of stories of agency and faith abdicated American minds and American movies at precisely the same moment.

Something had changed. A golden age had ended. When?

Why?

For weeks, for months, he swam in feeling. He remembered. He sat warm in the sun and walked cool on the shore. He hiked long, elevated mountain trails. He bristled at Columbia Pictures, still steamrolling his good intentions on *The Last Detail*. He raged soundlessly against the half-dozen D9s screeching and grinding outside his window. Hira at his side, he shut the office door behind him to better hoard lost causes, and cigar-smoked his concentration into the purer past. This is what he was now, surly and ecstatic, giant and decreased, less a man than an idea lost on a dreaming sea. Evenings, night, always found him alone, a light turned on above his head, walled in high cliffs of paper. Behind the paper sat a boy and his tide pool.

He read. To separate feeling from fact, his childhood romance from the Los Angeles that really existed, he read the histories Julie bought from used bookshops throughout the city, Long Beach to Hollywood. "I needed to find a library of the time," Payne said. "I needed [to find] the architecture. I needed what the L.A. crazies were preaching at the time, the politics. I needed everything on all those subjects, every one of them." He read Morrow Mayo's account of the Owens Valley water wars and Mary Austin's 1917 fictionalization, *The Ford*. He read the Department of Water and Power's official accounts of the crime. He read about the Tuna Club of Avalon, a members-only, big-money power club on Catalina Island—a book on the subject was the only book he bought for research; a rare find at Aldine's bookshop, it cost more money than he had to spend. Of course he read Chandler: *The Big Sleep* and *The Long Goodbye*. He read *The Day of the Locust* and *Double Indemnity*, and though they gave pictures to his memories, the quotidian evaded them. Towne was hunting for real-life details. "Everything seemed trite and untrue," he explained, "what you would call 'a Hollywood movie.'" These characters sounded like Bogart; Bogart sounded like a weary screenwriter; Towne wanted to know what people, real people, really sounded like in the thirties. What were their words? Their idioms? What was their humor? What *wouldn't* they discuss? He read *Ask The Dust* by John Fante—an L.A. novel he had never heard of—which his assistant got from the public library downtown—and finally found what he was looking for: "I just knew that was the way those kids talked to each other—the rhythms, cadences, racism." *Ask The Dust*, John Fante's hymn to the vanished Bunker Hill and the dreams of rookie writers, put the city in his ear. He said, "If there's a better piece of fiction written about L.A., I don't know about it."

There. He had the sights, the smells, the sounds. Per Hollywood and the D9s, he had a war to fight. From futility he simmered a lush lather of spite of longing, something to protest, a place to write from. He had the Owens Valley, a premise. He had his genre, the detective story, that had first attracted him in the pages of *West*. He had his time and place: Los Angeles between the wars, a time of innocence. Before Hitler. "World War II hadn't happened," Towne would explain. "And that kind of evil was not something that he [the detective character] would be used to dealing with. And I wanted to have that." And he had Jack.

Nicholson was playing tennis at Quincy' Jones's when Towne first proposed the idea.

"Look," Towne said. "We can't get *The Last Detail* going right now. What if I write a detective movie for you? It'll be L.A. in the thirties."

"Sure. Sounds great. What's it about?"

"I don't know." Then: "Water."

Jack would be Towne's detective. That right there gave him a clue to the character. Nicholson, Towne knew, was a popinjay, a clothes-horse. He loved his shoes, his vintage Hawaiian shirts, and leather jackets. Towne remembered Nicholson admiring himself in the mir-ror. "Look at my perfect teardrop nostrils," he would say, smiling. Towne's detective would have a little of that vanity. He would mind his hair, his fresh-pressed suits, his Venetian blinds. He would be class conscious, maybe a little Hollywood, and if those qualities op-posed traditional concepts of a movie detective—gruff, high-minded, ascetic—all the better. This detective would be different. Towne said, "[In] most detective movies I have ever seen—[and] in Chandler and even Hammett—all the detectives are too gentlemanly to do divorce work. 'If you want someone for that go down the block.' But I knew in fact that that's mostly what they did." For his detective Towne would go against genre; his detective *would* do divorce work. Unlike Chandler's Philip Marlowe, Towne's hero would do it for the money. That would give the character someplace to go, emotionally; it would give Towne the beginnings of a character arc. "I thought that taking someone like that," Towne said, "maybe venal and crude and used to petty crime and people cheating on each other, and then getting him involved in a crime which was really evil and allowing him to see the larger implications and then to draw the distinctions would be interesting." He decided, wherever possible, to counter movie myth with real life. "So I decided to do a movie about crimes as they really were," he said, "because the way they really were is the way they really are. I didn't want to do a movie about a black bird or anything. A real crime, with a *real* detective."

Philip Marlowe always understood the corrupt workings of the world around him. He was cynical to the point of immutability, a quality that allowed Chandler to serialize the character; readers would always get the same Marlowe almost exactly as they remembered him. Towne's detective, by contrast, would change over the course of the story. His detective would only *think* he knows the world. By the end of the story, his apparent immutability would capitulate to a new and terrible awareness of corruption his former self could never have imagined, and all his venality, his air of self-possession, would come crashing down. How could the fate of real-life ideals—he considered the D9s, *The Last Detail*—be anything else?

Of course there would have to be a blonde. In these stories there were always blondes, all the same, each in their own way. But in *this* story, flipping the paradigm once again, Towne would introduce the blonde as a femme fatale, then reveal, by the end of the picture, her actual goodness and innocence, not the other way around. That would be *his* twist on the convention. And in keeping with the fate of real-life ideals she, too, would have to be sacrificed. She wouldn't kill—as in detective movies of the forties—but *be* killed. The detective would lose the case, the woman, himself. He would lose, Towne came to realize, everything.

What had Robert Towne lost?

He had lost love.

They were in Jeff Corey's acting class. In the converted garage off Cheremoya Avenue. Jack and a cluster of eager students, hanging on his every gesture. And now the girl, Barrie Chase. She was a dancer, and she was beautiful.

"Hello."

"Hello."

She was not the blushing kind. Of all Corey's students, she was perhaps the most experienced, having worked the chorus of dozens of movie musicals before her ex-boyfriend, Stanley Kubrick, introduced her to Corey. Born into show business, her father Borden Chase, had written *Red River, Winchester '73, The Far Country.* "I grew up having to tiptoe because my father had to work at home," she said. "Don't yell when you go outside. No intrusions." To her shame, he had been for the blacklist. "My father was a patriot," she said, "so I know he did what he did out of love of country, but I don't believe that anyone has the right the take somebody's life away from him."

She and Towne went to Norm's, an all-night diner on La Cienega, for steak and eggs and talked about families. Towne's father, a powerful real-estate developer, was dubious about his son's interests. Writing for the movies was not considered a serious occupation; "It was aesthetically slumming," Towne said, "pandering for big bucks."

Her own father, Chase said, was, despite his success, "ashamed to be in the movie business. He always called himself a sellout." Chase's mother, a musician, regarded her Steinway and Bechstein pianos as her children, and addressed Barrie, her daughter, as "kiddo." Barrie would eye her from the far corner of their cavernous living room: "Don't you know my name?" she would ask. Years earlier Chase was with her mother at Googie's, a coffee shop on Sunset, when Gene Shacove, the famous Beverly Hills hairdresser, sidled into their booth, his eyes on the girl. But it was her mother who tried to pick him up. "You know," Shacove smiled back, "I want to go out with your *daughter*." Chase married and divorced him two months later.

Towne was shocked that she had already been married and divorced, shocked yet again that she had been married to a hairdresser—shocked that *anyone* would be married to a hairdresser—and shocked further to learn that after their divorce, he still did her hair.

In Corey's class they watched each other work. Nights they spent at Pupi's and Norm's scrounging cheap eats and listening to the Weaver weave. Towne, captivated by Los Angeles, narrated tales of its origins, the stories of its street names, Pico, Wilshire, Mulholland Drive.

Love came.

He introduced her to his mother and father, but she wouldn't introduce him to hers. "I don't speak to my father," she said.

She moved in. They lived off Westmount, near Melrose, with Towne's roommate, Jack Nicholson, who made a room of the garage. When Jack moved out, Towne's best friend from college, Edward Taylor, moved in.

One always found Edward at home. A tall, serene presence in love with literature and old jazz, he was quiet and kind, given to long hours of solitary contemplation. While Robert and Jack and Barrie went out, Edward, a Rhodes Scholar, stayed in, lit his pipe, and read his books, mysteries above all else. He had amassed a collection thousands deep. "It seemed like he had every mystery ever written," said Taylor's daughter, Sarah Naia Stier, "and he knew so much about it. He was obsessed with mystery fiction and L.A. history and he loved the hardboiled detective. That was just his heaven. " Taylor wanted nothing more than to meet the evening with Agatha Christie, and vanish into murder and a bottle of scotch. But sitting there in his tweeds, he could have been Sherlock Holmes, staring down an imponderable. "Edward was stoic," his friend Mike Koepf wrote. "Humor was his forte, and irony the breath he breathed in a world gone mad with ignorance. He was not a man to rashly storm the barricades, but more a man who ponders whether things are actually better on the other side."

Taylor and Towne were best friends, even closer than Towne and Nicholson. "They were in love," said Stier. "I always felt like their primary relationship in the world was with each other. They talked every day, their whole lives." Eddie would always say Robert had saved his life, having insisted on rushing him to the hospital just in time one horrible night—for stomach pains that revealed a ruptured appendix. Eddie, in turn, would play a vital role in Towne's creative life, time and again. "Everything Robert wrote, he ran past Eddie," Barrie Chase said. "They were in constant conversation about whatever Robert was working on." Despite his passion for and facility with stories and storytelling, Taylor did not share Towne's professional ambition or ambition of any kind; it was, perhaps, the one thing Taylor and Towne didn't share. "My father didn't seem to need to be successful," Stier said. He worked odd jobs, wrote grants, taught, nothing vocational. "He wanted to make enough money to just be comfortable." Towne, meanwhile, would not be stopped. "Robert didn't hardly leave his desk in those days," Chase recalled. "He would work around the clock."

"Robert," she would say, "let's go for a walk . . ."

"Not yet."

"You have to *move*."

"I will. Not yet."

"Soon?"

"Why don't you speak to your father?"

They fought. Talks of marriage became talks of separation. Chase took a job in Sweden, had a romance. Devastated, Towne pined. He exhumed the full inventory of his failures, and resolved to rescue, at all costs, the perfect future they had allowed to wilt away. When she returned to Los Angeles, he appeared outside her house on Mountcrest up in the Hollywood Hills, heartsick. It was his last chance.

They walked to the top of a hill and, at the edge of a cliff, stopped. Down below, the city streets, whose stories he once told her, kept running.

"You're going to kill me . . . ," she sighed.

"I want you to marry me. I want you to have a baby with me. I'll take care of you, I swear I will."

She sank. "It's too late."

"What do you mean it's too late? We're not dead yet. That's the only thing that's too late."

"I'm going back to Sweden. He asked me to marry him."

"Honey, please. . . ." There was nothing he could do. "Please . . . *please* . . . don't go."

Hutton Drive, night. Towne and his typewriter. His cigar and his dog. And his idea.

How to begin?

With the detective?

Begin with drought? A dried-up riverbed?

A murder?

Close by, Towne kept a postcard Julie had found him: Riverside, California, a promenade of pepper trees.

An aerial view of the great green city?

Night wore on.

Under Towne's desk lay Hira, the giant Komondor, toying with the phone cord he took for a water snake. Man, he thought, I never saw such purity in a living thing. Every walk, the same fire hydrant, the same look of happiness. At the most fundamental level, he thought, that purity is what people fall in love with.

Distraction—this was how it always started. "So much of writing," he said, "is trying to avoid facing it."

Hold the feeling, he told his heart. Hold the romance, the purity of Hira, the ideals of lost values. These would be the hidden qualities in his detective.

What to call him?

What about a name that hid those qualities, as he did? A hustler's name. Towne thought of a friend he and Jack had, Harry Gittes. Just pronouncing the name sounded vaguely insulting: *Gittes*; it was all in the nose. "Jake is a good name from the time period," Towne reasoned, "and it is also the name I have always called Nicholson. Jack's full name is actually John J.—so I took that, too, and it became J. J. Gittes, which seemed like a reasonable name, a real name. I tend to name characters that way, on the basis of their sound."

This was a detective movie. His femme fatale—not really fatale at all—would be virtuous. Nothing could be more virtuous than a good mother, Towne decided. A mother protecting her child. But from what?

On February 26, 1971, Towne had the idea of opening the movie at Gittes's office:

A woman named Marian shows up. Someone's been sending her a lot of money, she tells Gittes. Too much money. She shows him the statements—from banks all over Los Angeles. Gittes says he'll check it out. She leaves.

Later she comes back. She suddenly wants Gittes off the case. Strange.

In time another client, Dorothy Howland Bixby, appears in Gittes's office. She's worried about her ailing father. Once a great man, Mr. Bixby now bribes his caretakers to get him whatever he wants, including morphine, and perhaps even young girls. Will Gittes keep watch? Yes, he will.

On his watch, he sees Mr. Howland with Marian. His mistress?

Later Mr. Howland is killed, and Marian disappears. Police look for her. Gittes looks for her.

Dorothy Bixby suspects Marian's mother—she had a grudge against her family, presumably for something Mr. Howland had done to her in the past.

Then what?

Jake discovers that Dorothy is actually Marian's mother as well as her sister, and tries to reach Marian before Dorothy can get to her . . . because . . . ?

No. *Forget it.* Towne would have to try again.

What was the mother protecting the daughter from? What did it have to do with the Owens Valley, and what did any of this have to do with Gittes?

By March 6, Towne had latched on to the theme of sexual perversity and a working title: *The Picture Business.*

It opens in Gittes's office. Walsh, his partner, tells him a dirty joke. They head to the bathroom and Duffy joins them. He says he's got the pictures. They all gape. Duffy excuses himself to call his client, David Bixby.

Later, Dorothy Bixby comes to Gittes's office. She begs him to give her the pictures—they're of her and another man—and offers to double whatever Gittes's agency got for the photos. Gittes refuses. Mrs. Bixby pleads with him. Her husband is a homosexual, she says, explaining her infidelity; that accounts for the pictures. The news would kill her father, Mrs. Bixby says. Please. Gittes suggests she hire another agency to take shots of her husband in the act. A sort of Mexican standoff, he says. But she manages to win him over.

Later Gittes goes for a haircut and talks about horse races.

Back at the office, an old man, Mr. Howland, asks Gittes to find his lost dog. Gittes protests. He's in the divorce business, he said. But Howland offers a big sum, and Gittes takes the job.

Somehow—Towne didn't know—Howland frames Gittes. The old man makes it look like Gittes has run off with $250,000. Then Howland disappears.

Gittes is arrested and let out on bail. But Howland's daughter—Mrs. Bixby—believes he's innocent.

Gittes hunts down Howland and finds him with Marian, his mistress.

But before he can bust Howland, Howland is killed and Marian disappears. Gittes suspects Marian. Others suspect Gittes.

Gittes pledges to Mrs. Bixby he'll find Marian.

But Marian finds Gittes first. Someone's trying to kill her, she insists. But did she kill Mr. Howland? No, she couldn't have killed Howland: He was, she says, her father. . . .

How to prove it? They seek out the doctor who delivered her—only to discover he's been murdered. Eventually they get to Mrs. Bixby. She *is* Marian's mother, *and* Howland is her father. Marian is the child of incest. To protect the secret, she wants to kill Gittes . . .

What did any of this have to do with water?

"[The villain] must be the expert on who's [sic] opinion the city has come to rely," Towne wrote in legal pad. "How to tie in the daughter with the water. Public corruption with private scandal."

For a while Towne would walk in circles. He couldn't know who the characters were until he knew who they needed to become, and he couldn't know who they needed to become until he knew who they were. He wouldn't start to write scenes until he had a full scene-by-scene outline, and he couldn't outline until he saw his people in detail, what they thought they wanted and what they really needed. But didn't he have to have a good story first? Mystery plotting was a snake eating its tail: does character move the story, or does the story move the character? Towne would have to discover them both simultaneously, and proceed with caution, allowing one to inform the other, slowly, one short inch at a time.

He would outline constantly, throughout the process, continually hatching new ideas and returning to the drawing board to implement them.

It was overwhelming.

Mistakes were persistent, but they couldn't always be redacted without difficulty; if abandoned ideas once had narrative value, which they certainly did—otherwise Towne never would have outlined them in the first place—excising them would capsize all that followed.

"I wrote at least twenty different step outlines," he said, "long, long step outlines."

New ideas were like discovering a new piece to a puzzle; suddenly the puzzle would have to be disassembled and put back together again, and again and again.

By March 17 he had picked a last name for Marian: "Wells." There was water in that.

"Notes on Gittes," Towne typed.

Getting to know J. J. Gittes on paper, Towne would ask himself why—always why—and answer his questions in effusions of narrative prose and inner monologue he released like a free-associative novel:

"It wasn't," he typed, "that the limits kept you from getting hurt, or killed or even from losing too much. They kept you from getting lost." Gittes had to know his limits, what he couldn't do. Time and experience had narrowed those limits, and the same was true of his cohorts, Duffy and Walsh. They were all like the whore who would piss on a john's chest, Towne noted to himself, but would never shit on a chest.

Gittes had an enormous supply of charm, "almost rude quantities of charm," Towne wrote, and he knew his business and he knew his city but didn't know the first thing about grace. His years on the job had conditioned him to suspect the worst in people and, Towne noted, he was never proved wrong: "It was a great show, the city of angels. You could whoop and holler and have a hell of a time as long as you remembered that you were just a spectator." There were limits.

Those limits, Towne thought.

The limits of agency, of justice.

He thought back to Tony Silas, the vice cop who brought him his dog. His limit was Chinatown:

"What do you do there?"

"Nothing."

"What do you mean, nothing?"

"Well, that's pretty much what we're told to do in Chinatown, is nothing. Because with the different tongs, the language and everything else, we can't tell whether we're helping somebody commit a crime or prevent one. . . ."

Gittes would be lost in Chinatown, Towne decided. There are only two rules, two limits, he has: "Look out for your client and don't get tough"—Towne crossed out *"tough"* and wrote "lost in China-town."

He wrote: "The dream that died. The whole country had failed to put out. Why should L.A. be any different. End of a dream—"

Something must have happened to Gittes in Chinatown, something horrible. What was it?

Don't Get Lost in Chinatown. Was that a title? On April 19 Towne added a few others to the list: *Lost in the Sun, Deal Me Out, Last Chance, Jake's Limit*—the last three told of the gambler in Gittes.

Was he a gambler?

"Today his idea of gambling is gin at twenty-five cents a point," Towne began one outline. "Now that can add up, but thirty-five years ago when he had less to lose, Jake Gittes gambled for a lot more."

On June 21 he dreamed up a cast. "Gittes," Nicholson. Instead of

Howland, "Julian Cross," George C. Scott. His older daughter, now "Anita Cross," Jane Fonda.

Towne changed "Anita" to "Katherine." For her married name Towne chose the name "Mulwray." He liked the sound. Katherine Mulwray. It had languor and romance. And Howland had become Julian Cross. J.C. ("He must be a Christ-like figure," Towne noted, to hide the truth of Cross's evil.) That left her daughter, formerly known as Marian Wells. "Someone is going to want to exploit Marian Wells," Towne scribbled on a yellow pad. "Owens Valley farmers, or their relatives. Marian Wells has got to be a key figure in the whole attempt to hush it up."

Towne noted: "Gittes must come up against a conspiracy of sorts."

"Create the impression that corruption is everywhere," he scribbled. "'What's the point?,'" some character might say, "'You guys spend half your time convicting each other.'"

On June 28 Towne noted: "Water must be a factor—either a dam or an aqueduct—getting water to an area and speculating on the land." They're emptying the reservoirs at night to force a bond issue worth millions. Whoever finds out would be in serious danger. Is it Marian Wells?

Maybe not. "Perhaps the action takes place in the heat of summer—a drought—no water in the goddam city. A continuing annoyance as they go about the case.

"The water commissioner found dead in the harbor—man was looking for water anywhere he could find it.

"How to tie in Marian with the water supply—

"There's a drought & tempers are short. . . . Marian Wells must provide the key.

"She's the illegitimate daughter of the architect of the plan."

To himself Towne wrote, "My interest is in the kinds of crimes that society punishes—[the mother] will be punished, even crooked cops, but the business community will enjoy freedom from persecution."

"Julian Cross, The Sun King," Towne added to another pad.

The Sun King. Was it a title? *The Third Coming? The Julian Spoils?*

"If Marian is his illegitimate daughter," he wrote down. "He sleeps with her & it drives him—"

Then: "Julian Cross is an eminent criminal."

He's sinned against the city. He steals the water. And going by McWilliams's account of the Owens Valley scandal, the land speculators forced a drought. It was perverse. They destroyed their *own* land.

So would Julian Cross be perverse—twice. He rapes his land, and he rapes his child.

Then: "Katherine—*must* be upset about it. What if it's her sister, & she knows it."

She knows she's Marian's sister *and* her daughter.

Katherine, Cross's daughter, is protecting *their* child.

But what happens in the end? Does Katherine succeed in protecting her child? Does any mother?

Did his?

Helen and Lou Towne lived at 450 South Bristol Drive at the corner of Bristol and San Vicente in Brentwood, one of the most affluent neighborhoods in Los Angeles. Most days he took his lunch at the country club across San Vicente; she played cards and tended the dogs. An acknowledged beauty, Helen dressed in a prepossessing manner befitting her class, and Lou, since coming up in the world, in the finest handmade shirts and sweetest cologne. Lou—a big man in size and stature, a John Huston type—had made his money with Towne Homes, subdividing Simi Valley and Thousand Oaks, and though he had finally arrived, his striving for rank persisted. He was, some said, obsessed with notoriety, his and others'. His sons, Robert and Roger, screenwriters both, had not made names for themselves, and Julie, despite her Hollywood pedigree, had no fame—that wasn't good enough for Lou. Determined to surround himself with the "right people," he furnished his billfold and on one occasion palmed a reduced Joe Louis to appear at his housewarming party on Bristol Drive.

The Lou and Helen's home, Julie couldn't ignore, was eerily free of books. But what for another couple might have been a gaffe of decor was for the parents of not one but two writers a telling omission. "They had no sense of Robert's work," Payne said, "and almost no curiosity about his passion." They even went so far as to encourage him to see a therapist, Dr. Martin Grotjahn, to summarily address the problem. Towne wrote: "A writer was either a playwright, a poet, or a novelist—a screenwriter was a pimp." The criticism went both ways. "Robert always [implied] his father was a crooked developer," Payne recalled, and was at one time a bagman for L.A. mayor Sam Yorty. Preoccupied with winning, Lou on more than one occasion attempted to wrest control of Towne and Payne's personal investments. He was so relentlessly intrusive and, at times, so brazenly nasty, that Towne and Payne's actual financial manager was compelled to remark, "Lou Towne? Too mean to die." Dr. Grotjahn gifted Towne a copy of his book, *Psychoanalysis and the Family Neurosis.*

When Robert was a child his mother wrote poetry, he remembered, and read to him at night, but Bristol Drive was every inch his father's home, and Helen in every respect his father's wife. She had to ask his permission to buy herself a dress. "Lou Towne's outlook on women," Payne recalled, "was more appalling than anyone I ever met in Hollywood. He was emotionally sadistic to Helen." She was constantly apologizing for his drinking, "a bottle of vodka," Payne said, "before nine every morning." By lunch he was flattened. He would drink out the day in his segregated club, making passes, bullying waiters. Then he would pass out in the afternoon; a "nap," it was called.

Lou openly conducted an affair with his secretary and boasted to Robert about cheating on his mother. It was said he once slept with a Vegas hooker and the same night came home and slept with his wife. "He gave her guilt jewelry," Payne observed, and Helen would demurely insist that everything was "fine." She had a girlish giggle and apparently no memory.

"Nobody's getting me dinner . . . ," Lou would whine at home. "Helen . . ."

When he got too drunk and stayed drunk, Helen left town. But she always came back. "What can I do?" She confided to Julie. "I have no place else to go."

By the fall of 1971, some six months after he had begun, Towne was still writing outlines. Some he discarded incomplete. Others ended unsatisfactorily.

"'Chinatown' by Towne'" one began:

"Only a few years back, when Gittes was working for the D.A.'s office, he got involved in the tong wars. He had been forewarned by his superior, Leon Whitaker, not to fool around with any of the go-ings-on in Chinatown." If you had to go into Chinatown, Whitaker had told him, "do as little as possible."

Gittes had, to his lasting regret, ignored the warning. In the past he had discovered that one of the tongs was selling Cherry, a beautiful slave girl, to a rival faction. One faction enlisted Gittes to rescue Cherry. Gittes agreed, and Cherry was delivered to safety. Later, when Cherry died, tong wars broke out—first in Los Angeles and then the country. Whitaker was shot, and Gittes only barely got by though not without injury—an ax chopped off the pinky finger of his right hand. . . . In the years since, Gittes left the D.A.'s office for his own private practice, but the lessons remained: "For Gittes," Towne typed, "Chinatown has come to mean any place where he's on unfamiliar ground, a case, a country, any place where he can be taken by appearances." He vowed never to make that mistake again.

Cut to L.A. in 1937, a city in drought. . . . Citizens are pressured to approve a thirty-seven-million-dollar bond to divert and dam water from the north. . . . The water commissioner is found dead, drowned in an empty reservoir. . . . Meanwhile, Artemis Samples comes to Gittes with the suspicion that his wife is having an affair with Julian Cross. . . . Gittes tracks the wife to Cross's place, collects the proof. . . . Later, at a poker game, he learns Samples and his wife have been murdered—except they weren't husband and wife. . . . "Mrs. Sample's" real name was Olive Day—and Day's roommate, Marian (or should Towne name her "Marion"?) Welles (or "Wells"?) is missing. . . . At the Albacore Club (or Petroleum Club? Polo Club? Canyon Club?), a prominent judge asks Gittes to convince Cross to sell them the Deep Canyon portion of Cross's ranch. Gittes asks, Why me? On his way out, Gittes notices he's being trailed . . . He runs into his old pal, Luis Escobar who's looking for Marian, claming she's a sister of a friend, but smelling another Chinatown, Gittes declines to help him . . . He returns home to find, of all people, Marian herself waiting for him, afraid that whoever killed Artemis will kill her. "The girl's Chinatown," Gittes thinks, and hands her off to the police. . . . Later that night his phone rings. It's Marian. She's been bailed out. By whom she doesn't know. . . .

Once again Towne stalled out.

Forget it.

Dextroamphetamine. That had always helped. Ever since Towne was eighteen: One quarter of a 5mg tab just to get a "jump start" in the mornings.

On October 4 he started not with Gittes, but Mulwray:

It begins as ID profession Hollis Mulwray finds out the truth

about the water. . . . Later, Gittes is hired his wife, by Evelyn Mulwray. She thinks her husband is having an affair . . . Then Hollis
Mulwray is found dead. Looks like suicide, but Evelyn suspects he
was murdered by whoever wanted the dam. Unlikely, Gittes replies;
the whole city wants it . . . At the city morgue Gittes inspects the
body of a drunk, drowned in a storm drain. How is that possible?
There's a drought . . . At night he checks the river. Water is flowing in
from somewhere. Where? . . . Evelyn tells Gittes she's being watched.
Maybe they're afraid she knows what her husband knew . . . Gittes,
undercover as a dry cleaner, enters Julian Cross's compound, and finds
out that Cross, Mulwray's closest friend and Evelyn Mulwray's father,
did put the watch on Mrs. Mulwray . . . Gittes questions Cross. Why
is he spying on his own daughter? Cross is afraid she's seeing Luis
Ayala, a Mexican convicted of murder whom he believes has designs on his estate . . . Later, Evelyn and Gittes decided to confront
Cross: When they arrive, he's is hallucinating in his bathub. Opium?
Morphine? He grabs his daughter, crying. He mumbles something
about twelve bloody babies. Mrs. Mulwray translates. He means the
twelve months of the year . . .

Towne was in agony. Writing *Chinatown* was like being in Chinatown. A novelist could write and write—and indeed, Towne wrote
like a novelist, turning out hundreds upon hundreds of pages of
notes and outlines and dialogue snippets—but a movie is two hours;
in script form, approximately a minute a page. What could he afford
to lose? He needed to be uncompromisingly objective, but not so
hard on his ideas that he ended up losing what may have been good
in them—that is, if there was ever anything good about them to begin with. Was there? The question had to be asked. Was any of this
good, and if so, would anyone care? A civics lesson on water rights
and the incestuous rape of a child? From one vantage point, it was
dull; from another, obscene. Who would even make such a movie?
Columbia wouldn't even let him write forty *fucks*.

Maybe he was wrong to attempt an original screenplay. Acting as

both creator and executioner of this swiftly expanding entity, surg-
ing and swirling its squelchy way to incomprehensibility—it was
almost too much for one mind to hold, let alone master. And then—
worrying ahead—there was the dialogue. When—*if*—he nailed his
story *and* its structure, he still had to write the actual scenes. Who
says what to whom? And how do they say it? Precisely what words
do they choose to speak? Moreover, what don't they say? (This was
writing for the *screen*, after all.) A screenwriter had to ask: what
faces, behavior, gestures, clothing, and scenery can say that can't,
or shouldn't, be put into dialogue? And as for that dialogue, how
to be witty without being arch, wise without pretension, emotional
without sentiment, principled without pedantry?

In 120 pages?

He would have to borrow money. From whom? Not his father—he
had borrowed enough already. If only he were a faster writer. But
Towne knew what he was, and that was slow, and slow was expensive.

Edward Taylor would help.

After his workday at the University of Southern California, where
he taught sociology and statistics and wrote the occasional research
grant proposal, Edward Taylor would hop his motorcycle and head
home for a very quick dinner.

"Dad, where are you going?"

"To Robert's. To work."

Back on the motorcycle, he'd curl his way up the wide canyons of
Benedict to the hill on Hutton Drive, to Towne's office and his own
place, across from Towne at his desk, in a wingback chair Towne
had brought back from Spain. Lit by the downglow of an antique
parchment lampshade, Taylor propped up his feet on a footstool of
tufted red leather and was ready to go. At arm's length he kept a side
table prepped with his ashtray, drink, and yellow legal pads galore

for whatever ideas, bits of dialogue, or points for further research he and Towne ignited from their conversation. But by this point in the work, more research was unlikely: Since Towne had begun on *Chinatown*, he—with Edward's help—had gathered piles of information on the water wars, the orange groves, the powerful dynasties of Los Angeles's early years—everything pertaining and remotely pertaining to the story, and more. Too much, in fact: They had amassed a pile of nearly five hundred pages of outlines, notes, and character details. What they needed now was to cut and order, to figure out, once and for all, the plot, the exact structure of *Chinatown*.

Secretly Towne and Taylor had been meeting like this for years. On *The Last Detail* "Edward was in the room with Robert every day, seven days a week for five weeks," Julie Payne said, and whenever Towne pulled the latest draft of *Shampoo* from its drawer, she added, "Eddie would be there, working with Robert. He was a fixture in the house." Before that Towne consulted Taylor, his daughter Sarah Naia Stier recalled, on his *Godfather* additions, and as far back as the midsixties, on Towne's television writing for *The Outer Limits*. To Julie, Towne referred to Taylor as "my editor," but rarely spoke of his existence to anyone in Hollywood.

As in any partnership, the attribution of creative input remains an inexact science, the postscript of cyclical rounds of thought all parties involved can claim a part in; and considering that most creative partnerships, like Hecht and Lederer's, are properly credited on screen, there is rarely any need to investigate the question of authorship. It is openly shared. But in the case of Edward Taylor, whose intimate and ongoing involvement in the conceptualization and production of Towne's screenplays, whose cache of *Chinatown* notes—stacks of legal pads filled with Taylor's original scenes, plans for restructuring subsequent drafts, long swaths of dialogue, character sketches, synopses of projected material, and more—and whose in-person and on-phone discussions with Towne on a sometimes daily basis reveal him to be a generative intelligence, invited not merely to respond to the work as an editor would, but to participate in the creation and evolution of a script moment-by-moment from the project's inception, reveal Taylor's influence to be no different from that of any other cocreator—save for one thing: Towne held the veto power. But considering that he and Taylor collaborated (Taylor would say, protectively, "on *Robert's* scripts") for more than forty years, Towne must have said yes to Taylor's input at least half as much as he said no.

"To say Edward Taylor was Robert's 'editor' was an understatement," said Mike Koepf, who knew Taylor well and shared credit with him on several screenplays. "They had a working relationship that although it was secret was significant. [Taylor] didn't take the lead a lot, but when he approached a scene, he was always correct. He would never argue, never criticize. He would say something smart and it was so goddamned smart you'd have to take it. He had a great read on human nature. If there was something wrong with the logic, or against human nature, he'd pick it out really quick. Robert was the strong one and Edward was the weak one, but Edward was the brilliant one. I mean the guy was smart. Character psychology and motivation were his forte. The guy deserves credit, a lot of credit indeed."

"They would discuss down to the most minute details, down to the words being used," recalled their mutual friend and sometime producer, Lauren Weissman.

Taylor would propose to a subsequent collaborator that they should work together as Towne and Taylor had, with Taylor making "suggestions, not changes. You can then either accept them," Taylor wrote to this collaborator, "reject them or incorporate them in some altered form. I've been doing that with Robert for years. I don't get upset if he rejects a suggestion. I don't even get upset if he accepts a suggestion and then forgets that I was the one who made it."

"It was a given that Edward wrote the movie with Robert," said Taylor's stepdaughter, Katherine Andrusco. "Whatever Robert was working on, Edward was working on. Every day."

"Robert never wrote on his own," Payne said, "he never paid Eddie enough, and Eddie never asked for more."

Many in Taylor's family were at a loss to understand the terms of his arrangement with Towne, how Taylor could so comfortably consent to anonymity and what the precise nature of his contributions were. When pressed for details, Taylor himself was vague to the point of contradiction. To some Edward confided he had written full scenes in Towne's scripts; to others, he said he had only given suggestions. Sometimes Taylor insisted that working with Robert was a blessing; it had given him the means to write without having to interface with the business he hated; sometimes he protested he had no taste for glory and simply wanted to earn his keep, go home, and read; sometimes he complained he wanted to leave L.A. and get away from Robert for good. "So many times I would ask Edward about it," Lauren Weissman said, "and he would never define it. He was a gentleman to the core."

"Do you write dialogue?" his daughter, Sarah, asked.

"Robert writes the dialogue. I help with structure."

"What are you doing?" Andrusco asked her stepfather. "You can't *not* get credit. It's not fair and it's not accurate."

"That's not important. What's important is my friendship with Robert."

Taylor's genuine equanimity led his friends and family to wonder who, or what, he may have been protecting, and why. Taylor's widow, Virginia Kennerley, wrote that she "did brood for some time on what shameful secret there could be that accounted for Robert's remarkable and apparently unconditional, almost Svengali-like, hold on Ed." To Kennerley, Taylor always insisted that Robert "saved my life a couple of times," but was Edward thinking of the occasion when his appendix burst and Robert rushed him to the hospital?

Perhaps he was thinking of some kind of emotional rescue, an occasion when Robert showed himself to be a true and singular friend? There was the case of Taylor's ex-lover Veigh McElhatton, a schoolteacher still obsessively in love with him. She had sat around Hutton Drive every day during the writing of *The Last Detail*, "like a lump," Payne recalled, "horribly, horribly depressed." She had sprawling red hair, the creamiest white skin, and readily announced: If Edward wouldn't have her back she would kill herself. A psychiatrist assured Taylor that she was in no real danger, but when Taylor came home one day he found she had hanged herself in his closet. "And of course the police called him in for questioning," Kennerley recalled. "Robert was of the opinion that [Taylor] never really got over it, or so Ed told me." Towne saw his friend through this and other traumas, but would such kindnesses, Kennerley wondered, account for Taylor's unwavering, even self-denying allegiance? Was it an abortion Towne had arranged, years earlier, for another of Taylor's lovers? "Robert and Eddie enabled each other," Andrusco surmised. "They had fun, and they had secrets. And they'd known each other so long, they could be young together forever."

Taylor and Towne had been roommates at Pomona College. They shared a love of theater, literature, and philosophy and played in student productions of *The Crucible* and, according to their friend, actor Nicolas Coster, were, from the very beginning, mutually fascinated with the other's ability. "Edward, freely and without reservation, loved great talent," Coster said, "and Robert loved the great minds. It was a singularly deep love, those two." Their professional association began academically, in the form of term papers Towne passed through Taylor's brain. "Robert always liked people who were reasonably bright to edit his work, even as a college undergraduate," Coster said, "and Edward, with all his brilliance, was never patronizing." Even then Taylor was, according to Coster, "stunningly necessary" to Towne.

Taylor went off to Merton College, Oxford, on a Rhodes Scholarship, where he directed, in 1957, a production of *The Two Noble Kinsmen*, and fell in love with Somerville College undergraduate Virginia Kent (later Kennerley). She was playing Emilia, the lead. He was, as ever, "something of a mystery," Kennerley said. "I always wondered what was at the heart of this restraint." He carried with him, from house to house, a print of Albrecht Dürer's etching "The Prodigal Son." It confounded Kennerley. Why would this most elegant and deferential man, who gave so readily of his talent and intellect, who was so unanimously respected and adored, identify with this tale of woe? "Though he was an extremely good theater director and got good performances from all of us, there was a certain lack of confidence about him despite his brilliance," said Kennerley, who would marry Taylor nearly fifty years after they met at Oxford. "Every now and then you would catch him in a moment of not wanting to put himself in a leadership position." Their first relationship ended when Towne, in 1958, called Edward back to America to help him with *The Tomb of Ligeia*, a script he was writing for Roger Corman.

Returning to Pomona for a PhD in English, Taylor intended, upon graduation, to find work as a professor, which, a Pomona girlfriend recalled, "would have solved his money problem." Taylor's family—strict Southern Baptists come to California from Kentucky—"had nothing," she wrote. When his Pomona girlfriend got pregnant, it was Towne who paid for the abortion. "It happened at the same time Robert Towne's current girlfriend got pregnant," Taylor's girlfriend recalled, "so we both went to the same doctor in L.A." She and Taylor quarreled, and "Ed fled," she explained. "For a few months, he worked in an ice-cream store. And he and Towne were working on some grade-B movies." Taylor would not complete his PhD. "Yes," his former girlfriend added, "he was not ambitious in the sense that he did not devote himself to self-advancement."

To Taylor loyalty took clear precedence over the work. Years later, working with another very good friend on a script based on an idea Taylor had given him, Taylor would write to the friend: "I want never to hear another word about 'friendship.' A friendship of almost 60 years cannot be damaged by a disagreement over a few scenes in a script. I gave you this story to do what you could with. You are in charge. You can fire me. Wouldn't damage our friendship. Wouldn't even bruise it."

Towne, Taylor knew better than anyone, suffered from the reverse tendency. "His father was very successful," their friend Nicolas Coster said, "and I saw Robert competing with that image. He was fiercely competitive." By the time Taylor and Towne were living together in the late fifties, Taylor had seen enough evidence of Towne's ambition, professionally and recreationally, in work and in sport, to pull aside Towne's girlfriend Barrie Chase, and whisper to her a word of wisdom refined by many years of steady analysis. They were in the garage that doubled as Taylor's bedroom. "Be careful," Taylor advised Chase. "You don't want to root for Robert's success. Success will change Robert." It shocked the hell out of her.

Hutton Drive—Night: Towne and Taylor in Towne's office. Two writers.

What did they have?

A tangle of stories. There was Hollis Mulwray's discovery of the water scandal, his supposed infidelity, and his subsequent murder. There was the business of the fake Mrs. Mulwray, Ida Sessions, and her murder. There was the lawsuit Evelyn, the real Mrs. Mulwray, brings against Gittes, and his lawyer, named in homage to Nicholson's lawyer, Bressler. There was Gittes's gambling, his personal identification with Seabiscuit. There was the past: what happened to Gittes in Chinatown. There was the Albacore Club, its association with Cross. There was Escobar, Evelyn's former lover, their forbidden romance. There was Curly, a typical Gittes client, embroiled in a case of infidelity. There was the betrayal of Gittes by his partner Duffy. And of course there was the character once named Marian, the child of incest.

Upon closer inspection Towne and Taylor weren't simply navigating a bounty of subplots, but a cache of backstories. "Central problem I have," Towne noted to himself, "is with constant business of going into the past. How to keep from that." He answered his own question: "Try to keep the action ongoing—simple—"

Early in October 1971, Towne and Taylor attempted to reduce and combine their separate novelistic explorations of world, story, and character into the sparest outlines. "It was Eddie," Payne would say, "who got Robert to write his first outline. He wouldn't outline before *Chinatown*."

"ACT I," Taylor began one attempt:

1. Mulwray found dead—looks like suicide.
2. E[velyn]. says its suicide.
3. Gittes finds Ida dead—convinced it isn't suicide.
4. E. acts interested, but doesn't want police brought in—if Gittes can find who did it, fine, then they go to police, but she doesn't want more needless publicity.

ACT II

5. Gittes tracks down water scheme to Albacore Club.
6. Albacore Club claims innocence. Give Gittes proof that Mulwray was murdered—Evelyn did it. Offer bargain. Piece of the action if Gittes can prove that E murdered Mulwray—Gittes can."

The major plot points that followed were necessary, but their relationship to other scenes remained unclear.

Over the nights, weeks, months that followed, Towne and Taylor produced dozens of such outlines, each varying slightly from the last. They passed these back and forth between them, adding notes in each other's margins, crossing out dramatic loose ends, and discussing their findings before tearing off a fresh page and starting all over again, asking themselves throughout: Could they do it simpler?

Each time, no matter how far they got, they fizzled at the ending.

By November, Towne and Taylor had enlisted additional help. They sent an incomplete outline a friend who responded enthusiastically to the water-scandal material but found the tangle of subplots "formless and abstract." The friend advised: "You have to know how the story ends before it can be written. In a detective story you have to. Or at least I think so."

If Towne had an ending, they could, theoretically, work backwards. But how to satisfyingly end a story whose central precept, Chinatown, represented crushing futility? Most of the great tragedies end with a slim glimmer of hope or knowledge—the sense that the future may not be as bleak as the past. But what kind of glimmer could illuminate the pitch-blackness of total futility? If man's fate is indeed a Chinatown, a Sisyphean infinity loop, where does any story end?

Or begin?

Taylor would stay at Towne's house, grinding out failing possibilities, as late as three in the morning.

By 1972 Towne and Payne were nearly broke. "In those days" Payne said, "you could not pay Robert to write if he didn't want to write. He just wouldn't do it. He wrote only for love."

Warren Beatty would call Payne: "How's it going?"

"Slow. Robert won't put a word on the page until he thinks it's perfect."

"If he ever asks you what you think, don't say anything, because he'll stop."

And then, as it always had, the moment came. He handed her pages.

"What do you think?"

Julie glanced, but her answer was ready-made. "Shorter."

She hocked her diamond earrings.

3

It would be wise to meet Robert Evans for dinner.

Since their first dinner at Woodland, Towne had all but written off the idea of selling the script to Paramount. Potentially surrendering not only his vision of *Chinatown*, by taking Evans's money Towne would also be forfeiting control of the project's future, including the remote possibility that he would make *Chinatown* his directorial debut. It was, after all, a profoundly personal work—in a way, his whole life in sum—and he imagined, as a detective story, *Chinatown* would hold the audience's interest, even if he, as director, struggled to.

But these were dreams. Towne needed money.

In the five years since Evans had been anointed Paramount's head of production, he had managed, against all odds, to restore the dying studio from last place to first. But rather than bolster his credibility, the coup, which few could account for, made Evans a prime target. Those who wanted him to fail—be they competitors, enviers, or ex-lovers—would attribute Paramount's fairy-tale ascent to Evans's legendarily great good luck, but as Evans, borrowing from Seneca, liked to counter, crossing his ankles on the coffee table: "Luck, my friend, is where opportunity meets preparation." They surely met in Robert Evans. When others had balked, backing away from green talent and soapy material, he had bet on *Rosemary's Baby* and *The Godfather*. Those were, to use Evans's formulation, opportunities taken.

As for preparation, he would, in his words, "Do my homework." Indeed Evans was so thoroughly involved in his movies, so dangerously close to being a filmmaker himself, that he alienated not just Coppola but, working as hard as he did, his own wife, the star of his smash hit *Love Story*. Ali MacGraw, soon after marrying Evans in 1969, found herself, like Kay Corleone, in an unhappy ménage with a business empire.

Zipping between wife and studio, flattened by chronic sciatica, on top of a gurney, Evans was perpetually reduced and stretched thin, like a man in a farce. If he could merge love and Paramount, if he could fuse the woman and the work, he could continue his conquest of Hollywood with his home life intact. Thus would Evans make *The Great Gatsby—Ali's favorite book*-and cast Ali as Daisy. That's opportunity.

The preparation: Enlisting Truman Capote to adapt the novel, Evans assured the studio a prestige production, and himself, at last, a twin setting for his marriages, Ali and Paramount, but when Capote's script came back awful, both dreams sputtered to a stop. He needed to find his *Gatsby* a new writer.

And Robert Towne, pauperized from *Chinatown*, needed a job.

They met for dinner at Dominic's in West Hollywood.

"Love stories," Evans announced, answering his own question. "What I am looking for—what I've been looking for since I took the job—is the ultimate man-woman story. Why? Women don't want to see women. They want to see men *and* women. And when you get women to the theater, you get men. They bring 'em in. Love stories— they're good for business and they're good for people. Hollywood is America's single greatest export, its gift to the world. I want them to be proud of us. That's what I want. I want to give them romance." Evans leaned forward. He had a secret: "You know I've gotten more women pregnant than anyone in history. You know how?"

Towne laughed in anticipation.

"*Love Story*!"

Inclined by the nature of his profession to distrust executives, Towne found himself fighting a growing affection for Robert Evans—and losing. He believed what he said and his love of movies was urgently clear. That alone endeared him to Towne.

"I have something I'm working on," Towne revealed. "A love story."

"Go on."

"It's called *Chinatown*."

"Keep going."

"That's all I have." Towne elaborated as best he could. He told Evans about the water, about the detective who falls in love with the daughter of an eminent criminal, "and I have Nicholson. He wants to do it."

"Sounds perfect for Irish"—Evans's nickname for Nicholson— "It's set in Chinatown?"

"No. Chinatown is a state of mind."

"A love state of mind?"

"The detective's fucked-up state of mind."

Evans was lost. "I see."

"But the love story is Chinatown too."

"But it's not *set* in Chinatown?"

"No. Chinatown's a *feeling*."

Evans was still lost. *Rosemary's Baby* was about Rosemary's baby. *Love Story* was a love story, and both came from comprehensible source material—he could sell them—but this?

Evans hung in. He knew what Towne had done for *The Godfather* and how much Coppola had gained by it. So he broached the subject of *Gatsby*. Was Towne interested? It wasn't the producer's place to offer a fee directly to the writer—for that, he would have to go through Towne's agent, Evarts Ziegler—but Towne, whatever the figure, could expect a nice payday (one ultimately worth $175,000). And yet he turned Evans—and *Gatsby*—down: "So much of [the

novel] was in prose and so much of it was utterly untranslatable,"
Towne would reason, "and even if you could translate it, I thought it
would be a thankless task and you'd just be some Hollywood hack
who fucked up a classic. I felt that I had a lot to lose and very little
to gain."

Evans, Towne said, "was mystified" by his pass. He was also tan-
talized by Towne's game of hide-and-seek. In an industry where
writers are worth only what they're paid, Towne's rebuff silently
raised his going rate.

Evans bit. If the writer wouldn't do *Gatsby*, Evans said, maybe the
producer would do *Chinatown*, whatever it was (at least it had Nicholson. And a love story.) Evans would call Ziegler the next morning
and make an offer to option the unwritten script. If Evans liked the
finished script, a sale might follow.

Towne declined the offer.

Payne went to see Ziegler herself. They had run out of cash, and
Towne's agent, "a man of incomparable elegance," said his associate,
Marcia Nasatir, agreed to personally loan Towne ten thousand dol-
lars to help him through the writing.

Humiliated, Julie met Ziegler in the hall outside his office. It
was soon after Coppola had signed with Evans to write *Gatsby*, and
Ziegler was glowering.

"*Chinatown* is worth three *Gatsbys*," Julie assured him. "*Gatsby*
will never work on film. It never has. Robert's got a detective movie,
a murder mystery, and a blonde. How bad could that be?"

He handed her the check.

While the money dribbled away, Robert Towne descended.

Would he start with incest and then reveal the full extent of the water conspiracy? Or would he start with the conspiracy and reveal the incest second? The scandal in the present or the scandal in the past?

Julie recognized the signs. "I don't think writers work without anguish," she said.

Lost, he wandered down to Marcia Nasatir's apartment at the Villa d'Este—where he and Julie had sat out the aftermath of the Tate-Labianca murders—in West Hollywood. Nasatir could read. He trusted her.

She could see he was suffering, an Ancient Mariner, unshaven and bedraggled. He had with him a wrinkled albatross of pages.

"Water . . ." he would plead. "Or incest . . . ?"

"Incest?"

Towne nodded.

"Robert, will they make a movie about incest?"

In June 1972, Towne sacrificed half of his dream, to direct *Chinatown*, and accepted Evans's option offer. Twenty-five thousand dollars won Paramount the right to purchase *Chinatown*, should the script meet the studio's approval, for the terrific sum of $210,000, a figure that conveyed, to Payne, Evans's skepticism: "He never thought Robert would finish the script."

Julie exiled him to Catalina Island to get it done once and for all. It was the cheapest place she could find. At sixty-four dollars, she could rent an entire seaplane—room enough for Robert, Eddie, Hira, two IBM Selectric IIs, and provisions—and a room at the Banning Lodge, a funky bed-and-breakfast between Cat Harbor and Isthmus Cove, wasn't much more. The trouble was the restaurant, the only

place to eat in the area. It wasn't open on Sundays, so Julie would
have to fly out on the seventh day, every week, with food for all purchased, in part, with money Jack Nicholson delivered to Payne while
Towne was away. Money was that scarce.

On Catalina: Towne sat in his bungalow, before his Selectric, before his window before the sea.

He walked the coves, Hira at his side. He walked around the
Catalina Yacht Club, tanned by years of dust. Shielding his eyes from
the summer sun, he walked past the tiny clapboard ranch houses
that dotted the hillside, untouched for fifty years, and he walked
down to the shoreline and caught the friendly tang of eucalyptus in
the salt air. The old days. California.

As a college student, Towne had spent his summers on a tuna
boat four hundred miles from the shore, pulling the fish in by hand,
inhaling that salt air. For two months at a stretch the fishermen
would fix their watch on the water. They wouldn't take their eyes
of the sea. They would stare, all day, at the ocean surface, waiting
for a flash of color, movement, a tug on the line. Then they fought.
Sun-scorched and callused, they wore out their shoulders yanking
back a catch as heavy as three or four hundred pounds. Once a hurricane, rolling up cliffs of water three stories high, hurled the boat
up "and when [it] drops," Towne said, "it's like you're in an elevator
and somebody's cut the cable." On impact, every bolt and nut in the
ship squealed like a chorus of tortured rats "and you can't believe
the ship could possibly stay together." Some didn't. Towne knew of
the wrecks, the fishermen who didn't come back. "I always thought
that Hemingway's *The Old Man and the Sea* was about the creative
process," he said. "The old man was good enough to hook the big
fish, but he wasn't strong enough to reel it in. That's the tragedy of
it. He could conceive of a great novel but couldn't complete it, and
eventually he blew his brains out."

"Each script," Towne said, "is like a trip that you're taking." You
spend days, even years, watching the water, just watching. "And it's

the same thing with your brain," he said. The discipline wasn't so much the hooking of the fish but withstanding the hot hours, enduring, when the line comes back empty again, the panic of lost faith. Was this the time nothing would bite? There were fisherman who waited so long they never returned.

Towne was in Catalina for weeks.

"One afternoon," he said, "I was struggling with a scene and I heard the sound of a bagpiper right there in the center of the isthmus. I walked outside and looked down and about a hundred feet below there was a lone bagpiper playing. I don't know how or why he ended up on Catalina Island, but he would play about three times a week and you could hear that pipe for probably five miles out to sea."

He watched the still surfaces of numberless outlines, waiting. The bagpipes, the waiting, the sea.

Each time out, he and Taylor had outlined chronologically. And why not? Time moved forward, *Chinatown* would too, beginning with the past. But exposition, Towne knew, needn't be a strictly chronological concern: in a mystery, the events are quite often revealed in retrospect, by a detective in the present discovering the events of the past. The entire genre, in fact, was predicated on first concealing and then slowly revealing what had already happened. Why not begin in the present?

How could he have missed this? It was so intuitive.

If the past were already known, there would be no mystery to solve. Therefore he *had* to begin in the present—with the water scandal. "Then," he said, "I realized the past had to bubble up through this simple story about what the hell was happening with this water, and once I had gotten that notion right, then I had worked out about seventy percent of the structure."

At last he began to see it: Movement beneath the surface.

Every week, on his days away from USC, Taylor joined him in Catalina. "He spoke of himself as working *with* Robert," Virginia Kennerley explained. "If he gave himself a title, which he didn't, it would probably have been co-writer, but always the co-writer of Robert's script." When Taylor's friends demanded that he protest his anonymity, he would always say that Robert did the "actual" writing, by which he meant Towne originated the idea for the script and supplied most of the dialogue. "So what his friends saw as a problem," Kennerley added, "seemed not to have been one for Ed." And he appreciated the money Towne paid him.

Taylor was a kind of Hollis Mulwray, Koepf supposed. "Pure, righteous, within the law, cared about society, wanted to help, was altruistic—that was Edward." After the long night's work, before bed, he would pick up his book, fill a tall glass three-quarters full of vodka, and—head down—carry it into his bedroom. Then, turning the radio to the classical station, Taylor would close the door behind him.

In a rare public reference to Taylor, Towne called him "since college my Jiminy Crickett, Mycroft Holmes, and Edmund Wilson."

Heretofore all they had was outlines. But in Catalina they at last turned out a draft, a script.

And this time they made it all the way to an ending: Gittes, in the final chase, knows Evelyn is headed to kill Cross, her father, and rushes out to stop her, but he gets there too late; she's already shot him dead. Mercifully Gittes gets the girl, Evelyn's daughter, safely out of the country, and in a sort of epilogue, we see the Owens Valley crime go unpunished. The End. Taken together, it struck the bitter-sweet chord Towne was looking for. He said: "The one thing [Evelyn] had been trying to do—the purest motive in the whole film—was to protect her daughter. When she carried out this motive by killing her father, she was acting out of motherly love. You knew she was going to stand trial, that she wouldn't tell why she did it, and that she would be punished." But the bad guys would thrive. *Forget it*; they always would. "And, in a sense," Towne said, "that was the point. There are some crimes for which you get punished, and there are some crimes that our society isn't equipped to punish, and so we reward the criminals. In this case, greedy men displaced a whole community and took the land. So there's really nothing to do but put their names on plaques and make them pillars of the community." One of the final images of the first draft was just such a plaque high up on a mountain. Then a view of the valley, won with death, fogged below.

"They wrote the script out there on Catalina Island," Koepf said, "and the script they came ashore with was like 340 pages."

It's always the same story. The screenwriter, Towne said, begins "dreaming a dream. The job is to make a dream come true." As long as he keeps the dream to himself, it stays his own, as pure as it was intended. But for that dream to come true, the writer must sell the script to a producer, giving over creative control and, in most cases, standing by, hands tied, as the new owner of the material hires additional writers to alter the script. The basis for the revisions needn't be creative; the changing demands of actors, budget, location—any element deemed integral to the production—all necessitate amendments to the original. Then, Towne said, a "very tricky thing happens. . . . A director comes along, and you recognize that a transference has to take place, and he has to conceive of the film as his film." The writer's dream cedes to the next power, and, Towne said, "a natural antipathy between director and writer" sets in. "Classically a director gets the script from the writer and then says, 'Get that asshole out of here. We don't need him around.' If you think enough of a writer to gamble a year and a half of your life on what he's done, then presumably you should think enough of him to keep him around while you're doing it. This is done about as often as there are really good movies made." Perhaps less.

There is only so much any writer can do. While they sit in their little rooms, thinking of words, others are out there really doing things, making actual and appreciable change saving lives, planting trees, fighting bad guys, "trotting the corridors of power," Towne said, "and making sure they've put their own imprints in it." The uses of writing? At best they are indirect: "Everybody recognizes 'in the beginning is the word,' and all that fucking lip service, but I don't think it's in the nature of the writer's profession to go after that power." The writer is constitutionally disinclined to act. The inclination to create, to retreat to a world of the mind, where control is absolute, is itself a kind of abjuration, and among all artistic undertakings, few are more inherently abjuring than writing for the screen. It was almost foolish, Towne thought, writing *for* the screen, describing this thing for someone else to make, particularly when, as Towne said: "The image inevitably conveys more than the word." The screenplay is merely an industrial document, an idea for a movie, incomplete. In a way, self-destructive. "The only way a screenplay can be evaluated," he said, "almost by definition, is not on the page, but by viewing the movie it caused to be made. It certainly can be read and even enjoyed, but you're stuck with the inescapable fact that it was written to be seen." If a screenplay doesn't get made, does it make a sound?

Does the screenwriter matter? The unasked question pervades Towne's characters, instilling them with a sometimes noble, sometimes pitiful, futility of purpose. "It occurs to me," Stephen Schiff observed, "that all his characters are somehow projections of the screenwriter at his Sisyphean labor, that all of their virtues are the screenwriter's virtues, and all of their dramas are recasting of the screenwriter's own." They all have a job to do, and they do it well, but they end up nowhere, wiping the dreams off their faces in impotent rage or despair.

"It's a sucker's game," Towne said of his profession. "But sometimes you do get those moments when it all comes together. And that's exciting. Nothing can match that." "Sometimes"—a dreamer's word.

Los Angeles is their town. Sometimes.

4

Polanski could not return to Los Angeles. The canyons, the watercolor estates, the ruby red carpet into the Beverly Hills Hotel, the bending banana fronds—they all assailed his brain with Sharon, their swinging over the Topanga cliffs, pasta dinners on the beach, the scorched-poppy sunsets, drive-ins, cotton candy, Cracker Jacks, potted plants, baby books (the books in her hands, her hands turning pages, her fingers, her fingernails). Unlike Sharon, Los Angeles was still there. But his eyes couldn't see it. Where others saw crimson sunsets fade to pink, he could not stop her bleeding flesh from rotting to darkness, and though, in Los Angeles, there would be women and compassionate associates and the fondest friends, he would hear only what they wouldn't say: the pity, the admiration of his forbearance, their bracing attempts at wisdom. That alone would be too much. "For the world," he said, "it was an event. But what about me? My love was gone."

He would stay in Europe, based in Rome, in a villa big enough to hold every guest, girl, passer-through, as many as he could imagine. In Europe, with distance standing in for time, it was easier to forget. "In order to survive and function," his friend and sometime collaborator Kenneth Tynan wrote, "he has had to immunize himself against nostalgia." He had to keep moving, the faster the better.

He went to Gstaad. In Gstaad, high in the Swiss Alps, he could ski fast and forget. "I skied for four months," he said, every day."

He would invite friends to join him in Gstaad. "The measure of his loneliness," Tynan wrote, "is that he's never alone." He courted and slept with young women, some, he confessed, as young as sixteen (Switzerland's age of consent), and refused, whenever he was asked to account for his behavior, to admonish himself for it, claiming instead all manner of justification, citing their "untapped reserves of intelligence and imagination," how "they weren't on the lookout for parts" and other qualities not exclusive to sixteen year olds; "and they were," wrote Polanski in his memoir, "more beautiful, in a natural, coltish way, than they would ever be again."

Jack Nicholson came to Gstaad to join him on the slopes. Polanski's father, Ryszard, arrived from Poland with Wanda, his wife. The more he saw him, the more Polanski found himself becoming more and more like his father, overcoming, in a way, the emotional distance that had always persisted between them. Having survived the murders of their pregnant wives, both father and son, Polanski saw, were encumbered by a strain of unworthiness so oppressive it seemed innate, and the persecutory, profoundly Jewish superstition that every joy, every respite, would be paid for in the end.

When Polanski arrived in his father's hotel room in Gstaad, Wanda was playing solitaire. Under a soft light, his father was sitting on the edge of the bed, his eyes on the floor. He was crying.

"Why are you crying?"

"No, no," his father insisted. "It's just the music." Beside his bed, a radio. A German song. "O Mein Papa."

Oh, my Papa, to me he was so wonderful,
Oh, my Papa, to me he was so good.

Polanski sat beside him.

No one could be so gentle and so lovable,
Oh, my Papa, he always understood.

"After you ran from the ghetto," his father began, "and just before the final liquidation of the ghetto, they took all the people."

Oh, my Papa, so funny, so adorable,
Always the clown so funny in his way.

"They called all Jews . . . we were standing there . . . suddenly trucks arrived and they started loading children on those trucks. As this was happening, most were parents of those children, they started swaying and waving and moaning and screaming and crying and falling on the ground and tearing the mud from the ground . . . and the Germans were playing this song."

Oh, my Papa, to me he was so wonderful,
Deep in my heart I miss him so today.
Gone are the days when he would take me on his knee
And with a smile he'd change my tears to laughter.

Polanski would try to console him. "This can never happen again."

"Wait fifty years. You'll see."

In England, Polanski made a film of *Macbeth*.

On the morning of the murder of Lady Macduff's children, Polanski took one of the children aside and tenderly explained to her the particulars of the scene, where the screams would come, where she would be found dead, and how the blood he was painting on her face was only red paint, makeup, pretend.

"What's your name?" he asked, touching red onto her lips. "Sharon."

Polanski and Terence Bayler, in the part of Macduff, rehearsed the scene in which Macduff learns of the murders:

Ross: Your castle is surpris'd: your wife and babes, savagely slaughter'd.

Macduff: Merciful heaven! . . . My children, too?

Ross: Wife, children, servants, all that could be found.

Macduff: And I must be from thence! My wife kill'd too? . . . . All my pretty ones? Did you say all?

Bayler asked if afterward, he should keep walking in a daze.

"Yes, you should," Polanski said. "I know about this situation."

He dammed himself through exercise, working his body tighter against weakness. He built around his mind a wall of brittle knowledge, recalcitrant counterarguments, and cutting ripostes, and when journalists, invaders, came to the gates, he was ready with his responses, most of them antipsychoanalytical one-liners, to fight off the inevitable onslaught of inquiries into his past, the war, the dead mother, the dead wife and child, how they darkened his films. Why did he refuse to be analyzed? It would impede the creative process, he claimed. How to explain his obsession with violence? "The human is a violent animal." How had he managed to survive? This one was often laced with silent censure: How *dare* you survive? Why wasn't he still grieving? How could he be seen with other women? (Why were they so young?) Did he love them? No, he admitted. He couldn't love anyone. "I doubt if I shall ever again be able to live on a permanent basis with any woman," he confessed, "no matter how bright, easygoing, good-natured, or attuned to my moods. My attempts to do so have always failed, not least because I start drawing comparisons with Sharon."

He would not be treated as a science experiment or submit to anyone's theory of his mind. Theories were easy; the truth was that he was not equivalent to his tragedies but as variable as everyone else, if not more so. Polanski's mind came amplified by a creative muse so vivid that audiences unable to conceive the power of imagination had taken his films for his reality. Otherwise, why would they hate him so? Perhaps it was safer for them to try to contain the world's evil by attributing it to a single source—him, a witch in Salem—than allow for what he had learned too well: that chance is infinitely absurd and there is nothing we, with our little lightening-rod theories, can do to tarry the thunderbolts. *After all, even sitting here at some stage may be dangerous.*

"Shove off."

Though he was one of the most famous directors in the world, Polanski was then far from the world's most employable. In the aftermath of the murders, Hollywood kept its distance—"Roman was down for the count," Nicholson said—and whatever their merits, *Macbeth* and Polanski's follow-up, *What?*, further taxed his commercial and artistic appeal. The Playboy logo that introduced *Macbeth* (Hugh Hefner was a producer) drew laughs; the movie ran long; and its hyperviolence, some felt, detracted. And then there was *What?*—a raucous, absurdist sex comedy—whose very title was a blank check to critics.

Polanski needed a job, he needed a *hit*, but when the subject was broached in Los Angeles, it surfaced he was no one's first choice to direct *Chinatown*. "Robert and I couldn't understand how you could have somebody who was from Poland," Payne said, "who was a refugee, make a movie about California." But they had already tried for and lost Arthur Penn, "who didn't know what he was reading," Payne said, as well as Beatty, who, typically ambivalent, first showed interest, then joked it off. It was the Weaver who came to Polanski's rescue. He called his pal in Rome: He had just finished shooting *The Last Detail*, which Columbia, held to the fire by Nicholson, had at last sanctioned—with a script by Robert Towne, who had just written a new script for Robert Evans at Paramount. Would Roman have a read? They wanted him to direct.

No, Roman replied. He wouldn't go back to L.A. No.

So Robert Evans called him. "The script's a fuckin' mess, Roman. I need you here yesterday."

"I've got to go to Poland, Bob, for Passover."

"Fuck Passover, Roman. If you don't get here, we're never going to get into shape. I'll have Passover at my house."

Again Polanski declined. He wasn't going back. So Evans sent the script to Rome.

Polanski had always wanted to make a detective film; it was a genre steeped in the Hollywood he had grown up with. "Anyone who loves the cinema," he said, "wants to make each of the genres." He had read Chandler in Polish and loved Huston's film of *The Maltese Falcon*; there would be something magical in making a detective film for Paramount, like going home. Polanski had a particular fondness for Paramount's detective pictures, namely *The Glass Key* and *This Gun for Hire*, films rich in his sort of fearful atmosphere. He also felt, for Paramount, a supple sense of gemütlichkeit. As far back as the silent period, the studio had been famously and uncommonly welcoming to European filmmakers, a trend that lasted well into the postwar era. A haven within the larger haven of Hollywood, Paramount was home to directors Ernst Lubitsch, Josef von Sternberg, Rouben Mamoulian, and Billy Wilder, offering, uniquely, the same degree of artistic freedom that had nurtured them in Europe. "In almost direct opposition to MGM or Warners," writes film historian Thomas Schatz, "where the higher the stakes the more likely the studio boss and production chief were to be involved, at Paramount the high-cost, high-risk pictures involved the lease amount of executive control or front-office interference. Thus Paramount was something of a 'director's studio' where its prestige productions were concerned, and there was much less continuity in terms of style or market appeal between its top features and routine releases." There would be something right about going back to Paramount, back to work for Evans.

And there was the money—Polanski anticipated a much-needed mainstream success with a detective picture—and there was the love. After the murders, where others abandoned him, Evans and Nicholson showed undying loyalty to Polanski, the branded outcast. They would surely cushion the horror of returning to Los Angeles. There would be safety in Dick Sylbert, Anthea Sylbert, Howard Koch Jr., and Sam O'Steen, leaders of his intrepid *Rosemary's* band. And there was Warren.

Polanski didn't know Towne, but he came with Evans and Nicholson's imprimatur. Evans even offered to find Polanski a secluded house in the Hills, high up, away from gawkers and paparazzi, and big enough for the all-in parties Roman loved, with a pool and a view. And he wasn't kidding about Passover.

Of course the script that had been sent to him was a mess, but Polanski decided he would go to Los Angeles to meet about *Chinatown*.

"It was a bunch of friends," he said.

To get things going, Polanski, Evans, and Sylbert met Towne for lunch at Nate 'n Al's. Despite the comfortable deli setting, all were amiably agitated; exercising Towne's (expensive) right on the option, Evans had purchased a script that irritated everyone, and with the pleasantries behind them, the time had come to level with Towne: there was more work to do—a lot more.

Further, Polanski had found Los Angeles to be the heartbreak town he feared ("Every road I drove on brought the tragedy back to me"), and wanted nothing more than to offer his notes quickly and board the next plane back to Europe. Evans, foreseeing the showdown between writer and director, was on guard to keep both playing fair, though his allegiance was to Polanski; Sylbert, whose story sense was as valued as his art direction, was likewise inclined toward his friend, the director; Towne, the one who hadn't made *Rosemary's Baby*, was on defense, alone.

It would be a long lunch.

Where to begin?

Polanski. He assured Towne that he respected him too much to sugarcoat it. Though he appreciated that Towne had already gone to considerable lengths to narrow down the script from the hundreds of pages of the Catalina draft, it was still far too long at 180 pages. Evans and Sylbert agreed. The story was a bafflement of subplots; again Evans and Sylbert agreed (and, by the way, so did Nicholson, Evans explained to Towne). Gittes, Polanski felt, was lost in a horde of well-developed but auxiliary characters; again Evans and Sylbert agreed. And the title? Save for Gittes's backstory, the script had nothing to do with Chinatown or anything remotely Chinese. It didn't even have a single scene set in Chinatown. That wouldn't fly. Nor would all the civics. Polanski loved the scenes about the water scandal, but "in reality," he said, "the capitalist swindle with the water and land of Los Angeles doesn't bother anyone," and in their current form, he feared they would overwhelm the incest story, which, to Polanski, was *Chinatown*'s emotional core. And the ending? Evelyn kills her father? Be reasonable, Polanski advised. Why doesn't Cross "get away clean," Roman asked, "just like most bad guys really do"?

He was too tactful to say as much, but Towne felt even then that Polanski's objection referred to a tragic past that was more real to him than the script. "I don't mean this unkindly," he reflected, "but I think it was impossible for Roman to come back to Los Angeles and not end his movie with an attractive blond lady being murdered." Alongside the question of the ending, there hovered a larger concern: Had grief clarified or clouded Polanski's instincts?

Dutifully Towne considered Polanski's approach to the ending at face value, but explained that he was after something, he hoped, more complicated than desolate. Gittes tries, and, yes, fails to stop Evelyn from killing her father and ruining her life, "but he did succeed," Towne would say, "in getting her daughter out of the country. So the ending was bittersweet in that one person at least—the child—wasn't tainted."

"I felt this was too romantic," Polanski said. "Too much of a happy ending."

Towne looked to Evans and Sylbert for support. But they stood with Polanski. "We were really very critical to such a degree," Polanski recalled, "that Bob Towne was quite depressed." He regarded the draft in hand as the greatest thing he had yet written.

Reluctantly the screenwriter agreed to a massive revision, and the meeting adjourned.

Polanski, as soon as he could, flew back to Rome.

Towne, who had already spent more than two years on the draft, to say nothing of the many thousands of dollars borrowed and spent, who had willingly sold off his right to direct and his artistic control, was shattered. Shorter? It was already shorter. When would it be enough? When would it stop being his?

Had it already?

Forget it.

Leaving Nate n' Al's, Towne couldn't even claim the righteous honor of being wronged. No one had forced him to be a screenwriter.

By the time Polanski was summoned back to Los Angeles, in the summer of 1973, Towne's screenplay had gotten shorter, but was even more unsatisfying to Polanski than the earlier draft. Polanski was baffled, both by the story, a drama still too diffuse to captivate, and by a screenwriter who appeared, three years after embarking on his project, still at a loss to contain his own creation. If the latest draft had improved on the first, Polanski would have come back to town—this time to Dick Sylbert's Chinese deco place at the Lotus Apartments in West Hollywood—heartened by progress, but what with the antagonistic creative slog he saw ahead, his anguished Los Angeles, and the gloom of the Lotus's creaking floorboards and tiny rooms—more like an abandoned opium den than a Californian hideaway—his depression, held off for so long by avoidance and adventure, recurred and deepened.

And it wasn't all in Polanski's head; the city itself was undone by mourning. "It changed apparently beyond recognition," he observed. Since the murders the communal dream of social and political reformation that had illumed the sixties had blackened, almost on cue, at the decade's turn. The flower children, no longer children, no longer lined the Whisky a Go Go in their rainbow beads and tie-dye. They no longer fought proudly and smiled sunward; now, like Jack Nicholson, they raged and grinned and, come midnight, hid their eyes behind dark shades. In the morning, partied-out lapsed hippies woke up slumped against the Whisky wall in their ice-cold sequins and disco glitter, the nihilistic badges of Fuck-It-All America. What did the Bee Gees stand for? It didn't matter. Richard Nixon was president. "Sharon's murder and the landing on the moon changed everything," Polanski said. "When man walked on the moon, some romantic idea of the moon was over. I believed in romance when I was with Sharon. It was happening! I mean, *why it cannot be?* But the magic illusion of romance was gone." Memory was a despot that lived in his house and banged his pots and pans. It followed him to bed and sat on his head and shouted if he slept. It locked the door and cuffed his wrists and watched him try to run.

Polanski discerned the change in Los Angeles, "from really bucolic suburbs with quiet streets and houses left virtually opened, to an area of very dangerous living with people barricading themselves. Vengeance in all aspects. Not only crime on the streets but drugs and envy inside." The cause and effect of Sharon's murder was, to him, "the most dramatic change in the history of America," entwined as it was in Vietnam, its epidemic swirl of futility and rage. "The hippie movement has degenerated," he reflected, "but the degeneration came from the top, not from the bottom. When the kids began preaching new values, the Government tried to beat their ideas out of them. The reaction, from Berkeley on, was only what you could expect: violence." A civil war had been lost.

In satin shoes and cravat, cocaine doffed its hat and stepped into Hollywood in the heat of a cold sun, and promised, for a moment (and then another), a fraudulent dream too fast to refuse. Among its first casualties was the one who had called Polanski that night in London, the first to identify Sharon's body, Polanski's agent at Ziegler, Bill Tennant. Without even emptying his desk drawers, Tennant had simply walked out of his office, walked out on his wife, Sandy, and driven off, whereabouts unknown. It was devastating, to Polanski, to Tennant's clients, to the agency he left behind. "It broke Zieg's heart," Julie Payne said. "He was grooming Bill to be his successor."

Up on Mulholland, Nicholson welcomed Polanski, as he did all his friends, into his home. The place was pure Jack. Shelved with Sartre and Wilhelm Reich and Kerouac, his gods of death and sex and free living, ringed with artworks famous and unknown, and a killer view of the city, the house carried Nicholson's Beat loyalties into the seventies, and said that chez-Jack, the proverbial fridge was always full and the good times were on the house. On the coffee table there was a bowl of cash to take from—to remind his many friends and lovers that he was still, despite his earnings, very much the Weaver of Pupi's. There was also an opulent cocaine pyramid, pointing skyward in a help-yourself bowl in the foyer. For Polanski, it was a welcome change from the Lotus Apartments. At Nicholson's the ghosts were slower to find him. But when night came and the living room dimmed, city lights stalked the windows, and the mood moved down and away, to Sharon and to *Chinatown*. Polanski saw why he had come back: It was because he had never left.

From Mulholland, Robert Evans drove Polanski to see "a sexy house," white as powder, on Sierra Mar. Perched high above the city at the mountain fringe—"there's no more beautiful city in the world," Polanski said, "provided it's seen by night and from a distance"—its pool seemed to spill into the city Polanski regarded as a forgone joy, and its garden waterfall, when the house windows opened, could be heard from the downstairs office. There Polanski and Towne could work just steps from the pool. How appropriate that house's owner, George Montgomery, had played Philip Marlowe in *The Brasher Doubloon*, and that the house itself, a courtly Spanish sprawl, could have starred alongside him. Polanski rented it.

In an awkward jest, he presented Towne a book on the basics of screenwriting and inscribed it: "To my partner, with hope."

The heat was tremendous that summer of 1973.

Every day, beginning at eight in the morning, Towne would come to the little poolside office on Sierra Mar, his dog, Hira, in tow. Ventilation was scant, but Towne kept lighting cigars. Irritated and uncomfortable, Polanski hated the smell of tobacco and the giant hairy dog that made itself a bed on his feet. For three days he endured. Little was accomplished.

Procrastination.

Chit-chat.

Silent resentments.

"That's enough of that dog!" Polanski announced after another distracted day. Hira never came back.

But without the dog, they were out of excuses.

Rather than force *Chinatown*'s existing pieces together, the thing to do, they agreed, was to clear the table of all preconceptions and rebuild the story from scratch. That way they would see what was absolutely essential. The rest they would scrap.

They began by one-lining the script, writing single-sentence descriptions of essential story points at the top of eight-and-a-half-by-eleven-inch pages and posting them, in order, on the back of the office door. This alone was an undertaking. Not only was the pursuit of narrative economy intellectually taxing, but condensing the story forced Towne, at every turn, to sacrifice creative darlings he had nurtured for years. Removing them from his script at this point would be removing parts of himself.

Was that what Polanski was trying to do? Make *Chinatown his*? Well, yes. It was pointless to argue the line between ego and art, but at the same time, it would be impossible, with so much invested—two careers, two memories, two passionate visions of reality—to keep personal and aesthetic needs perfectly segregated. Mutual insult was inevitable. As the writer, Towne's job had been to dream out a script; as the director, it was Polanski's to wake him up. It didn't matter how Towne felt or what a scene meant to him; the best revision would care nothing for his heart's *Chinatown*, for all the thistle and eucalyptus he had once forgotten and written to reclaim. Those days were over—again.

So goodbye to his endless supporting characters, goodbye to the love story of Byron Samples and Ida Samples; Goodbye to Evelyn's affair with a mystery man and Gittes's looming jealousy, "which I felt would have been more interesting," Towne said; goodbye to Gittes's and Evelyn's protracted and suspicious courtship, her violent outbursts, his many faraway mentions of Chinatown; goodbye to Julian Cross's drug addiction; Julie's favorite scene, containing Cross's eerie aria to the sweet smell of horseshit; goodbye to the betrayal of Gittes by his partners, Duffy and Walsh, and his extended consultation with his lawyer, Bressler; goodbye to Escobar's jagged history with the Cross family; goodbye to Gittes's passion, Towne's passion really, for Seabiscuit, intended to contain Gittes's uptown ambitions;

goodbye to *Chinatown*'s multiple points of view: "You [should] never show things that happen in [Gittes's] absence," Polanski said; goodbye to the slowly encroaching paranoia, the hurricane of subplots that swirled around Gittes; goodbye to everything that wasn't water. Everything, Polanski decreed, had to move the water mystery forward; if they *could* cut it, they *should* cut it. But when it came to certain elements—namely, the love story (Towne wanted more scenes; Polanski, certain a good sex scene would suffice, fewer) and of course the ending—Towne and Polanski had two opposing definitions of "could." They fought. Their arguments were painful. Each was smart enough to see the virtues in the other's strategy; both were correct. Polanski explained he wanted Gittes and Evelyn to have satisfying sex because "it changes the rapport between them for the second part of the picture. Something serious starts between them." But, Towne countered, if she represents Chinatown, she can't satisfy Gittes. She's unknowable, impossible, a mystery.

Instead Towne had written a scene that brings them close— "There's something black in the green part of your eye," Gittes says; ". . . Oh that . . . it's a flaw in the iris"—but the scene following shows them *after* their clearly unfulfilling sexual encounter. "I hope it's something I said," Gittes says. Polanski's urge to gratify Evelyn, Towne pathologized; it helped him to argue his case: "I think perhaps, [Polanski] preferred identifying with the character when the woman praised him for making love well," he said. But if they don't have meaningful sex, Polanski returned, how could their relationship matter that much to Gittes, and therefore, to the audience? Good sex, which portends love, would give Gittes more to lose, a line of reasoning that reinforced Polanski's vision of a darker ending. And here Polanski used the same argument on Towne that Towne had leveled against Polanski's proposed rewrite of the sex scene: How Chinatown would *Chinatown* be if it ended, as Towne had written it, with Evelyn killing her father and their daughter escaping? It would be Chinatown enough, Towne maintained, to end, pulling back onto a wide shot of Los Angeles, to show the legacy of the water scandal corrupting the city into the present day. Having spent three years on these questions, he was indeed the expert, and having failed many times over, he knew what did and didn't work, but Polanski, the newcomer, was an expert *audience*, coolly objective to Towne's heated subjectivity; and each, armed with a mastery of story sense, could argue his case so compellingly that the glut of good sense led both writers astray.

They worked ten hours a day, Towne said, "posting [pages] on the door of the room and kept moving around the little slips figuring, you know, one way or another it would work. It was a little like monkeys on a typewriter."

It got tense. Nicholson swooped in for dinner and brought a TV into the office to lighten the mood. It didn't work.

Towne, turning away from the fight, would look to the window in time to see girls promenade down to the lip of Polanski's waterfall and plop prettily into the pool.

They would fight over individual words. Polanski simply would not relent. "People can go crazy sitting with me," he said, "because I like eliminating every unnecessary word."

"Bob," Polanski asked after one dispute, "do you think I'm a schmuck?"

"No," Towne returned, "You're a terrific .400 hitter, which means that I think you're right less than half the time."

As much as it provoked Towne, Polanski's stubbornness—or determination—also moved him. The director's vigor was partly utilitarian—"I have no time to think," he said, "to conceive and to analyze during the period of shooting. So I have to be sure that I can rely on what is written, and if I just film it the way I anticipated, I won't go wrong"—but as a man who had survived too much, the force of will he demonstrated in the office conveyed something of the "resilience," Towne observed, "[that] was rooted in personal history." For Polanski, an obsessive arguer, there was more than philosophical clarity on the far side of a debate; trouncing his interlocutor offered him a sportsman's rush and a quick surge of mastery. "Winning an argument," Susanna Moore said, "he would smile to himself," and why not? The world was chaos. He had long ago given up on God and the Devil, "divine justice, or any kind of plan in existence. We are born, it means nothing, we die." Cogent argument lent the nothingness shape, fleetingly.

After the murders the psychiatrist had warned him he would likely suffer four years of disabling grief. Then the pain would deaden and he would begin to function normally again. But the four years had passed, leaving Polanski to wonder at how an expert could be so wrong, and if he, uniquely scourged, was an aberrant case, stained forever.

By night he drew in waves of old friends—Robert Evans, Dick and Anthea Sylbert, Warren Beatty, Nicholson and his new girlfriend, Anjelica Huston—"the whole crowd," said Polanski's friend, the actress Nandu Hinds. "Those parties were a mob. Warren would be in the corner in the kitchen hiding from all these women, all these groupies, strange young girls that would come in and out and want to be part of the scene. I don't know who brought them or how they got there, but they always seemed to be there. They may have been fifteen years old but they looked older. There was drugs and sex of course, but nobody, no one, was hurting anyone. It was innocent." Friends would lie about the pool table and spill into Polanski's upstairs bedroom, pile together on the bed and giggle at porno flicks. "Roman loved people," Hinds said. "He was civilized and had a tremendous curiosity that more people should have. He'd look at people and analyze them always with a cute little wicked smile on his face." Polanski, for the first time, almost felt glad to be back in Los Angeles. "Once I was there," he said, "I began living again: parties, friends, girls. . . ." Towne said, "I don't think there was a day that we worked that we didn't go out and play at night. The mood at night was—it was the 1970s. We had a good time."

The spirit of communal enthusiasm those nights at Polanski's home on Sierra Mar nourished half dozen significant movies. At the top of their fields, all were working, and were scheduled to work, on projects they loved—movies that, if they weren't charged with political fervor, were playfully nostalgic for the genres they, as young moviegoers, had fallen headfirst in love with: Nicholson, after *Chinatown*, would costar with his friend Beatty in their friend Mike Nichols's film of *The Fortune*, written by Jack's friend from Jeff Corey's class, Carol Eastman. Then the Sylberts would join their friends Beatty and Towne's long-gestating production of *Shampoo*, directed by Hal Ashby, Towne and Nicholson's friend from *The Last Detail*. "This little group," Anthea Sylbert said. "We were working on each other's movies even when we weren't working on each other's movies." Where loyalties flourished, competition had no purchase.

Evans—making a rare appearance away from work—confessed that he still didn't get *Chinatown*, but frankly he wasn't worried. He was betting on talent, his friends, the surest bets in Hollywood. Others, however, were less sure of the movie's prospects. "Nobody I spoke with," Hinds said, "thought it would be any good."

"No one understands this script," Evans was reminded at one party.

"What's to understand? I got Irish, the Polack, and the greatest scribe in town. And the period," he added. "Los Angeles in 1937. You know what that is? That's a classic. *That's* romance."

Privately Evans had his doubts. "Evans knew Towne's father had tried his hand at being a developer," Peter Bart observed, "and felt his writing might entail working out some familial neuroses that were clouding the plot."

In the poolside office, the "working out" was not taking place. Polanski and Towne slogged through what was left of the story, suffering the other's excesses.

Edward Taylor, his existence unknown to Polanski (and, for that matter, Robert Evans), stayed away.

Polanski would shout. Solutions readily in mind, he rushed Towne to come around; Towne, for his part, procrastinated, deliberated, showed up late, took phone calls. Polanski lost his temper. Towne lost his back. "He put up more resistance in those meetings than the Maquis put up against the Germans in the Auvergne," Dick Sylbert recalled.

Polanski asked his writer: How could a movie called *Chinatown* not have a scene set in Chinatown?

Chinatown is a state of mind.

You can't set a scene in a state of mind.

I agree. Then we won't.

Then we shouldn't call it *Chinatown*.

(Dick Sylbert, paying a visit, suggested a compromise: One of the characters should like Chinese food.)

Depleted of patience, strength, conviction, Towne would nod absently and rise from his chair. "I've got to go home and take Hira for a walk now."

One problem they were dealing with: Gittes's discovery that Evelyn's daughter is hers by incest lacked the consequence expected of such a climactic moment. The news was simply delivered to Gittes by Escobar ("Do I have to spell it out for you? Maria is Cross's daughter") and didn't include Evelyn. Wouldn't it be better for her to be a part of the revelation? "Robert tried many ways and were always speeches that smacked of explanation," Polanski said. Nothing worked.

There was Towne's old girlfriend, lost to Sweden, Barrie Chase.

"Why don't you speak to your father?" Towne had asked her twenty years earlier.

One day she had told him. In 1949 Chase's mother discovered him in bed, "entirely naked," she said, with her twenty-four-year-old daughter, his stepdaughter. Wire recordings would reveal that Mr. Chase, sleeping with a .45, intended to kill his wife. Fearing for her life, Mrs. Chase made the scandal public, sought a permit to carry her own gun and have her husband's permit revoked. "If I stand without a gun and he has one, I am dead," she told the press.

On her way into the swimming pool one afternoon, Barrie heard her mother scream and halted. "Don't! Don't go in the water!" The underwater light had been torn out, exposing the electrical current.

On another occasion, as mother and daughter were driving from the house, the brakes went out.

One of the last times Chase spoke to her father he told her they were paranoid. No one was trying to murder anyone. "It's your mother who's doing this," he said.

Barrie Chase, Towne, and Eddie Taylor were in the converted garage, going over the details of the scandal, one evening in 195X. "Eddie and Robert wouldn't let it go," Chase said. Confused and fascinated, they had her explain it over and over, the relationships, the sequence of events, the threats:

"She was your stepsister?"

"My *half* sister."

"Your mother's daughter?"

"Yes. But I always referred to her as my sister."

"How old was she when—?"

"Twenty-four."

"And how old were you?"

"Sixteen."

"How did she find them, your mother?"

"Detectives. A raid."

"On her own *daughter*. . . . With her *husband*—"

"Then she found out my sister was pregnant."

That stopped them.

"Pregnant? By your father?"

Chase nodded.

"Would that make you . . . the baby's sister?"

"Or the aunt?"

"Sister," Towne said. "I think . . ."

"No," Taylor countered. "Aunt . . ."

"Sister."

"Aunt."

They took off.

"Sister!"

"Aunt!"

"Sister!"

"Aunt!"

"She's her sister *and* her aunt!"

There was maybe something there. But would a woman as coolly withdrawn as Evelyn Mulwray just come out and say it?

Arguments persisted on all fronts for another two months. "Robert was absolutely resistant to changing anything," Julie Payne said. Polanski had to fight to subdue, if not eliminate entirely, the disquisitions into Los Angeles politics that were personally and politically crucial to Towne. He was demanding universality from a story Towne had scrupulously grounded in specifics. "Initially," Towne said, "I was more specific about the story in Chinatown. I wanted what had happened to [Gittes] to be ridiculous—a humiliation—and instead Roman wanted to emphasize the tragedy, but he didn't want to be specific about it." But the more detail Towne revealed about Gittes's first tragedy in Chinatown, Polanski argued, the farther they would stray from metaphor and the harder it would be to emphasize the cyclical nature of Gittes's tragedy—and it had to be a tragedy, total tragedy. Polanski was still adamant about that. "My own feeling," Towne said, "is if a scene is relentlessly bleak . . . it isn't as powerful as it can be if there's a little light there to underscore the bleakness. If you show something decent happening, it makes what's bad almost worse. . . . In a melodrama, where there are confrontations between good and evil—if the evil is too triumphant, it destroys your ability to identify with it rather than if its victory is only qualified."

This was not the way the world worked, Polanski maintained. "You have to show violence the way it is," he said. "If you don't show it realistically, then that's immoral and harmful. If you don't upset people, then that's obscenity." Catastrophe happens, Roman would argue. That's life.

Towne, a romantic, advocated somewhere, for hope. It did exist.

Always? "I suspect that more people are just a mixture of good and bad," Polanski reasoned. "But then occasionally a serial killer comes along." He had a dark wealth of personal evidence to support his position, but arguing for unmitigated tragedy, he never invoked for Towne his memories of Warsaw or drifting the blood-scratched rooms of Cielo Drive, let alone the war in Vietnam or other devastations from recent history. In that office by the pool, Polanski never resorted to lecture on man's apparent delight in war, though he could have. Rather he based his position, privately, on a conviction he found in a memory, a happy one at that:

It was after the war.

He was a boy, no more than fourteen or fifteen.

He went to the movies. It was *Of Mice and Men*. Leaving the theater, Kraków's Kino Warszawa, Polanski couldn't leave the memory of Lenny's death. Replaying the ending in his mind, he wished, as everyone did, that Lenny could have lived. But, perhaps alone among those leaving the theater that day, it occurred to Polanski that it was unlikely he'd still be thinking about the ending, or that he'd retain the experience at all, if it hadn't hurt as it had: ". . . A field," George had promised Lenny, "of alfalfa."

Bang!

What made him remember, years later, the film with love, *was* the tragedy.

Julie Payne, who, as a girl, had been left alone with only books for comfort, went to see a doctor about the eye she had been worried about since she was a child—the same dark spot her mother, brushing Julie aside, had once decreed a beauty mark. The doctor, an eye specialist, told her it was a freckle. His colleague took another look. It was a tumor. "But don't worry," he said. It was benign "You were born with it." A flaw in the iris.

Two months after Towne and Polanski first began their revision, their arguments had reached unsustainable heights; they stopped speaking. Evans tried to referee but the game was over. "I would never work with Roman again," Towne explained, "nor he with me." "I would never work with Roman."

Polanski had erased Towne's elegy for Los Angeles. The very character of the city, lovingly rendered in place-names and native personalities and detailed changes in light and ambience, had been razed for an unbeautiful, blackly anonymous setting prostrated by menace and depravity. Towne complained to Evans, but Evans, a producer with a picture to make, had to press forward. Resigned to the natural course of production, Towne understood: There was nothing he could do. *Chinatown* was Roman Polanski's now.

PART THREE

The Mountain

PART THREE

The Mountain

1

Ali didn't even stop to take her clothes off. Emerging from the living room, she took one look at the pool, set among the gardenias and daisies and red and yellow rosebushes of Woodland, and dived in. She dived like she owned the place, like she had known Evans for years, and they had already courted and married and had a son, Joshua, instead of having just met ten minutes before, when he picked her up down the street, at the Beverly Hills Hotel. When she surfaced, smiling his way before diving down again, her eyes did not show the cunning of a beauty greedy for reactions—Evans was fluent in actresses—but satiation, peace. She loved it here. Woodland— Evans's home, and for a time, hers—was paradise.

Evans and Ali MacGraw divorced four years later, but Woodland's fountains still arched into the pool, the moon still rose over the projection room, and Evans, a ripping pain from sciatica down his back, still watched, from his bed, her ghost diving in, smiling, diving back down. He regarded that night and all their nights to follow with the unforgiving eyes he turned on a film flailing in postproduction, blaming himself for the dream he had in hand but couldn't hold. There were so many things he should have done, but now there was nothing he could do. It was over. She had gone off with Steve McQueen.

Evans knew it was his fault; he had left her first, many times, but not for another woman. For his boss Charles Bludhorn, chairman of Paramount, his first love. "I'm a failure in many ways as a man," he confessed, "because of my obsession with what I do." Bluhdorn guarded Evans as jealously as a teenage lover, calling him away from Ali in sickness and in health, to tend to studio matters, to *The God-father*, to *The Great Gatsby*, which now would star not Ali, but Mia Farrow. One of many casualties of the divorce.

"If I can negotiate with the North Vietnamese," said his friend Henry Kissinger, "I think I can smooth the way with Ali."

"Henry," replied Evans, "you know countries, but you don't know women. When it's over it's over."

Alone, he kept the same schedule he had when he was married. He woke late, in time for lunch, and went to bed, with the help of sleeping pills, long after Hollywood had punched out. In between he was a man attached to a phone. His home, at one time, had exactly thirty-two, an average of two per room, but his favorite—a relationship that would last longer than any of his marriages—was the one he kept in bed, propped up on a pillow between his Rolodex and his view of the pool. Writers had the blank page; Robert Evans had the dial tone. All his imagining—his multilayered thinking about scripts and how to get them into movies—began here, on the phone, with slightly more than nothing, just a phone number and a hunch. What about Faye Dunaway for *Chinatown*? What about Jane Fonda? Would she come for dinner this week? He wanted to talk to her. He wanted to hear *her* ideas. . . . These invitations were stepping stones Evans would place across dry riverbeds. Then he would step back, survey his progress, and ask, Will those get us to a movie? What else do we need? Are we ready for the flood? Daniel Selznick said: "He had the same thing that my grandfather and my father and other people who created the business had. How do you define it? It's a crazy hunch, some combination of brains and instinct gambling." Savoring the process ("Come for dinner tonight, Roman. We'll keep talking. . . ."), he thrilled to the deliberate accumulation of stepping-stones, along the way, asking, always asking, Has my dream changed? Has yours? Are we still having fun?

This is what Robert Evans, head of Paramount, did for a living: It was why he lived. A gambler, he bet on his taste, his talent for talent. The filmmakers were free to do the rest—almost. Unlike his colleague, the estimable John Calley of Warner Bros., Evans—though he made an exception for Polanski—rarely gave away final cut. "Unlike most of my counterparts," he said, "I don't get involved in the executive end of the business. I get involved in the making of the film, which annoys a lot of people." But it wasn't power Evans was after; he wanted some small say in the dream he got off the ground. As producer, midwife, and Medici, he wanted to stay close. "He's the best producer I've ever seen," said Dustin Hoffman. "He has the best taste, the best memory, suggestions for cutting." To others, like Coppola, he asked for too much.

Hence the fine line he had to walk, like a responsible parent, keeping an eye out but never spying, or appearing to. Hence the distance he kept from the studio itself. Most days he wouldn't even go in, but worked from home, taking and making calls and receiving his friends, the filmmakers of Paramount. He also rarely went on set, where he knew he would slow things down (or unnecessarily speed things up) and generally create a self-conscious disturbance detrimental to the artist's concentration. So he stayed at Woodland, watching dailies in the screening room under the moon just beyond the pool. Why leave paradise?

He would bring the meetings to Woodland. The talent business was the people business, and the best way to get the best people, and the most talent from them, was to remove the proverbial office desk, welcome all into the living room for a chilled glass of afternoon of wine, and give them a good time. From those good times came hunches, and from those hunches, more stepping-stones, more movies. "See, I was never a star-fucker," Evans said. "I always writer-fucked. And people always star-fucked. I didn't believe in that. If it

ain't on the page, it ain't going to be on the screen." He was a salesman, but he sold with heart.

"Help Yourself," could have been chiseled over Woodland's
sumptuous front doors, and, during Evans's reign, the same sign
could have hung over Paramount's famous front gate, for Evans's
personal and professional policy, the secret to his success with
friends and film, was: Give. Give to get. Caviar? What *kind* of caviar
do you want?

Designed in 1940 by John Woolf, favored architect of Judy
Garland, Vincente Minnelli, Fanny Brice, Cary Grant, and George
Cukor, Woodland was a prime specimen of Southern California Re-
gency, a relaxed stylistic descendant of eighteenth-century France.
Evans first laid eyes on it in 1956. He had just been spotted, loung-
ing poolside at the Beverly Hills Hotel, by Norma Shearer. It wasn't
so much that he looked like her deceased husband, the legendary,
doomed producer Irving Thalberg, who had died twenty years earlier at thirty-seven; it was the way he powered the telephone. Though
she couldn't hear him from her cabana across the pool, she could
see Irving's passion in Evans's intensity and enjoyment, his fullness
of attention to what she presumed (correctly) was a business call.
From that hunch Shearer would persuade Universal to cast Evans,
a twenty-six-year-old former actor then working as an "executive
clothier"—he was in women's pants, he liked to joke—as Thalberg
in *Man of a Thousand Faces*. "She taught me everything about Thalberg," Evans said. They were instant friends. Together they strolled
into the hills behind the hotel and discovered the estate, the century-
old sycamores, the cozy splendor of 1033 Woodland Drive. "Robert,"
Norma said, "Isn't it beautiful?" She could see what the place did to
him. One day, she told him, you're going to live here. It was just a
hunch, but he was Thalberg, and she knew Thalberg.

A decade later, in 1966, Charlie Bluhdorn, seeking a throne room
for his prince, instructed Evans to find a house where they could do

business and pleasure incognito. Evans took his new boss to Woodland. That was it. For $290,000, the place was his, theirs. Then came
the improvements, each tailored by Evans to Evans's specifications:
"Paramount put at least a million into it," Evans said. "An army of
60 studio engineers, carpenters, painters, electricians, bricklayers,
built outbuildings, and expanded the pool house into a screening
room with state-of-the-art projection facilities and the largest seam-
less screen ever made—16 feet wide." Inside the projection room
a fireplace was just visible, across the pool, from the white marble
fireplace in the living room. "There were more deals made in my
projection room than there were at Paramount during those days."

Of his home he said: "I know it's self-indulgent, but it's indicative
of my work. I care about nuance. . . . I am a perfectionist to the point
that it's difficult to work with." One of his girlfriends, feeling a lack
but not minding, explained that with Evans "nothing's rushed, no
love or passion expected. You don't feel you are with somebody."
He was a lover boy, always marrying ("Maybe they fell in love with
the house and not with me"), but preferring always something better; his last night of monogamy ended with his first wet dream. "I'd
rather have one week of magic . . . and a lonely six months," he said,
"than just an okay six months. One week of greatness. No, I'll go to
a great *night*, rather than just a decent month."

It was how he made movies, partied, lived. Women knew it. Evans knew they knew it: "My past," he said, "works against me."

And so most nights he stayed home to work with it. Better to
dream and remember than live with less, and like a florist before a
drought, he built Woodland out of memories, alternating with the
art more personal photographs than could wilt in his lifetime. "And
in my contract," he said, "I had that I never had to go to any awards
shows or dinners or charity functions. I never went out to parties or
events. I stayed with my pals, maybe watched a film and discussed
film." That's how every night at Woodland would end—if it didn't

end with a party—on the other side of the pool, with a screening in the projection room. "Talent," Evans would say. "*That's* what it's always been about for me."

He had done it for his father, Archie Shapera, a dentist.

Archie worked hard, seven days a week. It was the Depression, but Archie never knew anything else; he had toiled his whole life, since he was boy, taking extra work to support his parents and three sisters. "Because his father had been an indigent, a nonprovider, his family always came before his dreams," Evans wrote. His practice was on the corner of 133rd and Lenox Avenue up in Harlem, and at least one Sunday a month, Robert would help him count his earnings, separate the bills into nine stacks, one for each employee, and see a beautiful black nurse squeeze his father's hand and whisper something comely in his ear. Maybe Archie dreamt too. "It was," Evans wrote, "my only glimpse into what could have been a secret life."

Father and son would walk home through the streets of Harlem, Robert, a cutup, doing his Cagney, Bogart, Gable, and Archie, a good man and king, a white dentist to a black community, gathering hellos as they passed.

"Hiya, Doc, how's it goin'?" "Sorry, I'm late, Doc, I'll bring the two bucks on Monday!"

"What do you think about me being an actor?" the boy asked.

He laughed. "Sure, sure."

Robert knew his father could have been a great pianist. Once he had played Carnegie Hall. But now played only at home, on the Steinway "he killed himself to get," Evans said. "My father never had a break."

In December 1941, in a cab home from the Polo Grounds, they heard that the Japanese had just bombed Pearl Harbor. That night a family meeting was called at Uncle Abe's luxurious eighteen-room apartment overlooking Central Park. Riding the elevator with his father, Evans could tell that the old man, mysteriously ashamed, felt a sorrow older than the coming war. Archie, his head low, whispered a lesson his son would never forget: "The wealthy will get wealthier and the young will die."

Dreams: as his father wanted to become the man his father wasn't, so did Evans resolve to become the man his father couldn't be. "My dreams," he wrote, "would become realities no matter what."

"I'll live."

Woodland. The Georgian silver, the Etruscan art, the jade figurine (a gift from Kissinger), the Biedermeier furniture, the Dalí, Picasso, Monet, Modigliani, Toulouse-Lautrec paintings, the nudes by director Jean Negulesco, the Porthault bedsheets, the potted poufs of fresh white roses, the Rigaud candles his butler, David Gilruth, kept burning day and night. Too perfect? No such thing. Evans installed a tennis court, designed by Gene Mako, the best in his class. To further seclude the property, Evans moved the front drive to back of the house. It traced the shady perimeter of the estate, giving visitors a taste of what was to come, before curling round the fountain in the driveway to Woodland's front door. Behind his bedroom Evans kept an office and a secluded Jacuzzi, for his sciatica and for fun. After all, if Evans, with his delectable good taste and matchless bonhomie, could draw the finest talent to Woodland, he could also produce the most beautiful women. He was in all senses a producer.

He was interested in people. He always had been, even before he got the big gig at Paramount. "When he came out to Los Angeles," his friend, the *New York Times* journalist Peter Bart recalled, "Evans didn't just want to know agents and Dick Zanuck. He wanted to broaden his circle of friends." They were introduced by a mutual friend, the screenwriter Abby Mann. Bart was a Swarthmore graduate and fellow New Yorker, and Evans, an independent producer on the make, immediately impressed him; Bart liked him too. Evans was voraciously attuned to Hollywood art and commerce, and for all his drive and cunning, there was something innocently old fashioned about him. He had a weakness for romance.

"I want to write a piece about you," Bart told Evans.

Evans wasn't so sure. "I don't need any more ink. They know I played Thalberg."

Bart wrote it anyway.

Picking up the *New York Times* on August 7, 1966, Bluhdorn—whose Gulf + Western had just acquired Paramount—chanced on Bart's story (and a dashing photo) of Evans, then thirty-six, peddling film properties, fielding a midnight frenzy of phone calls from his room at the Beverly Hills Hotel with the panache of an international spy. "The Beverly Hills man was not a secret agent," Bluhdorn read, "merely a movie producer named Robert Evans hot on the trail of some promising movie material." Bluhdorn, who knew nothing about the movie business, read on. "In the old days the search for 'properties'—novels, plays, short stories—was a relatively sedate affair. The agents would put a finished work up for grabs and the studios would enter their beds. Today the market for likely properties has gone wild." United Artists and the Mirisch Corporation spent $750,000 for rights to James Michener's *Hawaii* and novelists Harold Robbins and Irving Wallace were getting a reported million for the movie rights to books they hadn't written yet. "While the old-time producers may sit in their offices and read the synopses of forthcoming novels . . . the younger men are out beating the bushes." Bart's article described the elaborate, clandestine schemes Evans juggled on his winding way to a deal: "In order to get 'first look' at material, Evans has, in effect, constructed the nucleus of a spy system in the New York publishing world." His enterprise was phenomenal, his strategy sound: "If you own a good story the stars will call you," Evans told Bart. "The directors and writers will be at your door."

In a matter of days, he was summoned to Charlie Bluhdorn's office in New York. They had never met before, never even talked before. But Bluhdorn was a gambler too.

"I vant"—the thick Viennese accent—"you to run ze ztudio office in London," Bludhorn decreed.

No trial period, no apprenticeship—straight to power.

Hollywood was dubious but after four months in London, Evans had squeezed out Paramount's single hit of the year, the inauspicious but profitable *Alfie*. A little movie with no stars.

"Evantz! Peck your begs! You're movink to Los Angeles. You're going to be ze head of ze ztudio!"

Evans returned to Los Angeles in 1966 the laughing stock of Hollywood. *One paper called* him "Bluhdorn's Folly"; *Hollywood Close-Up* went for "Bluhdorn's Blowjob." He was too young, too green, too good looking (a former actor!) to shoulder the compound responsibilities of production head. Theories abounded. There was speculation that Bluhdorn had installed Evans to be his fall guy; if Paramount continued to plummet, he, not the chairman, would suffer the humiliation. Some said Bludhorn, blinded by fatherly feeling, had found the scion he had always wanted. ("It was girls," Julie Payne speculated, "Evans bird-dogged for Bluhdorn.") And yet no one was more surprised to find Robert Evans behind the big desk than Evans himself. Of course he had played Thalberg in the movies, but overseeing an entire slate of Paramount pictures, year after year? In need of a consigliore, he called Peter Bart.

"Peter, I need you at Paramount."

"What?"

"I don't trust anyone. I trust you."

"Evans, I'm a journalist."

"You know the business."

Disney, Warner, Selznick, Hitchcock, Wasserman—Bart had interviewed them all. As the *New York Times*'s man in Hollywood, a turf then underexplored by major news outlets, most of which regarded movie journalism as gossip, Bart practically had the beat to himself. No one outside Hollywood knew Hollywood better. "The *Times* sent me out to Los Angeles to cover the political changes," Bart said, "but they said specifically, they don't want to cover Hollywood, so don't cover that stuff." He did anyway, and in the course of his reporting, saw what was really going on: the industry was in a state of panic. "You'd have to be brain dead," Bart said, "not to realize that the studios were broke and you could go in there and really have an impact."

"You read, Peter," Evans explained. "You have taste. That's what this is all going to be about—taste."

"And their taste?"

Evans had that one sewed up. "We won't tell them how to sell and they won't tell us what to make." A pledge of freedom—Evans had Bluhdorn's support on that.

"What's the worst they can do?" Evans asked. "Peter, what have we got to lose?"

They went to Palm Springs, to Riccio, their favorite restaurant, and spread their cards on the table: In 1966 the studio was deeply in the red: *Is Paris Burning?*, a critical and commercial disaster, went a million over budget, and so had *El Dorado* and *This Property is Condemned*; and *Oh Dad, Poor Dad, Mamma's Hung You in the Closet and I'm Feeling So Sad*, over budget by $2.175 million, had been shelved for a year. In fact, over the last decade, Paramount had produced only a handful of worthy films: *Breakfast at Tiffany's*, *The Man Who Shot Liberty Valance*, *Hud*, and in 1966, *Seconds*. How had the studio survived? "We were," Evans said, "up to our necks in shit."

Alfie had taught Evans something, though. Modest of budget and conception in an age of road-show spectaculars and notably starless—the film *made* Michael Caine, not the other way around—*Alfie* was proof positive that some big movies had humble beginnings.

"It's back to basics," Evans explained to Bart in Palm Springs. "It doesn't matter how much money you throw at the screen. If you don't have a script, you've got nothing."

Evans's assertion ran against the grain in midsixties Hollywood, where a gerontocracy in crisis was fighting the small screen with grand expenditure, the more-is-more strategy of the road-show economy. Bluhdorn's own taste wasn't much different: He went in for lavish musicals and war epics, the sort of cast-of-a-thousand-stars productions he, along with many of his generation, identified with Hollywood glamour and prestige, like his Paramount pet, *Darling Lili*, a World War I musical staring Julie Andrews and Rock Hudson, a project Evans and Bart abhorred.

"What would happen," Bart schemed to Evans, "if we bought in really interesting commercial projects and brought in arty directors to make them? Instead of dealing with grumpy old people like Henry Hathaway and Howard Hawks, we could be dealing with bright young people."

It was a dream proposition for Robert Evans: commercial security, a whisper of art, the old genres revisited, classicism modernized. The glamour Bluhdorn mandated they would deliver; the kiss would still be a kiss—but maybe, this time around, a little French.

Battle plan in hand, Evans and Bart returned to Los Angeles and divided to conquer. Evans, the front man, would handle the studio politics, Bluhdorn, the board of directors; he would handle the personalities in front of and behind the camera; he would honey-darling the agents, put the movies together, and see it to it that they came out right. Bart, his right hand, would read like crazy. He would sniff out movie material, work with writers to develop ideas, and court talent into Evans's hands. It was perfect. "There was not one moment," Bart said, "I can ever recall, not ever, of anger or tension between Evans and I."

Back at the studio, Bart said, Evans struggled to "clean up Bluhdorn's faux-pas," the wreckage of tone-deaf films they inherited, while Bart scouted for material. Meanwhile, new bad-idea movies, many preceding Bluhdorn's takeover, kept breaking their concentration, clogging the pipeline. *Paint Your Wagon, On a Clear Day You Can See Forever, Skidoo*—how were they supposed to release these things? In the fall of 1969 Paramount hit a new low, by one count a $22 million pretax loss. Among recent releases, only *The*

Odd Couple turned a good profit. Film production was down; most soundstages were occupied by television shows, their staff and crews imported by the networks, orphaning Paramount's own reserve of office personnel and film technicians. Against the wall, Bluhdorn let go of close to 150 of his own employees and began to talk about selling off half the lot—which would nudge production onto location and divest filmmakers of the in-house expertise of the studio's own wardrobe, set design, and lighting departments, the prepaid advantages and convenience of working at home. Without a studio lot, it would be harder to control the elements, harder to schedule. Each production, like an independent film, would be assembled from scratch, everything would move slower and, accordingly, fewer films would be produced. Fewer risks would be taken. The films themselves, colored by the realities of actual location, would likely assume naturalistic qualities—by no means a defect, but to Evans, compelled by the aesthetics of romance, the greenhouse splendor of on-the-lot production—"I've been to Paris France and I've been to Paris Paramount," Ernst Lubitsch famously observed. "Paris Paramount is better"—selling half the lot was a tantamount to half a goodbye. But where Evans felt the loss, Martin Davis, senior VP of Gulf + Western and Bluhdorn's second in command, saw fast cash. The romance of Paramount? "These kids," he rationalized, "aren't going to the movies to take home dreams." Davis was no dreamer. He was, Peter Bart said, "the worst dirtbag who ever lived."

Half the lot—the features half, not the television half—went up for sale in October 1969. Months later, Bluhdorn found a buyer in Società Generale Immobiliare, a huge Italian corporation with Vatican (and mob) ties. In April 1970, as the terms of the sale were arranged, Evans and Bart and two dozen associates were relocated off the lot to a small building on 202 North Canon Drive, a few paces from Evans's table at the Bistro in Beverly Hills—a nice neighborhood, but no matter how they tried to spin it, the buyer and the move sent a humiliating distress signal to Hollywood.

Paramount's board of directors, meanwhile, kept pressuring Bluhdorn to close on the Italian deal—and fast. In the coming year *Love Story* was the only film Paramount had slated for production.

Under the gun, Evans and Bart would carpool to the offices on Canon Drive. "That hour with Peter to and from the office," Evans said, "was where we got our best work done." Driving from Woodland to Rexford, Rexford to Sunset, exchanging views of last night's readings, last night's screening, synchronizing their aims for the meetings ahead, no phone calls, no interruptions, no single compromise disrupted their focus in their war room on wheels. How would they get Roman Polanski into *Rosemary's Baby*? Bart had a plan: "I talked to a friend of Roman's," Bart explained, "and learned that the way to get Roman's interest was skiing and girls." For the former they had *Downhill Racer*; the latter, Robert Evans. How to get Coppola into *The Godfather*, a book he shrugged off? "I knew [Warner Bros. executive John] Calley had dumped Francis and he was broke," Bart said. "I was the only person who was unpleasant enough to talk Francis into it by reminding him of his fear of poverty, reminding him of his tuition payments." Bart actually kept a notebook of all the lies he had to tell: "Lies," he said, "are the way to get a movie started: 'So-and-so's *really* interested.'" Among their early endeavors, only *Love Story*, a project so treacly it made them wince, was consciously assembled to make money. Their original director, Larry Peerce, was the sort who satisfied the Palm Springs mandate, but when he expressed an interest in politicizing *Love Story*—he'd make the character of Oliver into a Vietnam vet—Bart and Evans, in the ride to work, nixed him in favor of Arthur Hiller.

And then Ali MacGraw dived into the pool at Woodland, and in December 1970, *Love Story*—and Robert Evans and Peter Bart—saved Paramount. Going forward, Evans and Bart would have nothing to prove. "We had," Bart said, "total freedom." They were, Evans said, "*Pishers* no more." The garden gates opened, and Charlie Bluhdorn—joining their parade, *Love Story*'s explosion, the sensational audience reaction, the advance dollar signs, the Christmas cheer, the foregone vistas of more and greener meadows rolling out ahead of them—rushed a box office in New York, hollered to the theater manager, "Raise the fucking prices, don't just stand there!" and planted a kiss on Evans's cheek. Bluhdorn—who, for all his bluster, loved Evans like the beautiful and beautifully assimilated version of himself he dreamed he could be but knew he never would—was crying. "America," he murmured, putting an arm around Evans's shoulder. "Imagine, twelve years ago I was walking the streets selling typewriters door-to-door."

Gulf + Western retained control of Paramount, but henceforth it belonged to one man—Robert Evans.

And so it began. From Bart and Evans's Palm Springs decree blossomed a truly miraculous run of acknowledged American classics. At the studio Evans called "the Mountain," Polanski, Coppola, Peter Bogdanovich, Robert Towne, Hal Ashby, Nicholas Roeg, Michael Ritchie, Gordon Willis, Alan J. Pakula, Dick Sylbert, Anthea Sylbert, and others produced some of their most defining work. In the first half of the seventies, among the major studios, only Warner Bros.—with *Deliverance, American Graffiti, Klute, The Exorcist, Mean Streets*, and the works of Stanley Kubrick—approached Paramount's epochal record of artistic and commercial achievement. Bluhdorn himself attributed it to the spirit of purposeful collaboration, exchanging profligate productions and runaway salaries for small budgets and personal fervor—the films filmmakers wanted to make. Sharing in the risks, Bluhdorn saw they really would save money by making art. "And when these people don't feel like marionettes pushed around by big studios, they become live," he said of Paramount's filmmakers. "They work like slaves for themselves." Removed from the lot, Paramount's offices at Canon Drive assumed the personality of an independent production company. "The minute we moved," Bart explained, "everything changed. We lost all the committees, and it came down to a tiny group of us. We were all working faster, more closely together. Everything began to get a little sizzle and all of a sudden good projects began to come to us." In the summer of 1972 Bluhdorn hatched the highly improbable, almost utopian idea for the Director's Company. Within a limited budget range, about thirty million dollars to be distributed over a dozen pictures, the three Director's Company directors Coppola, William Friedkin, and Bogdanovich would have complete artistic autonomy and on a nonexclusive basis to the studio. The Director's Company was Paramount's gift to star auteurs, a deal clearly and in every way biased toward filmmakers, so much so that it earned the ire of Paramount executives certain Bluhdorn was giving away the store—which he was.

"You von't belief vat I've done," Bludhorn enthused to Paramount executive Frank Yablans, the fiercest, crassest one of the bunch. "An impossible dream, an impossible dream!"

Yablans, based in New York, was not paid to dream but to guard the bottom line.

"I think it's shit," Yablans barked. "I think it's the worst, stupidest, dumbest idea I ever heard in my life. And I'm not gonna have any part of it. Why don't you just give 'em the company, Charlie? What the fuck are you paying me for?"

The mood at Canon Drive was far sunnier. "Evans and I loved the idea," Bart said. "These good little projects started coming to us." In 1972 Friedkin stalled, taking work elsewhere, but the Director's Company allowed Coppola *The Conversation* and Bogdanovich *Paper Moon*, masterpieces of Paramount's—and indeed Hollywood's— most progressive, art-forward venture of the 1970s.

Floodgates opened. The river rush of corporate money and the latitude, conferred upon studio leaders like Evans and Calley, to conduct business as they saw fit fostered an industrywide reflowering. But it was due to the particular style and charisma of Evans, and the bestowals of his Woodland estate, that he and Bart consistently attracted and maintained artists inclined toward the manner of glamour and classical ideals adjudged Old Hollywood. It was different at Warner Bros. John Calley—to his great credit—freed directors from his own (highly refined) inclinations. He didn't have a style: "I was really comfortable with directors," Calley said. "We started doing pictures without producers almost immediately. Directors had to run the fucker." (Bart, walking with fellow journalist-turned-producer Howard Stringer, spotted Calley in Beverly Hills one sunny afternoon, and Stringer remarked: "Do you ever notice that when John Calley passes he leaves no shadow?") Not so Evans, who favored painterly beauty and moods less suited to the faster film stocks and portable technologies of the Vietnam years than to the across-a-crowded-room yearnings of World War II, of his youth. Thus would *Chinatown*, set in the seductive past against the smoke spirals and ivory Plymouths of the late thirties, assume for Evans a special gleam (despite its messy script, still without an ending). It was his homecoming, a victory flag he staked on the mountaintop. It would also be his first film at Paramount not just as executive but as producer. If Evans was king before, now he was king-emperor.

In 1973 Evans declared the film the maiden voyage of his newly inaugurated Robert Evans Productions, Bluhdorn's thank-you bonus for saving the studio. Under the terms of Evans's highly unusual new deal, he would produce his own pictures for Paramount, one a year for five years, and simultaneously maintain his position as Paramount's head of production. It was a virtually unprecedented arrangement. Not since the estimable Darryl F. Zanuck, thirty years earlier, had such a sweetheart deal been offered to a studio chief. With unfettered access to studio finances, manpower, and production and marketing resources, Evans the executive could conceivably direct unlimited assets to Evans the producer. What couldn't he do now? His *Chinatown* would want for nothing.

Others feared their films would go hungry. "Bobby has to make a choice," Warren Beatty confided to Bart. "Either he runs the studio or produces pictures." Beatty's unease was echoed by many at the studio, most vocally by Frank Yablans. Though Yablans was, in the words of Paramount's IDTK Charles Glenn, "a genius of film distribution," responsible for the revolutionary release strategy of *The Godfather*, his clumsy power plays and blatant and incessant boasting—"I saved Bluhdorn's ass," he would claim—ruptured his relationship with Evans to such a degree that Bluhdorn's 1971 promotion of Yablans to president was roundly considered the boss's way of just shutting Yablans up. The promotion was troubling to no less than Yablans's brother, Paramount's West Coast sales manager, who took it upon himself to prepare Evans for the coming storm: "This is never going to work," he warned. "Trust me—Frank Yablans is crazy. I should know—I'm his brother. He's doing well where he is, but he'll never be able to handle this much power." The next day Yablans fired his brother.

Demanding the same right to produce as Evans had, Yablans even insisted that Bluhdorn give *him* a percentage of *Chinatown*. When Bluhdorn, the peacemaker, consented, Yablans called Evans to renege. Taking his name off the picture, Yablans said, was the right thing to do-a ploy, Evans thought, to get him to do the same. "Are you out of your mind?" Evans returned. "I'm not taking my name off this picture. I'm gonna be a producer. I'm gonna produce this movie."

Retaliating, Yablans backed John Schlesinger's *The Day of the Locust*, a 1930s Los Angeles–set production, shot at the same time at the same studio as *Chinatown*, that he hoped would give Evans's film a run for its money. Literally moments after Yablans attached first assistant director Howard Koch Jr., to battle-plan his intricate production, Koch, bounding through Paramount's Canon office, heard Evans call his name from down the hall. "Howard! Get in here!" Inside Koch discovered Evans and Polanski, weary from rewriting with Towne, sitting on Evans's couch. They had all worked together, happily, on *Rosemary's Baby*. "Howard," Evans continued. "I'm taking you off *Locust* and putting you on *Chinatown*. I want you on *my* picture." The round went to Evans.

When Yablans learned that *Time* magazine was planning a cover story on Evans, he demanded that Evans convince *Time* to share the cover with him: "If you don't deliver the cover," Yablans insisted, unsuccessfully, "I will make every hour of every day of your life so miserable you'll wish you were dead." Evans brushed him aside. He was Paramount's chosen one, and he had a picture to make.

2

Jack Nicholson was making late-night calls to Faye Dunaway's hotel room in Madrid, where she was shooting *The Three Musketeers*, imploring her to keep her schedule open; he wanted her for *Chinatown*. She was interested, but she wanted an offer from the studio first. Assuring her the official offer was imminent, Nicholson kept calling Dunaway's hotel phone, tantalizing her with choice morsels of Evelyn's mystery and glamour. Days later the offer still hadn't come in. And he kept calling. Keep waiting, he said.

"Jack," she protested. "Why should I wait for something that might not be real?"

"Dunaway, it's real, and it's worth waiting for."

Back in Hollywood the hustle was on. "Bobbeeeeee"—it was Creative Management Associates' star agent, Sue Mengers, on the phone with Evans—"I need an offer for Faye by the end of business Friday. Otherwise she's going to Arthur Penn for *Night Moves*."

"I gotta talk to Roman first. Let me get back to you tomorrow."

It was unquestionably a high bar, but in the six years since *Bonnie and Clyde*, Dunaway's breakthrough, she had yet to approach the same level of success. Was it bad luck? She had been underserved in *The Arrangement*, miscast in *Little Big Man*. Perhaps it was that she was not so easy to cast. In the days of Jane Fonda, Dunaway's hard and perfect porcelain face, her almost alien beauty, belonged better to Hollywood's more aestheticized past; she was born (too late) for

Sternberg. But *Chinatown*, being a period film, and touching the kind of high style seventies Hollywood rarely ventured, seemed, potentially, a good fit.

Evans called Polanski. "We're gonna lose Faye if we don't move. What's going on with Fonda?"

He laughed. "She doesn't understand the script."

"Who does?"

The next morning Evans called Mengers. "Bluhdorn wants to go with Jane," he said, lying. "But you know me. I want Faye."

"Of course you do, honey."

"What can I do? It's Bluhdorn's money."

"It's Robert Evans Productions isn't it? Tell the studio to take a flying fuck."

Evans loved Sue Mengers, "Mengela." he called her; it was half Yiddish endearment, half Nazi salute to Josef Mengele. Though they played on opposite ends of the table—he the buyer, she the seller—their affection for each other and for the game itself superseded the bruises left over from seven years of high-stakes negotiations.

"Can't do it."

"Fuck you."

"Fuck *you*, honey."

Evans laughed. He lived for this. "I love you, Mengela."

A regular presence at Woodland, she loved him too. Though he knew she'd never say so.

"Talk Jack into Faye," Mengers persisted. "Then tell Bluhdorn Jack wants her. He'll go for it."

"Bluhdorn would go for it—for fifty thousand."

She slammed down the phone and called back later. "Bobbee, if I tell Faye that number, she'll drop me and I won't blame her."

"Mengela, it's Faye we're talking about, okay? She's not easy."

"She's a great actress."

"Great, but not easy."

"*Bonnie and Clyde—*"

"Was seven years ago. . . . There's no money in the budget for it. Got it?"

"Got it, prick."

She slammed down the phone and called back later. "Bobbee?"

"Yes, Mengela."

"We'll take it."

"Could be too late," Evans purred. "I think we're moving forward with Fonda."

"You son of a—"

She slammed down the phone again, and Evans called her the next morning: "Was up all night with Jack and Roman"—it was true—"They're all worried Faye's gonna be difficult. But she's got the part."

"Deal closed?"

"Closed."

"Bobbee?"

"Yes, Mengela?"

A giggle. "There was nothing for Faye in *Night Moves.*"

"Mengela?"

"Yes, Bobbee?"

"Fonda passed."

"You son of a bitch!" She was laughing as she hung up.

That month Evans read with relief the revision of *Chinatown.* It was shorter, streamlined, and it moved. "There are lots and lots of people and they all know that Roman structured the screenplay," Julie Payne would say. "Draft one is Robert's; draft two is Roman's. But it was not Roman's way to ask for credit." Polanski said, "I could have arbitrated [Towne's credit], of course I could have. I didn't want to go to that fight with Bob [Towne] and the Director's Guild. Not my style. But indeed if you look at the first two drafts, you will see." He explained; "When I was young I didn't attach much importance to the credits. I didn't even credit myself as an actor in *Vampire Killers*. I didn't think much about money at that time. I needed as much money as I needed. I think we were all less materialistic in those days."

The new "Polanski" draft was focused on its inalienable essence: Jake Gittes. He was in every scene. True to convention, the audience would never know any more or any less than their screen detective but would uncover the mystery as he did, clue by clue. Additionally Polanski had tossed out Evelyn and Escobar's affair along with their tangential subplot; he cut many of Gittes's lowlife vulgarisms and class consciousness, reviving in their place certain hard-boiled characteristics common to–the genre; he removed scenes with Cross's goons and long expositional dialogues between Evelyn and Gittes— strewn confusingly with red herrings and dense conspiratorial fogs right out of *The Big Sleep*. Where once the character of Byron Samples—also cut completely from the new draft—accompanied Gittes on his investigation of the retirement home, now Evelyn goes with Gittes; the change enhances their complicity, their love story, and leads nicely to bed.

In Towne's first drafts, Gittes's motivation is blurred in the smokescreen of twisty misdirects. After Evelyn drops the lawsuit against him, what does the water scandal matter to him personally? In the Polanski rewrite, however, an answer is offered as an outraged Gittes, in the barbershop, defends the integrity of his profession, an indication that for all his sleazy divorce work, a nobler detective is waiting to emerge. The water mystery is his opportunity to do good—which, in a flourish of chilling irony, he will blunder by hindering rather than helping, near the climax of the Polanski revision. In the original Evelyn masterminded the showdown with her father; in the Polanski revision Gittes instigates it, creating a new scene that further demonizes Cross. Rather than tremble and repent when confronted, or wither under a narcotic haze, as he did in Towne's early drafts, Cross here stands firm and fully justifies his crimes: "You see, Mr. Gittes," he growls in the new scene, "most people never have to face the fact that at the right time and the right place, they're capable of anything." The line suggests his is an evil beyond even those evils he has already committed and echoes an oft-pondered query of Polanski's. "I often ask," he said many years later, "is it possible under the right circumstances for anyone to be capable of any act, however evil?" He had reason to wonder.

At long last, and in only a few weeks, the script was in order. The mystery plot, reduced to the essentials, dominated; it was, finally, coherent. And yet, still—to Robert Evans's consternation—*Chinatown* had no ending.

Howard Koch Jr. and Dick Sylbert squeezed into Koch's little brown Audi and took off to look at Los Angeles, Koch behind the wheel, Sylbert in the seat beside him, turning his Minox through open windows as they scouted locations. Born and raised in Los Angeles, Koch was the ideal coscout and driver for Sylbert. As a boy, working as a one-man liquor delivery service, he had scoured the city with his *Thomas Guide* of maps, acquiring Los Angeles one secret at a time.

They found that much of Hollywood proper wouldn't work. "Hollywood Boulevard was in bad shape," Koch said, "and we needed to bring back a little of the romance of what the city used to be like." Every day for weeks, Koch brought those memories to the *Chinatown* scout, suggesting throughout this or that street, alternative routes, buildings he had passed many times but never had an excuse to examine, like the row of courtyard apartments between Fountain and Sunset on Crescent Heights, an ideal setting for early in the film when Gittes, perched on the rooftop, snaps a few shots of Mulwray at the apartment Sylbert would name El Macondo—after the city in *One Hundred Years of Solitude*. Just to be sure, Koch and Sylbert climbed the red-tile roofs at 1400–1414 Havenhurst Drive to examine the view themselves.

In a city famous for erasing its history, it was a particular challenge to find locations that predated the film's period. Sylbert said: "You're always looking around to get rid of a television antenna when you should be thinking about something else." But even more than era-appropriate, Sylbert-approved locations had to "rewrite the script in visual terms": They had to correspond to what he called visual structure. "You cannot write music without structuring it," Sylbert said, "You cannot write a play without structuring it. Why should you be able to design a movie without structuring it?"

Long before the scout, Sylbert began by making up a set of aesthetic rules for *Chinatown*. They would foretell the visual experience of the entire picture. "You say to yourself, Okay, *Chinatown* is about a drought, so all the colors in this picture are gonna be related to the idea of drought," Sylbert explained. "And the only time you're gonna see green is when somebody has water from the grass." He added, "The reason [the buildings are] white is that the heat bounces off them." This white/heat dialectic Sylbert would call his "home theme," the notion from which all subsequent visual concepts would emerge. "And not only will they all be white, they'll be above the eye level of the private eye. Above eye level means for the private eye that he has to walk uphill. It is always harder emotionally to walk uphill—you know the old expression, 'Man, this is really uphill.' You then decide what the colors are going to be and why they're going to be that way, and what the range should be. Let's say, from burnt grass, which is a terrific color, to white, which you know you're already gonna deal with, to umber. Umber is interesting because it's the color of a shadow. And in a movie like this, the more shadowy the better. And then you're gonna use certain kinds of repetition: Spanish building, Spanish building, Spanish building. . . . And you use all architectural space for what you want to do. You use the layers, the planes . . . use everything you can. All these things are available to you to structure a movie. Even opaque glass. You know what's interesting about opaque glass in a mystery? You can't quite see who's behind it, and it looks like frozen water," which Sylbert would correlate to *Chinatown*'s power structures: the coroner's office, the morgue, the Hall of Records. All of these Sylbert would re-create in the studio. The sky would never have clouds; that might indicate rain. In keeping with the drought, the sky would be as white as a Spanish building, except when Gittes is out at sea, surrounded finally by water. Then, Sylbert decided, "It should then be the most intense cerulean blue imaginable."

Sylbert would keep the secrets of his visual structure from Polanski. It was not his custom to trouble the director, who would be consumed with the manifest content of story. If Sylbert did his job right, as he had on *The Graduate*, *Rosemary's Baby*, *Carnal Knowledge*, and the others, all Polanski would have to do was place the camera and direct the actors. Sylbert's work would be only subconsciously experienced—"My whole philosophy of production design," he said, "is that what I do is so real that you can't tell the difference"—in the many subtle shifts of color, texture, shape, tone, and contrast that were, like phrases of a symphony, visual variations on a theme, in this case, drought and its ancillaries, water, flora, sun. There were zero accidents.

"What kind of ointment is that?" Elia Kazan, Sylbert's first feature director, had asked of one of Sylbert's sketches for *Baby Doll*. Sylbert had drawn a fluted column beside an old rocking chair, and on the floor a squeezed-out tube of ointment.

"Gee, I don't know," Sylbert answered the master. "What kind of ointment *is* that?"

"It's pile ointment," Kazan improvised.

Lesson learned—and never forgotten. In a Sylbert film, if something was in the frame, it was either because Sylbert put it there or

because he allowed it to be there. All other design departments on
the picture reported to him.

Koch drove Sylbert east—the farther east they drove, the older the
Los Angeles got—to Echo Park Lake, unchanged since the thirties,
where Gittes would spot Mulwray and his "girlfriend," and then
on to a hilly neighborhood above Echo Park, to 848½ Kensington
Street, a lime green apartment split by a central bungalow corridor,
ideal for Ida Sessions, the actress posing as Mrs. Mulwray. "It was
picked," Sylbert said, "because it was completely symmetrical and
had a long narrow passage in the middle of it, so that you looked
at it and said, 'There can't be any problem here.' But once you got
into that narrow corridor, the opposite happened, because narrow
corridors produce anxiety. And then, of course, you get to the door
and the glass is broken."

They drove east to Pasadena in search of Evelyn Mulwray's
house, "and we looked and looked and looked at house after house
after house," Koch said, and finally found a sprawling white estate,
on a hill, of course, off California Avenue. Inspecting the property,
Sylbert was pleased to find no other buildings were visible from its
massive lawns. "Because in [1937]," he explained, "the whole image
I was after was that there was nothing out there. I chose the place
because one can see in a straight line from the backyard through the
house to the front entrance."

Koch and Sylbert boarded a helicopter for a look at Southern
California's orange groves. But not just any grove would do; Sylbert
was looking for the narrowest possible corridor of orange trees to
"squeeze the tension of the chase scene." They found it in the town
of Fillmore.

Sylbert, scanning the vista, lost in thought, would whisper his
tentative assent. "Yes . . . I think . . . It *could* work ."

"Do you want to keep looking?"

"Yeah, let's look some more. But I think I like this—"

"It's good, isn't it?"

"I think so—I just want to give Roman some choices."

Locations secured, Koch and Sylbert would shepherd Polanski on his technical scout, his chance to examine the setting for story and camera.

"Okay," he would say, laying hands on Koch's shoulders, "You are Jack. I am the camera." He would step back to measure the view from an imagined wide shot. "Howard, you go over there, to that rock, I'm going to pick you up *here*, and"—panning with the "camera" he made of his hands—"follow you *there*, and then—Dick, stand there—you're Faye—you come to that chair—no, *that* chair."

"Here?"

"Yes, Dickie. Good. This is good for the camera."

"Can I check?"

"Yes! Come! Check!"

Koch would take Sylbert's position.

"Oh, yeah," Sylbert would say, assuming Polanski's vantage, "I like this. Good."

Koch would listen very closely. As first AD, it was his primary responsibility to "hear and see everything and learn to anticipate," he said, "everything that the director needs, complete it on time and within budget, but that's not enough. It's got to be good."

Koch walked in the Canon Drive office with the schedule. "Whaddya got?" Evans asked. "Roman doesn't work fast."

Koch didn't need to be told. He remembered *Rosemary's Baby.* "I've given him sixty-eight days."

"Great."

"He can shoot this in sixty-three, but knowing Roman, if I give him more time than he actually needs, he'll be relaxed."

"Whatever you want."

It was a tribute to Evans's investment in *Chinatown*, and to the studio's investment in Evans, that Koch allotted so much time to preproduction—twelve weeks. No less important than rewriting the script, this time to rehearse and "rewrite" cinematic concepts was, far from an indulgence, an indispensable touchstone of working for a major Hollywood studio inclined to quality, a supportive entity—a combined bank and playground—with the means, and, under a benevolent production head like Evans or Calley, the willingness to finance the many art and technical departments to make the best, most considered creative choices. Or as Evans put it: "I did what I needed to do so they could do what they needed to do for Roman." Accordingly, Sylbert could afford to pay scrupulous attention to every period detail. He and his assistants could search out authentic props and set decorations that, to the discerning eye, or to those who remembered 1937, would help *Chinatown* transcend the retro, the nostalgic, the revisionist kitsch, and arrive, per Polanski and Sylbert's sound judgments and childhood memories, at a naturalistic glamour based always in character—that took time—perhaps not as mistily romantic as Evans or even Towne might have preferred, but just as elegant.

"Dick was very attracted to glamour," his wife, Susanna Moore, said. He and his identical twin, Paul, were born in New York to a pants cutter and a milliner, Lily and Sam.

"Lily just gave birth to tvins," Sam Sylbert, with his Yiddish accent, droned into the hospital telephone.

"Don't *vorry*," came his mother-in-law's voice, "maybe von of dem should die." She meant it.

When he began to support himself, painting sets for the Metropolitan Opera, Sylbert was sure to send a little money to his father. He would waste it on useless goods and lose it on horses. "Dick thought his father wasn't very smart," Moore reflected, "and his mother very difficult. He couldn't get away fast enough." Designing for Hollywood, Sylbert would commit artistic patricide film after film, redecorating, as his friend Mike Nichols had, all traces of his origins with a design sense as cosmopolitan as his social circle. Coming to Hollywood in the midsixties, he found the "world I'd stepped into was elegant—a world of people who preferred life in Europe. Darryl Zanuck, [Charles K.] Feldman, all of them. . . ." They collected the most beautiful art, the cubists, the fauvists, the French impressionists. "What did strike me was their taste and their commitment to the work—all they ever talked about was movies." Not money, Sylbert noted, but art. "Even Jack Warner, who was an ignorant self promoter, was interested in only one thing: making movies." These were Sylbert's people. When their golden age ended, he found their likeness in Evans, Polanski, Anthea, Warren Beatty, Joan Didion . . .

"I vatched you on the Academy Avards," his mother told him on the phone the morning after he won for *Who's Afraid of Virginia Woolf?* "You looked short."

Anthea Sylbert was burdened with her in-laws, Sam and Lily Sylbert, whenever they came to Los Angeles. As soon as they arrived, she said, "Dick and Paul would sort of disappear." At first Anthea tried to play daughter-in-law and hostess, but in time their chronic dissatisfaction wore down her goodwill. Adopting the twins' technique, she moved them into the Beverly Wilshire and kept her distance.

As a girl Anthea was always afraid. When she heard sirens screaming up the apartment walls, she saw New York on fire and her building burning to the ground. "I made an enemy," she said, "to control my fears." She named him Mr. Crack. She dressed him all in black. He had a crooked top hat and a cane and hunched like a miser out of Dickens and followed her out of the apartment and to school, into the classroom, to the desk behind her, to lunch, to recess, and, at the end of the day, back to the apartment, "but my room was magic," she said, "so if I could make it to my room, he couldn't come in there, so I would close the door and laugh at him."

"I don't know," Anthea reflected, "what I was so afraid of. Nothing ever happened to me."

She often dreamed she was queen of her own island, a paradise of obedient people who did exactly as she told them. Reality was somewhat different.

During preproduction on *Chinatown*, Faye Dunaway was rarely on time to her fittings. She was scheduled to arrive at Western Costume at 3:30, where Anthea—deputized to her brother-in-law once again as costume designer—Lilly Fonda, the head of Western's custom-made department, and Fonda's assistant had been waiting, costumes in hand, for more than an hour. Anthea, whose restlessly analytic mind kept her up at nights, enshrouded in paper towers of research, eliminating what was wrong from her costume sketches, worrying her design ideas to perfection, had no patience for this or any other strain of unprofessionalism.

Should she leave and set a precedent? Irene Sharaff once waited an hour for Sinatra, she remembered, and as soon as his car drove up, she walked out.

"We'll be here until eight now," groaned a fitter.

Anthea had squandered not a moment of preproduction. From Dick's visual narrative, she had produced a wardrobe as rigorously adherent to *Chinatown*'s color scheme as it was to history. Foremost, there would be no blue ("I'm not fond of blue anyway," she said. "On screen, it screams"). She never designed from fashion magazines—they gave a false picture of everyday style—but she made a telling exception for the character of Gittes, preserving some element of Towne's conception of him as a class-conscious dandy. "I thought he would be interested in fashion," Anthea said. "The one who would be noticing what the stars were wearing when he went to the races." This insight would come only to the most caring viewer, and of course to Nicholson himself. Her designs would be, paradoxically, obsessively rendered and invisible. "I used to even think about what was in their pockets," she said. "There are those people who had one key. There are those people who have three keys. There are those people who have five keys. They're different and they come from different places."

Designing costumes to Anthea was sending covert, subliminal information—"telling you who the character is before he even opens his mouth"—not drawing attention to her own originality and craftsmanship. Accordingly, Anthea insisted—as Dick Sylbert did—on subduing period clichés. Like red nail polish on Evelyn.

"No," she said to Polanski. "This woman is old money. No woman in her bracket would do that."

"You don't understand. People know this time because of the movies, not because of what was real."

It was the only time she conceded on *Chinatown*. "Roman was smart," she explained. "And he would listen. And he was appreciative, so that when you did something that he liked, he would let you know you had."

Chinatown would refrain from the generic tropes of thirties movies for looks Anthea drew from primary source material, the personal (not professional) photos procured from friends, of citizens of Los Angeles and the San Fernando Valley in 1937 (not '36, and not '38). For Cross, Anthea cribbed William Mulholland's style directly from newspaper photos, and, for Evelyn, borrowed from memories of her mother. "I was born in 1937," she said, "so I had all those photographs, but there was a not a friend who I didn't ask for their albums of photographs. I was looking at *everything*." And she would never design without a photo of the location—to be sure the clothes worked in context. Did she want a particular design to blend into the background? To contrast? In conjunction with Dick Sylbert, Anthea's consideration of the total image was so complete that she refused to delegate any extra's clothing, as many would, to her wardrobe assistants. She selected them herself. "It's like doing a painting," she said, "nothing should pop out of the painting and nothing in the painting is arbitrary." She had done her graduate work in Art History, "so my idea of what things should look like had to do with looking at paintings more than anything else. [I learned from] professors like Julius Held at Barnard who taught you how to look at a painting and determine from what you saw and what they were wearing, their social status, their economic status, the place, all of that. Clothes will tell you all that. They tell you how to solve the puzzle."

Faye Dunaway arrived at Western Costume at five o'clock, an hour and a half late, in a flurry of feeble apologies. "I'll pay for the overtime from my own money," she announced, collapsing at Anthea's feet in mock-theatrical supplication. "I'm so sorry. I should have watched the time."

"You're ruining my budget."

Dunaway threw off her jacket and jeans, stepped into a skirt, and checked herself in the three-way mirror. An assistant put a beret on her head.

"Great," she said.

An assistant tilted the beret.

"Careful. I don't want it to become a real beret. I've already done that" (*Bonnie and Clyde*).

Dunaway changed into a black silk crepe dress with cape sleeves. "It's cold in here," she said.

The air-conditioning was shut off.

She changed into a gray suit with belted jacket. She changed into a gray pleated mid-calf skirt and black turtleneck.

"Perfect," Lilly Fonda said.

Anthea ordered on a black hat and stepped back to study the results. "It's still too much crown for the screen," she said. "Let's take out half an inch here."

Evans had authorized the deluxe treatment. Sparing no expense, Anthea had ordered vintage silk stockings from Paris and rented period jewelry so expensive that full-time guards were required to chaperone it. She knew hardly anyone would note their authenticity; it was likely that these details, largely hidden under coats and dresses, wouldn't even appear on screen. But Anthea hoped they would tell Dunaway's body something about the character and bleed their way into the performance. Time would tell.

At seven o'clock the night watchman appeared. All said their goodnights, and Anthea repaired to the nearest bar for a glass of white wine and guacamole and remembered. There was so much to admire, she thought, about the way women used to dress, their sensitivity to caliber and detail. Even the middle-class women of the thirties had a respect for clothing absent from the current vogue, à la Dunaway, for jeans and a jacket. Can anyone say, with precision and certainty, when a golden age begins and ends? Can they be separated from the bronze? Or are they the colors of the rainbow, consigned to secret delineation? Once upon a time, there really were wardrobes, distinct pieces tailored to each separate occasion, shoes for lunch, the right shoes for dinner. There were hats. There were hatpins. Engaging the beauty and romance of clothing had dignified behavior, she thought, bettering the way one thought and felt about oneself and the world. "Today," she said, "with all our pretensions of being free, we really are more rigid and uniform."

Polanski cast *Chinatown* out of the offices on Canon Drive.

Chatting with the director for nearly an hour, the actor Jesse Vint assumed, quite reasonably, that he had been called in for a big part, and when Polanski climbed onto the desk with his Polaroid and started snapping Vint's picture—then, reevaluating the light, climbing down to flip the Venetian blinds and climbing up again—the actor was convinced the part, if he got it, was even bigger than before. He was mistaken.

"Where are you from?" Polanski would ask from behind his

Polaroid. "What have you been working on?" He turned to his secretary. "Where am I going to put this guy?"

In the orchard, Polanski decided. After all that, Vint would play a small part, an irate farmer with a few lines.

Polanski's stack of Polaroids kept growing. "For me," he would explain, "the right casting is always more important than having the perfect actor." He wouldn't have to audition them, only study their faces.

Richard Balakyan, sitting before the Polaroid, had never seen a director take so long to see an actor for so small a role.

"This is the way people work, I suppose, out of Europe?" he asked.

"Yes, yes."

No, actually. It was the way Polanski worked, the way his whole crew would work, doing in prep what would be impossible in life, exercising absolute jurisdiction over chance.

And yet, days and actors later, there remained one small part the director wouldn't—or, so he claimed, couldn't—cast.

The pain down Evans's back, his leg, was impossible to locate in time. Did it start when he lost Ali? When he won Hollywood? Had it always been there, waiting? It had certainly increased since *The Godfather*, in the days and nights since he lifted Paramount from the grave. Now it never left him, and there was nothing he could do about it save bed rest and choice injections from Dr. Lee Siegel, aka "doctor feel-good," who brought his syringes to Woodland, or occasionally to Canon Drive, though Evans, as *Chinatown* neared production in the fall of 1973, was not coming into the office much anymore. It was the pain, he said, that kept him home, on gurneys carried in and out of cutting rooms. It was the pain, he assured Bluhdorn, after Frank Yablans reported Evans's absence to the boss ("Doesn't Evans had a legitimate doctor somewhere in his Rolodex?"

Yablans asked). It was the pain that kept him up late, up early. That kept him from fucking.

"Take a sniff," one woman said to him in bed, unscrewing the top of a gold cylinder she wore around her neck.

"Is it what I think it is?"

"It'll help."

With Ali and their son, Joshua, no longer around, there was no one he needed to hide it from.

And why hide it when no one else was? Hollywood hadn't hidden the marijuana, why hide the coke? Rather, why not show it off just a little—because coke *was* expensive, a status symbol, a sign of box office ability? And when it gave energy, the energy to create, to fuck, why not, as Evans's bedfellow had, recommend it to one's friends, or as Nicholson had, give it away in little vials for Christmas? Why not, when nothing else worked, and it drained the past away?

"It's a miracle," Evans told Bart. "You can't believe how much better my back is."

"Bob, you don't take cocaine for your back. You take it for energy."

"*You* take cocaine?"

"I love cocaine. What I can't believe is that *you* love it."

Evans, Bart knew, ordinarily had no interest in drugs. Even pot confounded him. When Hal Ashby, an inveterate marijuana smoker, slowed production of *Harold and Maude* to a stoner's pace, Evans threw up his hands and dispatched Bart to jumpstart the director. "Evans was too interested in work and getting laid to be distracted by drugs," Bart said. "And I loved him for that. I started doing coke because it was wonderful, but for Bob it was innocent."

On October 7, 1973, Jack Nicholson wrapped *The Passenger*, a strenuous production under Michelangelo Antonioni—to Nicholson's mind, a most uncollaborative director—and flew home from Spain physically and emotionally depleted and glad to be home.

Nicholson loved Los Angeles. He even loved the earthquakes. "People comically impugn the L.A. sensibility," he said. "They think it's kookie. But it's based on breadth. We have an open view of things that comes out of the topography." Since he first arrived, in 1954, he took to the big-sky freedoms of the natural landscapes—"Where else could you have all these mountains and desert and still be in the dead center of one of the greatest metropolitan cities in the United States?"—the great western spread of desert, ocean, and ideas that made Los Angeles, for him, "the only truly modern city," an expanding urban possibility unlike the comparatively confined New York. Nicholson was instantly at home in Los Angeles, its pace of life swayed to the type of languid hangouts he commandeered as a young man, at Pupi's, and later as a movie star, in his yawning living room atop the Santa Monica Mountains. "It would be a shame if these mountains get developed any more than they are now," he told one journalist from his living room window. "We'd be dead. Once the spine of the Santa Monica Mountains is gone, there really is no Los Angeles any longer. This is what makes the difference between here and 55th and Fifth—this desert/mountain/land-by-the-ocean look. It's what gives it what it has. That's what *Chinatown* [is] basically about."

He was in Western Costume with Anthea Sylbert a day after getting back, for wardrobe fittings, one of his favorite parts of making movies. Jack savored clothing. His vintage Hawaiian shirts, the spectator shoes with eyelet-worked brown leather, gleefully mismatched in the heedless California style, were charged with memories. Top to bottom, he dressed himself in loyalties: This piece a gift from his lady, Anjelica; that one from his great pal, Harry Dean Stanton; a stalwart bomber jacket, picked up on location, thrown over a Lakers T-shirt; "a black porkpie hat that I'd gotten from the freeway in a motor accident that involved a priest"; those spectator shoes, the trademark image of one of his father figures from back in New Jersey: Shorty, as Jack called him, married to Jack's much older sister, Lorraine. "A very dapper dresser," Nicholson said, "he participated in all the Asbury Park Easter parades on the boardwalk."

His namesake, the man who may have been his father, Jack rarely saw.

When he did see Shorty, it was in bars. Once Jack watched him swallow thirty-five shots of Hennessy. "But I never heard him raise his voice: I never saw anybody be angry with him, not even my mother. He was just a quiet, melancholy, tragic figure—a very soft man." Jack's mother, Ethel May Nicholson, ran a full-service beauty parlor out of the back bedroom of their house—and worked all the time.

"You're on your own," she told her son. "All I expect is that if you get into trouble, you'll tell me about it."

It was perhaps too much freedom for one so young. "I always knew there wasn't going to be anybody to help me and emotionally support me," he said "that whatever I did I'd have to do on my own." He built a second family of friends he culled from sports, acting, and girl chasing—team efforts all. In sandy feet, he romped around the Jersey Shore with the guys, talking the big talk of little men, pranking, clowning, dreaming those long summer days of the sweet rumor of Manhattan, the big breast of the East. Then a little basketball, maybe shoot some pool to the music of a beatnik soliloquy from Jack, who just discovered the undying combination of black Ray-Bans and Camus. They were big mellow days and, with a girl, bigger nights: "Did you? With *her*?" The big smile. But as good as the kiss was, it was just as good telling the guys about it the next day, the next year. Over the years Jack kept them close with a lasting, even romantic, code of courtly devotion. "I come from a small-town environment," he explained, "and I remember my childhood impressions that, if you were a conniver or a fink or whatever, everybody knew about it and you were a louse for the rest of your life." He stayed Jersey, but he read about the world.

Nobody ever *needs* you—he read and revered the existentialists—"You've got to remember that," he said. "You're alone, that's it. Friends are a boon, love is a boon, contacts with other human beings and events, these are all boons. You've got to do your part as well as you can." As soon as he got to Hollywood, Jack more than did his part, traveling in packs of like-minded artists and cinephiles he harvested from Jeff Corey's class. "The only way I've been able to eat all these years," Jack said, "is through the help of friends. I figure I owe them something." He graduated onto Roger Corman's sets, his pal Monte Hellman's sets, and then, eventually, into his pal Dennis's Hopper's *Easy Rider*, where overnight he became a hit, but he might easily have ended up as a writer or director instead. For his pal Bob Rafelson and the gang at BBS—a leading young production company named for Bob, Bert (Schneider) and Steve (Blauner), producers of *Easy Rider*—he'd written *Head, starred in Five Easy Pieces and The King of Marvin Gardens, appeared in A Safe Place,* and directed *Drive, He Said.* He was an artist. The benefits of movie stardom were lovely but limited; the ensemble's regenerative feed was Jack's first priority. "As an actor," he said, "I want to give in to the collaboration with the director because I don't want my work to be all the same. The more this can be done with comfort, the more variety my work has had." Got a good idea? Jack was game. Even if it was what he called a short part, Jack would take it. Film was, after all, a group undertaking. And he never forgot where his group came from.

Money? Consider the bowl of ripped-up fifty-dollar bills Jack kept on his coffee table. People, laughing, would ask, What's with the torn money in the dish? "And I started to realize," he said, "that I was creating a work of art. It was sculpture, as much as that Salvador Dalí piece over there. In fact, of all the things that are in this room—the Picassos, the Francis Bacon, the Magritte–this bowl of money is the one piece of art that always draws the most comments and attention." He invited anyone to throw money in. That too was a collaboration.

"There's something about the familiarity with which he greets all souls," his friend and costar Karen Black said, "the way he assumes people are present. It's a sort of grace he grants others." They would talk about it:

"You know, Jack, some people, you just can't find them."

"Blackie, they are there. If you search, you'll find them."

The remnants of traditional family—ex-wife, Sandra Knight; daughter, Jennifer—were harder to integrate, the terms of Jack's loyalty mercurial, his to define. For women the dance—go away, come close—was exhausting, charming, exhausting. It made the dancers dizzy. Then they got hurt.

But a noble deed was often all it took to win Jack's friendship for life. The day he met Robert Evans, early in 1969, Evans offered Nicholson, then unknown, ten grand to play a short part in *On a Clear Day You Can See Forever*, the actor's first big Hollywood movie.

"Pal, you don't know me," Jack whispered to Evans in his suite at the Sherry Netherland, "but I sure know who you are. Could you do me a big favor?"

"Shoot."

"Ya see, I just got a divorce. I gotta kid, gotta pay alimony, gotta pay child support and I'm on empty. Could you make it fifteen?"

"How about twelve-five?" Evans said.

Nicholson never forgot it.

Chinatown would be a family affair. Jack found a small part (later cut) for his friend Harry Dean Stanton; he brokered the casting, which had been Polanski's idea, of his girlfriend's father, John Huston, to play Noah Cross; and of course, J. J. Gittes had been named long ago by Towne for one of Jack's best friends, Harry Gittes. On the periphery Nicholson's circle extended to the Sylberts, whom he had worked with on *Carnal Knowledge* "When the Ant does your costumes," he said, "you don't have to act as much." That was, Anthea thought, the perfect description of a job well done—and the feeling was mutual. "Jack was easy to dress," she said. "He never argued and went along with everything. There is no Jack Nicholson when we worked. There was only Gittes. Who is Gittes? That's the way we did it."

Gittes's hat, Nicholson decided, would be an integral part of the performance. "I've always been one of the top wardrobe men in the business," he said. "I spend hours at Western Costume." But *Chinatown*, coming after a run of stylistically informal films, most of them set in the politically insurgent present, gave Nicholson his first chance to look elegant on screen. "No one had worn a regular suit in the movies for a long time," he said. "No one had had real short hair for a long time. And that was one of the things I thought could be fresh with a movie." It was a leading-man look, his first.

Reviving lost standards of cinematic beauty was Nicholson's retaliation to the glut of televised imagery—horrible with news of Vietnam and banal with sitcoms—that he felt was further coarsening the national sensibility. He called television called the cancer of film. It was the death instrument of our times, philistinism in a box. He would note how televised broadcasts of his films were destroying, while claiming to preserve, the art form that was his life and livelihood. "The overall concept of a film is the story," Nicholson explained, "the pace at which it's told, the progressions, the aesthetic viewpoint. The object is to make all of that a part of an audience's life, for that period of time. But on television, you are turned on and off. They can make you different colors." The forthright glamour of *Chinatown*, he felt, would be a welcome uplift to an increasingly cynical age, but he also knew his mission was doomed: "It's a demographic principle," he said. "Don't bet against it if it's good for television. That's what America's become." *Chinatown* was the lifeboat he boarded with his friends, film artists, and sailed too late into the wreckage. "I know," he said, "I'm not going to win." But he sailed anyway. "I'm a romantic," he confessed, "because I allow myself to believe that things could be better, could be more than they are. Because I allow myself to want that."

The orchard, fifty miles out of Los Angeles, still looked like old Southern California—mountains, wide valley, and eucalyptus—for a moment. Then: Row after row of Valencia orange trees, acres of trees, of pristine runs of thick, dreaming green seized by cables and generators and Winnebagos and a swarm of production personnel. This was *Chinatown*'s first location, October 15, 1973.

The early-morning hour-long ride out to Everett Ranch, Polanski and Evans spent laid out, side by side, in the back of a station wagon, the director nauseous with worry, the producer burning with sciatica, both chuckling, despite their agony, at the pretty picture they made: two grown professionals stricken at the starting gate, about to roll film on a picture Polanski hadn't finished casting and still didn't have an ending. The director had practiced his usual first-day psych-up, shoring his conviction that, yes, he knew what he was doing, he was good, sometimes the best, and the film was going to be a success. It was imperative that he convinced himself; if he didn't, he knew the crew wouldn't be convinced either. "And I've learned that [the affirmations] must be said without the slightest hesitation in your attitude," he explained, "or they won't put up with it. They'll tell you, 'Go fuck yourself.'" This shield was his preemptive riposte to all the adversity he would face on a film, from the actors, who might fight him, to the critics, who would accuse him of encouraging hyper-violence they tied, somehow, to Sharon's murder. And so, that first day, Polanski would become, "psychologically invulnerable," against them all. He said, "If I've learned one thing about filmmaking, it's that it requires not only talent but the stamina to resist all these attackers."

Already at the location, Nicholson and Sylbert, leaning under the shade of a tree, watched as the station wagon pulled up, dislodged Robert Evans on a stretcher and a wobbly Roman Polanski, who doubled forward and promptly threw up in the dirt.

Nicholson was close to stretcher-ready himself. He was dead tired. Working with Antonioni on *The Passenger* had been a grueling experience, brittle with creative cross-purposes and autocratic rulings—which Nicholson accepted, in the spirit of collaboration, largely without protest—and having arrived in Los Angeles only two days earlier after twenty hours of flying, he came to Everett Ranch on no rest. He was also anxious, though he didn't wear it the way Polanski or Evans did. The first day of shooting was always a minefield of concerns for Nicholson. He was still discovering for himself Gittes's secret, the tragic flaw that would lead Jack, the actor, to comprehension. But not total comprehension: Full knowledge of the character, for Jack, would curb the precious likelihood of spontaneous discovery he needed to save for the camera. He could only plan so much. And yet, without sufficient preparation—and coming from *The Passenger*, he hadn't the time—he hadn't yet located that secret semiknown place in Gittes, a place to start, and married it to the same in himself. For he was "at least 75% of every character I play." But he was also, he knew, "slow to inspire." On the first day of shooting, he was closer to 90 percent Jack and 10 percent Jake. It would take him about two weeks, he estimated, to "crawl completely inside the skin and brain of a character." But in the meantime, what would he do?

For ten years he had managed to keep off cigarettes. Jake Gittes brought them back.

"You believe in aliens?" he asked Jesse Vint.

Vint, cast as the grove's crippled farmer, searched Jack's face for irony. There wasn't any. This was just Jack. "Do *you* believe in aliens?"

"They're here. They're here today. Right now. Taking us over. One by one."

"You putting me on?"

Vint remembered that great scene in *Easy Rider*: Jack, with Hopper and Fonda around the fire, improvising a stoned monologue about extraterrestrial life. He was clearly high in that scene, a tour de force of subconscious release. Was he high now? Or did he really believe this stuff?

Never one to miss a debate, Polanski had drawn close to Nicholson's lecture, listening intently. Stanley Cortez, director of photography, was slow to set up the shot, leaving cast and crew ample time—too much time, in fact—to talk about aliens.

"We only have this location for three days," Sylbert reminded Evans, who didn't need reminding.

"We'll get it."

Evans was disinclined to Cortez from the first; he had pushed for Gordon Willis for director of photography. He wanted the broodingly romantic look Willis brought to *The Godfather*, but Polanski, having so enjoyed his work with William Fraker, DP on *Rosemary's Baby*, resisted. Evans feared reteaming them. Two kids in a sandbox, they had pushed *Rosemary* behind schedule, and Evans wouldn't let *Chinatown*, the first Robert Evans Production, run the same risk. Yablans and the rest of Paramount were watching the production carefully, waiting (or in Yablans's case, hoping) for Icarus to fall, and any perceived indulgence of time or budget—Evans was trying to keep the latter to three million—would be characterized as his fault. Cortez, then, was a compromise; Polanski could get behind the cinematographer of Orson Welles's *The Magnificent Ambersons;* and to Evans, the faded glamour, the sumptuous camerawork of *Ambersons* portended well for *Chinatown.* At sixty-five, Cortez was, after all, familiar with the period he remembered well, and even if he wasn't as comfortable with the new Panavision technology as a younger cinematographer might be, at least he would bring a degree of stylistic reportage to *Chinatown.* But how long would they wait for it?

Cortez was laying boards on the dirt to smooth, theoretically, the camera movements. But the dirt wasn't a flat surface.

"He's putting down a dance floor?" Koch asked. "He should be using rails."

Assistant producer and production manager Doc Erickson had his suspicions. Cortez, he knew, was figure of considerable influence at the American Society of Cinematographers and "had his name on a number of films," but he "had *not* done that many pictures" as director of photography. Whatever Cortez's facility with black-and-white, Erickson could see, watching Cortez set up the shot, that he had comparatively little experience with color.

Another director might have exploited his downtime to reconceive the shot or storyboard upcoming setups, but Polanski, who stopped storyboarding after film school, had already completed his preparation. He knew, basically, where he wanted the camera. But there was no point, Polanski reasoned, in attempting to plan for every contingency; committing to a shot in advance would be as senseless as reverse engineering, "like ordering a first class suit by a leading tailor in Paris, then trying to find a person that will fit it," he said. "I do it the other way around." Adjustments to the proverbial suit would come from watching the actors discover the fit, "letting them rehearse and seeing that instinctively they find the right places, the right attitudes, the right readings and the right body language. . . . Only then do I start thinking of filming it, deciding when and how I'm going to place the camera." In the interim Polanski would hold off the actors. Why warm them up only to let them cool down? He'd wait—for Cortez to give him the go-ahead—and in the meantime reexamine certain technical details.

"Get your clubfoot from wardrobe," he told Jesse Vint. "I want to see your walk."

A crutch under one arm, Vint hobbled along.

"No, no. You're too athletic," Polanski called back. "Here's the thing. When a person is born with a clubfoot, what happens during the growth is the skeleton becomes deformed and they will compensate."

Vint's character would appear only briefly in the film; amid the chaos of the scene, an altercation between Gittes and the farmers, the particulars of his handicap would likely be lost in the melee, but to Polanski there were no minutiae.

Polanski took the crutch, and Vint watched astonished as Polanski's frame adapted, just as he had described, to the clubfoot. He walked to and fro, Vint thought, making the anatomical readjustments of someone born with the deformity.

"Why the hell aren't *you* doing this part?" Vint asked.

"I'm already doing a part," he replied inscrutably, returning the crutch.

When the time finally did come to shoot the scene, Polanski instructed Vint to give it everything he had.

"Hit Jack on the head with the crutch," he said. "Hit him hard and don't hold back."

"Hear that, Jack?" Vint turned to Nicholson. "Roman said it. Not me."

"Don't worry about it, Vint. Do what the boss tells ya." Ready for the take, Nicholson put out his smoke. "Let's go."

It was so hot, unseasonably hot for October. They would have the location for three days. Both too much time and too little.

"Quiet!" Howard Koch shouted, calling the set to order. "We're ready to go." Then: "We're rolling."

Polanski held stone still next to the camera lens—any closer to the actors and Koch would have to forcibly pull him out of the scene.

"Speed."

Perfect silence down the orchard, the eucalyptus in the foothills, the mountains at the farthest reaches of the landscape, and for three still seconds the Tierra Rejada valley sounded a million years younger.

"And . . ." Polanski murmured. His focus was absolute; he was a rifleman staring down his kill.

A hot breeze, the sound of secrets whispering the oranges.

"Action!"

Vint raised the crutch and whacked Nicholson over the head, knocking him down, Vint flung onto him and they tussled in the dust. The violence was real, but Jack kept acting; more, fastening onto the rage, feeding on it. "He cannot stop," Polanski observed. "He goes into a kind of fit . . ."

Polanski, involuntarily acting alongside them, his expressions changing, his shoulders twitching in step with Vint's lopsided shuffle, absorbing the drama like a scene written in Braille, until his body touched a falsehood and recoiled. "Cut!" He was Polanski again. "Cut."

He crossed to Vint. "You think that's a hit? That's not a hit."

"You hear what he said, Jack?"

Jack heaved himself up from the dirt. "Go ahead, pal. You can't hurt me."

Polanski jumped back to the camera, and they went at it again. Vint thwacked Nicholson dead to the ground.

"Cut!"

That was it.

"Good!" Polanski said. "Now Jack."

They would go in now for Jack's closeup, a shot of him knocked out in the dirt.

Polanski, the camera hovering over his shoulder, leaned over Nicholson's face. "Don't look," he said. "Close your eyes."

Studying the results—Jake's head haloed in bits of bark and leaves—Polanski cleared the brush from around Jack and reexamined the picture—Jake's head framed against the empty brown dirt—and reconsidered yet again. Polanski selected a green walnut off the ground and placed it beside, but not too close to, his actor's head. He then added a brown walnut to the composition. He moved the green walnut two or three inches to the side and Jack opened his—

"Close your eyes."

He moved the walnut back. He then let an ant crawl onto his finger and lowered it onto Jack's face.

"Roll camera, please. . . ." Polanski backed out of frame. "Jack, eyes closed. . . ."

The ant crawled over Jack's nose, along the bridge, up to the forehead. . . .

Polanski to the operator: "Did you get it?"

"Didn't get it."

"We'll do it again."

Polanski crouched beside Jack, scouring the dirt for another ant. "Eyes closed. . . ."

"Jesus." Jack chuckled.

Roman found his ant and edged it onto Nicholson's face. "Roll camera," he said, backing out.

"Rolling."

From out of frame, Polanski watched the ant seem to climb up Nicholson's cheek, change its mind, and climb down off his face.

"Cut."

Polanski ducked back into the frame to adjust the ant.

"So," Jack drawled, "let me get this straight—"

"Eyes closed."

"When the ant gets it right, we've got a take?"

"That's correct."

Jack smiled too big. "How long are you gonna hold on this shot, Roman?"

"A second. Maybe two. Roll camera, please."

Polanski stepped out, and all eyes were on the insect, the costliest ant in human history.

It went on for forty minutes. Then Polanski, satisfied, thanked the crew. He had gotten what he wanted.

Evans had watched the whole time. This kind of care, this patience for creative suggestion and experiment, was what he wanted for *Chinatown* and each successive Robert Evans Production. It would be up to him to draw the line, but this ant wasn't it; he knew exactly what it would cost to produce a Polanski-Nicholson-Sylbert production, and as pissed as Frank Yablans might be with these dailies, Evans would stand and fall with his filmmakers. He didn't always have to understand them—in fact, in the case of *Chinatown*, he didn't understand much—but he also didn't try to. Why should he tell Polanski how to use his talent? Evans had hired an artist to make those decisions himself, that's what he was paying for, and he would do everything he could to keep the Mountain behind him, behind them. That he also happened to *be* half the Mountain didn't hurt.

There was a low thunder of hooves. Heads turned.

From out of the farthest trees approached a tall rider on a white horse. It was a startling sight—what appeared to be a long lean old man under a wide white hat, heedlessly approaching the film set as if it were his own. The crew, who had stopped working to behold the stranger, heard him haw-hawing in the distance, bellowing in happy Spanish to the orchard hands as he passed by. They watched him, drawing near, gallantly doff his hat to a few grips he seemed to recognize or who seemed to recognize him.

"God," someone said. "John Huston."

He was the guest of honor at a long redwood table, set for lunch, under the kind orchard shade. Polanski, host and conductor, took the head; Huston and Nicholson were opposite, and on the bench beside Jack, Anjelica sat quietly. She was never one for set visits, with good reason: They left her feeling extraneous, like she was interrupting an intimate exchange, but her father had asked her to come to *Chinatown*. And of course there was Jack.

[SPACE BREAK]

He was her dream well before they ever met. In 1969, as the most hopeful and, she thought, most beautiful decade faded out, she saw him in *Easy Rider*, and went back a second time to see him again. In his ease and humor and exuberance and his princely smile, spanning the screen like a victory flag, she saw a man she could love, and—in a way, like the rest of the world, already did.

She saw him again, for the first time, in April 1973. Her stepmother, Cici, brought her along to a party at Jack's. It was his birthday. He was thirty-six.

"Good evening, ladies," he said, opening the door, the evening sun singing in around him. "I'm Jack, and I'm glad you could make it."

She had dressed as she always did, *con amor*, with discretion, allure and commanding good taste, in a long black evening dress, open down the back. So much back.

As soon as he saw her he saw class. He was New Jersey. She was a princess, nobly descended from a Hollywood king, John Huston, himself the son of Walter Huston. Royalty did not impress Jack, but there was no turning his eyes from the aura of quality, aristocratic in merit, that at twenty-one already shone from her formidable grace and bones, her valiant nose, long and fine, like a beautiful bayonet or a cherished family tradition.

That night they danced for hours in a small moon of candles, and he asked her to stay the night. Cici went home alone.

The next morning Anjelica passed Robert Towne on her way out. Jack didn't drive her home. He didn't call her that day or the day after, but days later, to invite her for dinner, a date he later called to cancel for, he claimed, a previous obligation.

"Does that make me a secondary one?" she asked.

"Don't say that. It's not witty enough, and it's derogatory to both of us."

That night, out with friends, she saw him at a restaurant with Michelle Phillips, an ex-girlfriend.

This was the Jack dance. Come back, go away. Come back.

In those years she followed him everywhere.

In New York, a night before she was to leave for London, they spoke frankly of old loves; unraveled his slipknot of infidelities, Michelle Phillips; his need for so-called freedom; her mother, the plangently beautiful Enrica Soma, called "Ricki"; and she told him she loved him. Holding her, he told her he loved her too. When she arrived in London, she learned that the night she left New York he had slept with another woman, and though he had never promised to be faithful, saying he loved her must have been his promise of something. She confronted him. "Oh, Toots," he answered, "it was just a mercy fuck." Weeks later they wandered the green around the Serpentine lake in Hyde Park—he had to fly to *The Passenger* the next morning—and when he told her he hated to leave her it thrilled her. She tried to imagine marriage, as she had as a girl at St. Clerans, her family's estate in Ireland, covering her eyes with a veil and dream-walking the grounds as a fairy-girl bride, but she quickly came to: There was always present the vortex of a darker past, what had been done to her and Jack as children, what they had done to each other as adults, and would probably, even against their will, do to each other again. In Barcelona they met again. They talked of Regina Le Clery, his friend who had just died in a plane crash at Orly Airport, and again of her mother, killed in a car crash in 1969, who managed her father's many trangsressions ably, like a deposed queen burying a broken heart; and they talked of ghosts, memories that lace the eye; and he fell asleep fingering the pearls, once her mother's, she wore that night to bed; and following him to France, she discovered he had slept with another woman.

She became a detective, snooping for evidence wherever he had been, the bureau, his wallet, the little table by his bed. It was agony.

She became, not for the first time, her mother's daughter and buried her heart.

The symmetry, the nonaccidental coincidence of repeated history, was not lost on her, nor was the incontestable power of Freudian law. Gittes should return to Chinatown, and she should love this Irishman Jack, an actor, writer, director, so discernibly in communion with her father, an actor, writer, director, two genial cheats laughing, leaning in across the long orchard table, to light each other's cigars. She was no more than a prisoner, as all children of parents are, subject to a story of love written for her long, long ago.

Nor was the cycle lost on Jack. A movie fan, he had loved Huston, "my idol since childhood," well before he had loved Huston's daughter. When they finally met, Jack saw John—forthright, sophisticated, adventuresome—exactly as Jack had dreamed him to be: "I consciously knew for a certain period with John that the greatest guy alive was a friend of mine," Nicholson said. For one who never really knew his own father, Nicholson felt a singularly rich devotion to the old man. "He's one of those people in life whose approval I seek," he said. It was a feeling Huston, in his way, returned. ("Jack's a virtuoso," he would offer.) His own father Huston practically never saw until he was fifteen. He mirrored this relationship with Anjelica when he was off filming, providing, in lieu of sustained fatherhood, brief location hello-and-goodbyes squeezed between takes. "And since he had never played a father," Huston said, "he never assumed that role with me. We were more like brothers or good friends." And so would he be brother and friend to Nicholson, betraying limited fatherly feeling, rousing him instead with tales of his conquests and memories of the old days. "When John Huston dies," Nicholson said, "I'll cry for the rest of my life." He meant it.

Huston had cast Anjelica in her first starring role in his 1969 *A Walk with Love and Death*. She didn't want to the part. "I felt that I had to do the movie to please him," she confessed, "which is certainly not the way to go into any project." She hated the way he made her look on camera and cried through the production, and when she tried to move out of his hotel, into accommodations with crew folk her own age and where her crush was staying, Huston prohibited her. He wanted her close.

John Huston's sometime lover Eloise Hardt paid a visit to Ireland and saw Anjelica, per her father's direction, ride a horse at high speeds through very cold and dangerous terrain. It was, she felt, sadistic. Some kind of punishment for something.

"John," Hardt said, "she's going to die on that horse."

He replied, "She wants to be an actress."

Helpless and revolted, Hardt watched Huston "practically do [Anjelica] in in order to get her out of the business." She would attempt to forgive him, as Anjelica would, when he showed as much tenderness. "But the more you loved him," Hardt concluded, "the less respect he had for you."

Hardt returned to Los Angeles in early 1969. She was home the night her daughter, home for Christmas break, pulled up their driveway at 8962 Cynthia Avenue and a black car rushed in behind her, a man jumped out, shoved her daughter into his car, and drove away. Two days later the body was found in heavy brush off the 8800 block of Mulholland Drive, beaten and stabbed in the neck and chest. Two clues—the size and proliferation of the knife wounds and the crime scene's proximity to recent murder sites—pointed to Sharon Tate's killers. But the murder was never solved.

Four weeks after her daughter's death, Hardt received a phone call from Anjelica. She was sobbing: Her mother had been killed in a car crash. Hardt actually could not speak; the news lobotomized her. "I couldn't get through my own pain to answer," she said. "It was like I was in some kind of nightmare that was never ending."

Anjelica's eyes were as deep as the richest black oil; they told of legacy, the ages of subterranean refinement preceding her actual birth, and the long dinners at St. Clerans when, too early, her father would drill her for the benefit of his treasured guests, the likes of Sartre and Steinbeck and Pauline de Rothschild. At one dinner she testily upbraided van Gogh. "You don't like van Gogh?" her father blustered. "Then name six of his paintings and tell me why you don't like van Gogh." Of course she couldn't. "Leave the room," he commanded, "and, until you know what you're talking about, don't come back with your opinions to the dinner table."

He scared her. But she clung to his leg all the way from the house to yet another car that would take him from away St. Clerans for more months of moviemaking, for it felt better, she came to believe, to fear him at home than love him from afar.

Allowing Nicholson and her father to trade laughs in the orchard, Anjelica would concede that for all Jack had of the old man, there was something in him that brought back her mother, "a certain kind of square earthed presence," she said, a resolve that felt to her—if he could lay off the girls—almost like permanence. That was the Jack she alone knew—and hoped for.

That Jack and Jake's love interests, Anjelica and Evelyn Mulwray, daughters of power and paragons of class, were both fathered by John Huston and his image made for an electrically intimate "triangular offstage situation," Nicholson said, for John Huston and for Jack.

It was less useful for Anjelica.

"So . . . ," her father boomed across the table to Nicholson. "I hear you're sleeping with my daughter"—Anjelica reddened violently—"Mr. *Gitts*."

4

At Woodland, after the Nate 'n Al's hot-dog dinner, *la spécialité de la maison*, Evans and Towne walked their drinks around the pool to the projection room where Evans finished his nights. Surrounded by floor-to-ceiling photographs, a memory mural of loved ones laughing and triumphant—Alain Delon Kissinger; Evans's brother, Charlie, and sister, Alice; his son, Josh; the banditos three, Jack and Evans and Warren, along with the women, the impossibly beautiful women, daisy-, dream-, and dagger-eyed, but none more beautiful than making movies—he and Towne sat silently in spacious black leather chairs, staring down the screen for the first results of their labor. At last it was finally that time: the dailies.

Evans, wrestling his sciatica, picked up the phone by his seat and told the projectionist they were ready.

Window curtains closed and lights dimmed and Evans was not pleased with what he saw. The photography was much harder, more naturalistic than he had imagined. Where was classic Hollywood *noir*? Polanski had bleached his exteriors in blinding sun. Even the orange grove he had dehydrated completely to desert. Forsaking Towne's remembered Arcadia, he was shooting a city scorched by the hell of his own memories. "I don't like sunlight very much," he would confess. "In the subjects I like to deal with, sunlight is . . . alien." Evidently Polanski wasn't understanding Los Angeles; he was scorning it. "Roman was just letting everybody know how he felt about L.A.," Nicholson said. "It was a place where blood always flows." Was grief blinding him? Towne certainly thought so.

"What's with the ending?" Evans asked.

A question mark, in place of an exact location in Chinatown, upset the otherwise perfect call sheet. Evans wanted it resolved.

"Talk to Roman," the screenwriter said, and left.

This was the job, Towne knew. Paid to fall in and out of love. Paid to lose.

At least he was back on *Shampoo*, scheduled to begin filming soon, in March 1974. *Shampoo* was a tender spot for Evans, a project he had let slip away. Beatty, naturally, had taken it to him first and, as predicted, Evans loved it, and would have paid almost anything to be in business with Towne and Beatty, but Columbia, racing to catch up with Paramount and Warners, made Beatty a terrific offer that Evans claimed Frank Yablans refused to let him top. It was a sign of Yablans's mounting dissatisfaction and Evans's uneasiness as producer–production head, losing the Mountain a project stacked with some of Paramount's closest friends.

Thus would Evans, losing ground at the studio and in the *Chinatown* dailies, pick up the phone and call the lab. He had an idea. A way, he thought, he could improve *Chinatown*.

The Santa Anas were blowing the last days of October 1973, swathing the city in lethargy and an unright argument of fog and sun tense Angelenos inherited from the sky. It was the Santa Anas, Raymond Chandler had written, that made "meek little wives feel the edge of the carving knife and study their husband's necks." In Malibu, Joan Didion felt the winds change. Sensing a noxious turn to the air, she felt smoke in the far hills, sirens in the canyons, and "woke in the night troubled not only by the peacocks screaming in the olive trees but by the eerie absence of surf. The heat was surreal. The sky had a yellow cast, the kind of light sometimes called 'earthquake weather.' My only neighbor would not come out of her house for days, and there were no lights at night, and her husband roamed the place with a machete. One day he would tell me that he had heard a trespasser, the next a rattlesnake." It evoked for her the famous last scene of Nathanael West's *The Day of the Locust*, when the burning Gomorrah is dealt, somehow, the fate it deserves—for its sprawling invasion of the land, its Hollywood hedonisms, and repudiation of the American East. The bad winds: the city's guilty paradise tax. "The city burning," Didion wrote, "is Los Angeles's deepest image of itself."

The cast and crew of *Chinatown* sat the winds out in the red Naugahyde booths of the Windsor Restaurant, where they were shooting a scene with Gittes and Evelyn. But in the aura of Faye Dunaway, the winds followed them inside. She was so brittle, some said, out of some kind of Method adherence to her character, Evelyn; others sensed profound insecurity. Whatever the source, she was at this early stage already niggling Polanski to change this or that word, give her more makeup and then less, keeping the crew waiting, then interrupting takes ("Roman, I need to start over"), and even refusing, according to one Teamster, to flush her own toilet. No stranger to actress pathology, Polanski tried, at first, to receive her with tendresse, but in no time found he couldn't win.

The crew finally did turn against Dunaway, and her delusions came true. They hated her. She regarded their every creative impulse with suspicion, and in her paranoia—knowing, perhaps, that Jane Fonda was once Evans's first choice—seemed to resist on principle.

"Ugh. Here she comes."

"Fuckin' Faye."

"The Dread Dunaway."

Polanski saw signs of an actress who hadn't prepared. Evelyn's nervous pauses and double-backs were Dunaway's stalls, he suspected, to cover for not having learned her lines. "I think Jack and Roman had great patience with Faye," Koch said. "They knew she was brilliant in the scenes, but boy, was it hard to work with her." Styles clashed. Dunaway had expected to discuss Evelyn with Polanski, but claimed they never did. "The word *motivation*," she said, "was never mentioned." Customarily Polanski stayed clear of such discussions, allowing the actor to formulate the character on his or her own and for the camera, but the isolation left Dunaway even more insecure, cut off from answers and feedback, and Polanski's many technical notes—what she called his "rigid, dictatorial approach"—tested her further. "A director like Polanski wants you to get your adrenalin up," she explained. "But your adrenalin is already up."

A few days before, Koch had called Dunaway, out with the flu, to check in.

"Hi, Faye. It's Howard. How are you doing?"

"I don't talk to assistant directors."

"Okay," he said, and hung up.

Polanski and Cortez set up a shot of Nicholson in a booth, over Dunaway's shoulder. Beside the camera, Polanski called action. The camera sputtered. A technical error.

"Cut," Polanski said. "Right away, right away."

But Dunaway summoned her personal makeup man, Lee Harmon, who came rushing in with Dunaway's Blistex, applying away. Her hairdresser, Suzie Germaine, appeared with an aerosol can and started spritzing.

"Give me those things," Polanski yelled, and snatched them away from Harmon. "I'll do it myself when you need it."

Polanski reset the camera and went again. A strand of Dunaway's hair caught the light, he called cut, and summoned her hairdresser to smooth down the hair. But in the next take the hair popped up again and Polanski reached over and plucked it out.

Dunaway's eyes flashed, and Howard Koch Jr. snapped to attention. "Lunch!"

"I don't believe it!" she cried. "I just don't believe it! That motherfucker pulled my hair out!"

Screaming ensued, Dunaway leveled Polanski with obscenities, and Polanski exploded.

"I am the *director*!" He lectured her on the politics of production, how the film belonged to the filmmaker, not to the actress, that it was his job to know everything and hers to submit to his reason whether she agreed or not.

She blew out of the restaurant and after lunch refused to return. Production shut down.

An emergency meeting was called Freddie Fields, head of CMA, one of Hollywood's toniest boutique agencies. In contrast to the giant William Morris Agency and in tandem with their Sunset Blvd. neighbor Evarts Ziegler, Fields and Begelman needed to keep CMA growing, and as such were early to understand they required young agents to lure young talent. As Ziegler had turned to Bill Tennant, Fields and Begelman leaned on Sue Mengers, who would cultivate for CMA a tremendous roster of next-generation filmmakers: Barbra Streisand, Peter Bogdanovich, Ryan O'Neal, and with the blessing of her pal Robert Evans, Ali MacGraw after she'd left him. On the day of the meeting, it was Fields, Dunaway's early benefactor, who received Robert Evans. Not Mengers.

"Fire Polanski," Fields pleaded. "You know how he works. He's crazy. You'll thank me for it."

"He's not crazy. He's a genius."

"Faye can't work with him."

Evans distained Fields—a liar and, Peter Bart surmised, sociopath. Not that Sue Mengers was above lying, only that when she did, Bart said, "she did it with a wink." Agenting was war for Fields; for Mengers it was fun; she thought in relationships, he in deals; and though both strategies proved equally successful, Evans favored hers. It was a decidedly modern, poststudio approach to humanize, as Mengers did, her clients. In the contract days, the agent would be more likely to move talent wholesale and let the studio manage the rest. But since the dissolution of those contracts, as each individual movie became its own negotiation, the agent-client axis acquired deeper intimacy. No longer was it chic to *own* the talent, parent-to-child; new agents, in keeping with the antipaternalistic spirit of the day, befriended them. That was one of Mengers' strengths. "Sue couldn't read a contract if her life depended on it," said one agent. Fields, trained in the previous generation, didn't understand this.

"I'll give you Mark Rydell," he told Evans at their next meeting, in Paramount's conference room, as Dunaway and Polanski looked on. "He'll get you out of this mess."

"Fuck you, Freddie."

"Don't be stupid. You wanna recast? You're a week in and you're gonna lose Faye."

"I'm gonna keep Faye and I'm gonna keep Roman. That's the way this is gonna go."

"I can't work with him," Dunaway blurted. "He tries to control my every move."

"It's called directing," Polanski explained.

"See?!" she complained to Fields. "He's crazy!"

Evans cut in. "Faye, you did something that wasn't very nice—"

She started screaming. Roman, behind her, rolled his eyes at Evans.

If ever there was a studio head gifted at seduction, it was Robert Evans. He had Woodland, his partner in seduction, to enhance the enchantment, and it was there, surrounded in fresh white roses and firelight, its glow kissing up his Picassos and Dalís, that he smoothed Dunaway's furrowed brow, creaming her with praise—sincere praise; she was, he knew from the dailies, doing the best work of her life—finally tempting her dreams with an Oscar or a Rolls Corniche, "One or the other," he said, "I personally guarantee." She came back.

One crisis immediately gave way to another.

"What is this?" Polanski asked of the dailies. He was in the screening room of the Canon Drive office, surrounded by his team, the Sylberts, Koch, Cortez. "This reddish tint. We didn't shoot this."

Polanski went down to the lab to see how they were printing the film. "Why is everything tinted?"

"Robert Evans requested it."

"He did?"

Polanski raged into Evans's office. "Why did you do this? Everything looks like ketchup."

"I wanted to try. Just to see—"

"Well, now we know and now we go back."

Later, Polanski and Sylbert would laugh about this interference. Evans's artistic convictions, "were sometimes quite naive," Polanski reflected. Knowing he had transgressed on the tinting, Evans retreated, and the intended naturalism of the *Chinatown* dailies was restored.

But the issue of Stanley Cortez persisted. In dailies Polanski flinched at the effects of all that waiting around. "Cortez's style and his use of light were old fashioned," he said. "He used a lot of light, lot of projectors, and he didn't use much reflected light. I wanted it done with [contemporary] means, for the world [of the film] to photograph as it looked then." Evans conceded they needed to find someone else.

"Bob, you tell him," Polanski said.

"He's your cameraman. You tell him."

It was a painful conversation. Cortez, to Polanski, "was always this charming, wonderful man." That he seemed to take the news so well made it even harder.

Evans then brokered Polanski's introduction to cinematographer John Alonzo, whom Evans wrested from preproduction of *Young Frankenstein* early in November 1973. Alonzo, who had documentary experience shooting film for *National Geographic* and Jacques Cousteau, working fast with a minimum of equipment and a maximum of natural light, was comfortable with new Panaflex camera technologies and had ably served Paramount on *Harold and Maude*.

Polanski spoke to Alonzo only briefly, explaining that Cortez's work was too slow and the results too pretty and he wanted something grittier.

"He wants reality," Alonzo told to his eighteen-year-old daughter, Gorgiana, over dinner. "He wants the soft red tile to look soft red, and he wants the blood to look like blood."

With only Saturday and Sunday to prepare for his Monday shoot, Alonzo spent the weekend catching up on dailies at Woodland, then setting up a projector in his own living room and running prints of *Knife in the Water* and *Repulsion* to discover for his own eyes Polanski's version of realism. He saw that even *Repulsion*, for all its surreality, maintained a matter-of-factness that made the horror hit harder.

Monday came, and Gorgiana, who was beginning her freshman year at Cal State Northridge, drove her father to Paramount on her way to school, briefing him, in the car, on the library research she completed over the weekend, a "précis of the city," she said, along with Carey McWilliams's account of the Los Angeles water wars, to give her father "a quick appreciation of the topic he would be working with." What he learned floored Alonzo.

"They stole the water?"

"Yes."

"And this is how we have Los Angeles? A crime?"

"Yes, I guess so."

When Alzono arrived at the studio backlot, at the barber-shop set arranged just off Paramount's New York street, Evans was already there, in tennis clothes, to make sure Alonzo's first day went smoothly. Alonzo took a quick look at the crew and lighting plan and waved Richard Sylbert into a conference. Such was Sylbert's production expertise that Alonzo could address him the way one would a producer.

"I work with a very lean crew," Alonzo explained. "If you want to pay these guys, that's fine, but I won't be needing them."

Sylbert nodded. "Okay, I'll let them know."

"I don't know how Cortez works, but I'll sweep the floor if I have to."

Sylbert then conferred with Evans, who handled the request without issue.

The Santa Anas, meanwhile, were not respecting the sunny skies—known on set as "Koch Weather" for the miraculous deal the AD seemed to have struck with God—needed to maintain the film's thirsty look, a concern Doc Erickson took to Alonzo.

"How can you do this?" Erickson asked, meaning shoot the overcast view through the barbershop window. "It won't look like it's summer out there."

"Don't worry. I can handle that. I'll blow out the window."

Alonzo's high esteem for Polanski, based until then solely on his work, dramatically increased when he saw how the director operated in the field. It was obvious Polanski had amassed an uncommonly sophisticated cache of production expertise, that he had reasons, the greatest reasons, for everything, would take the time to explain (in somewhat fractured Polish-English) those reasons, and was, despite his intensity of focus, compassionate to all, not only "cognizant of the cinematographer's problems," Alonzo wrote, "but . . . aware of the art director's problems. He knows lighting, as well as direction." Indeed English was Polanski's sole deficiency, and where he couldn't get the right word, he would motion at Alonzo or toward the crew in sweeping gestures that had them laughing even when they weren't confused. Once Alonzo discovered Polanksi spoke Italian they cut short their English and started in with Italian, which Alonzo then translated back into English for his crew. From there they communicated easily: "There were out-and-out arguments at times," Alonzo reported, "but good healthy ones, because they were logical, rational, without egos involved."

They grooved. "Polanski would pick out a set-up in a specific place," wrote Alonzo, "using a specific lens and we'd compare notes about why this way or why that way. Sometimes we'd get into a debate and draw the compositions on the floor of the sound stage with chalk. He would insist that this was better composition than that and, by golly, most of the time he was right." The new fast lenses freed up Alonzo to use less light. "I have an idea," he told Polanski, "that if we shoot the remainder of the picture with a 40mm, 45mm or 50mm lens, whenever possible, this will give the picture a very subtle look—not a distorted look. It won't be *A Clockwork Orange*. We'll shoot the closeups with a 75mm lens, maximum. We'll use the zoom lens only to trim 4 to 6 millimeters with a dolly—never strictly as a move. If you'll let me stick to that approach, I think it will influence the atmosphere of the picture in a subtle way." Polanski agreed. Because Alonzo worked so fast, Polanski was always comfortable, if need be, to ask him to modify the setup, even after it was ready. But once Polanski had made his decision—after he allowed the actors, in rehearsal, to find their blocking, and, consequently, determine the final placement of camera and lights—he would stick to it and insist the actors do the same. Requiring his actors to hit their marks precisely, Polanski defended the rigor of his frame and Alonzo's lights, which won Polanski more of Alonzo's heart.

They were shooting in one of the city's oldest neighborhoods, Angelino Heights, a hilly enclave of Victorian and gingerbread houses in turn-of-the-century colors, soft red and orange, turquoise and sea green, ornate wraparound parapets, and spangled Moorish filigrees ,the grand promise of an earlier Los Angeles. Since then, most had faded. The lawns had browned. Money had evacuated farther west.

The lime-green bungalow apartment at 848 East Kensington Road, where Gittes finds Ida Sessions dead on her kitchen floor, was locked and the key was missing. The production had been waiting for a solution, costing Polanski valuable time at the location. He was, "exasperated," according to L.A. Times reporter Priscilla English.

"Bernie!" called Howard Koch in the big voice that earned him a Nicholson nickname, Bullhorn. "Bring a hammer!"

Polanski wouldn't wait any longer. He made for the front door, ready to smash in the glass with an empty Coke bottle.

"No! Not that way, Roman," Koch shouted. "No, Roman, the *back* door."

But Polanski was already breaking in. "I like it," he told Koch, reaching in for the doorknob. "See? That's the way the murderer got in."

Polanski stepped over the pile of broken glass and walked inside. "Bernie! Bring a broom!"

"Hey, guys," Polanski said to the crew behind him, "keep this glass, okay?"

Nicholson, hands in his pockets, strolled up in a gray suit and fedora. A Latino boy tugged at his sleeve. "Hey, mister, do you know what kind of mystery this movie is about?"

"Yeah, I do."

"Well, what is it about?"

The kid trailed him into the bungalow.

"It's about murder—and ladies."

Inside, Diane Ladd as Ida Sessions, was stretched out "dead" on the kitchen floor. Polanski hovered over her body, inspecting it for realism.

"I want it like this," he said, helping her elbow up to the side of her face. "And the leg"—he bent the leg unnaturally and stood up to assess the results—"it is right."

Ladd had been on the floor, sensing something ominous. "Everyone thought Roman was replaying the death of his wife," she recalled. "It was a very scary day."

A production assistant produced a jar from a high shelf and passed it off to Polanski.

"Roman, what is that?" asked Ladd.

"Ants."

"No, Roman, please, no ants, please!"

She was terrified, but he was laughing.

"Okay, okay," he said. "Kill the ants!"

"Kill the ants!" someone shouted.

"Kill the ants!" echoed down the line.

"Roman," Ladd said, "I need some cotton. For my ears."

"Cotton for Diane!" Polanski called behind him.

"Cotton for Diane!" echoed down.

"Do you know *why* I need cotton?" Ladd asked Polanski, not wanting to appear wasteful.

"Because you are a Method actress and you don't want to hear anything because you are dead."

Watching Polanski conscientiously arrange props in the shot, turning a head of lettuce into and away from the light, then checking with Alonzo for his reaction, USC student intern Maggie Parker observed a change, the impress of creation, come over his face. "When it came to 'This is what I want' Roman was so focused and intense," she said, "but he never created tension. [When he wasn't concentrating] He kept things light and fun." A fan of Polanski's work, Parker had called his office every day, talking to Thelma Roberts, his secretary, asking to please let her, a twenty-year old film student, observe the workings of a Polanski movie up close. Finally, Thelma arranged a meeting with Polanski. A former film student himself, he consented to let Parker observe on the condition that she never miss a class and get her degree "or I couldn't step foot on the set," she said. He gave her a front row seat, right next to script supervisor, May Wale Brown. "Everyone was so wonderful to me," she said. Parker was amazed how by thoroughly Polanski and his crew, the entire *Chinatown* production really, welcomed her every day, especially considering they didn't have to. Moreover, she was tended to. They took her as seriously as she took them. Bernie Schwartz, key grip, would go out of his way to ask Parker if she had any questions. "I got to have a hundred wonderful big brothers," Parker said. "I felt like they would protect me, like if I dated somebody who wasn't nice to me." The mood of joy and inclusion, she learned, was the emotional byproduct of three

people on a film set: the director, star and the first assistant director. "[Howard Koch Jr.] and Roman and Jack," she said, "kept that
crew happy." Happy, and then, again, the look of creation setting over
Polanski's eyes: "When you see somebody like Roman using everything available to him to express his vision," Parker said, "you realize
[filmmaking is] about the details. This is the most all encompassing
art form in the world—musicians, painters, costumers, cinematographers, actors, every kind of talent—and Roman was a master of all
of them. He was on top of every single detail in the frame of every
single shot."

Nicholson hung around as they worked. Other stars would retreat to their Winnebagos, but Nicholson, enjoying the atmosphere,
would settle into Polanski's director's chair, his feet kicked up on the
one in front him, and peruse the sports pages, a lighted Camel—he
wouldn't quit again after this movie—in his hand. Sure, it was work,
but he loved it; he loved film sets. Five years of movie stardom since
Easy Rider and he still relished the low hum of intent professionals,
the camaraderie, the team spirit of group creation. "I look at acting
as a team effort," he said, "where everyone's doing their best to try
to make the team win. I don't want to sit in my trailer. I'm there to
work and have fun. There's also the professional dynamic of it. It's
good to disarm people by coming on the set with a non-star, let's-
have-fun attitude." As long as they wrapped on time (he had Lakers
tickets, dinner reservations at Dan Tana's, a drink at the Rainbow),
he could sit there all day. No more lines needed memorizing; he
had already prepared. The trick now was to relax and receive the
stimulus, to enjoy. He loved the storymaking process as much as he
loved acting, and here he was, here they were, making another story
for the world. "And it's just like I've always said," he explained, "that
John Wayne—an actor—was more important to the mass psyche
than any single American president. . . . And in that sense, I consider what I do to be writing in a very modern sense—the modern
writer is the screen actor." Not a bad way, he thought, to spend one's

life, banging around with friends, writing for the world. Why go back to the trailer?

"Jack," Polanski said, "was one of the easiest actors I ever worked with. Everything seemed natural to him. He never ever interfered with my directorial decisions. He felt comfortable." If power was one of *Chinatown*'s central themes, its personal effects should be reflected, even subtly, in Nicholson's performance, "so I had him talk differently to each [character]," Polanski said. "He talks differently to John Huston, different to Faye, differently to the other characters."

Directors had asked Jack before to talk faster, and though they were probably right, the technicality of the request rankled him. When Polanski broached the subject on *Chinatown*, Nicholson recoiled.

"No, no, no," Polanski said. "No, wait a moment."

Grinning. "Yes, Roman. What is it?"

"Look at this script. It's a hundred-and-whatever pages long. In order to have a movie at a screenable length with the amount of things that you have to say, for no other reason than that, you have to talk faster."

He took the note, no problem—he always would—but there was a fair amount of ballbusting along the way:

"Roman, I don't think I should stand here."

"Stand there! *That's* where you should stand!"

"Roman—"

"Stand there and say your fucking lines! Roll camera, fuck you, action!"

He looked straight into the camera: "Hi, I'm Jack Nicholson and I'm making a movie."

Unlike working for Nichols and Rafelson, working for Polanski was a technical challenge for Nicholson. "I saw immediately that I wasn't going to be able to do the kind of character work that I'd have done with another kind of director," he said. "Working like this doesn't allow you the time or the rhythm—in other words your interior monologue is broken too often by 'now I've gotta move' and 'clear the mark' and 'check the light' and 'make the turn' and 'match the look. The interference is too frequent to allow the character to grow on you as you work with it over the weeks." What kept Nicholson afloat was the knowledge that all the niggling details were somehow serving Polanski. Even if he didn't always understand it, his respect for systems and methodology, his trusting adherence to the director's vision, were, Koch said, "total and complete."

But the Lakers were the Lakers. One day on the Paramount stage, setting up for the scene in which Gittes is kept waiting in the Department of Water and Power, Polanski was staring down the artificial "afternoon light" through the Venetian blinds, testing changes in the angle of the blinds to produce the precise feel of the waning sun. "It was a tough shot," Koch said, "tough to get focus because we were panning from Jack's face to the photographs on the wall." Nicholson, standing by as Polanski tinkered, was getting restless; there was a Lakers-Celtics game he needed to see and since they were in Boston it was probably getting close to the fourth quarter.

He turned to Alonzo. "Is this shot about me or the Venetian blinds?"

As Polanski toiled, Nicholson dashed to the TV in his trailer to catch what he could of the game. He reappeared when called, urging Polanski, who had already kept the crew overtime, to wrap for the day. Polanski refused and the Lakers went into overtime and Nicholson kept running to and fro from his trailer and Polanski seemed not to get any closer.

Nearing seven o'clock—uncharacteristically late for the production—Polanski was finally ready, but there was only a minute left in the game.

"I'll be right there," Nicholson told the second AD.

The minute stretched on.

"Where's Jack?" Polanski asked Koch.

Koch appeared at Jack's trailer.

"Bullhorn, it's overtime," Jack said. "I'm not leaving now. There's thirty seconds left in the game. Just tell Roman I've been waiting for an hour and a half. Let him wait for a few minutes."

The game went into double overtime.

"Where is he?" Polanski asked Koch.

"Roman, it's double overtime."

"What the fuck is double overtime?"

Roman didn't care; he ordered them to tear Jack from the TV. But Jack wasn't moving.

Outraged, Polanski grabbed the nearest weapon, a mop, and stormed the trailer to smash in the TV, but the trailer wasn't tall enough inside to get the mop up, so cracking it on the TV the screen he didn't do much damage, but Polanski kept smashing. "You know what you are?" he was shouting, smashing. "You're a fucking asshole!"

Tossing the mop, Polanski yanked the TV from its perch and flung it out of the trailer. It smashed all over the stage floor.

"Who do you think you are?!" Jack screamed.

"I'm the director, and I'm trying to get the fucking shot!"

Jack threw anything he could at Polanski,—his hat, his shoes, his tie. He stripped his pants and threw them, he threw his jacket and ripped off and threw his shirt. Then Roman started throwing his clothes at Jack. They were down to their underwear, screaming at one another and Jack bolted from the stage and Polanski ran after him.

"Wrap!" Koch yelled.

Jack sped off in his car; Polanski jumped in his and chased him out of the studio.

They locked eyes a few minutes later at a red light at Gower and Sunset, Jack in his old VW, Roman in his Mercedes, "smiling like a monkey." Both in their underwear.

"Fucking Polack." Jack laughed.

Polanski started laughing. Getting out of their cars in the middle of the street, they guessed the crew had figured they'd both quit the movie. That made them laugh even harder.

"Let's not tell anyone," Jack said. "Keep 'em guessing."

Jack got back in his car and disappeared down the road, thinking how great it was to have this lunatic, a great artist, for a friend. "That's a fantastic relationship to have," he would say.

Up in Bel-Air, at the Stone Canyon Reservoir, Nicholson was nervous about the nostril-slitting scene.

"It will be okay, Jack," Roman kept saying, suppressing a smile. "Don't worry."

But Jack knew Polanski, He knew he wouldn't hedge it, that for the effect to look real the blade had to appear to actually slice his nostril, and Polanski wanted the whole thing on camera. Special-effects supervisor Logan Frazee suggested a prosthetic nose for Jack then reconsidered—he knew in close-up the makeup would look fake. Versed in all manner of mechanics, it was Polanski who came up with the solution.

"Okay," he said. "I do it."

He envisioned a blade with a hinged tip. On impact the hinge would give and a hidden tube on the off-camera side of the knife would squirt a gurgle of blood onto Jack's nose. But the hinge would have to be weak or the blood might be real.

"Jack, Jack," Polanski said. "Don't worry."

Polanski had cast himself as Nicholson's assailant. It was, he claimed, Robert Towne's suggestion. To his casting associates he protested he had done his due diligence searching for the right actor to no avail, and while it's true that Polanski cast many smaller parts at the eleventh hour (casting director Mike Fenton had busloads of actors hauled to location), some in the crew, relishing the mischievous off-camera rapport between Nicholson and his director, suspected that the part must have appealed to Polanski from the beginning.

Frazee built the prop, a nine-inch switchblade that didn't quell

Nicholson's worry. The thing looked so real, and despite the tests there was no telling if the spring hinge, at the fearful moment, would respond precisely as demonstrated. Further, Nicholson knew Polanski was a daredevil on skis and raceways, and had a hunch he expected the same of others. Nicholson inspected the prop; the hinge, he saw, went only one way. That was unexpected. Cautioning Polanski to be sure to slice in the right direction, Nicholson asked him to please be careful, but Polanski put the prop back in the actor's hands. "Jack, please," he said. "Before every shot, make sure the thing goes."

"You little fucking Polack. You better watch what the fuck you're doing."

Polanski only smiled.

They got the shot in the first take; the effect worked beautifully.

But Polanski kept going. Koch said, "I think we ended up with about twelve or fourteen takes. I'm not going to say that Roman just loved doing it."

Watching Polanski play with Jack or attack production problems, Koch saw in his fevers of frustration and excitement "a little kid who was fighting, fighting, fighting for what he believed in. Roman had all this dark stuff that you knew he was always overcoming, but [directing *Chinatown*] you could see this was his life coming through." Then something would change. When the shot ended and the lull returned, Polanski would walk off, not far, but away from the chatter. He would fall silent. Alonzo's daughter Gorgiana, a familiar visitor to the set, would see him "alone, staring off into space." During these episodes Alonzo would tell her not to approach.

"Why?" she asked. "What's wrong?"

"He has flashbacks."

After the day's work, at home on Sierra Mar Drive, Polanski would turn on the television and watch the Watergate hearings, like everyone else in America.

During the hearings the citizenry became a detective, obsessed by a crime with infinite clues. It was a tawdry and sinister episode and ultimately a coup de grâce. The hegemonic sanctity of all American institutions—with the notable exceptions of Hollywood and the music industry—went down with the president, ending, historian Andreas Killen writes, "the greatest prolonged boom in the history of capitalism." That year, a year Killen called "a genuine low point in U.S. History," something that had been ending for years was suddenly over. There was the 1973 oil embargo and subsequent depression; the '73 failure of the Vietnam War, the longest in U.S. history, with more than thirteen hundred MIAs unaccounted for; the January '73 report in *Time* that airplane hijackings had reached epidemic proportions, and the disturbing number of passengers aboard those flights who, incredibly, found themselves siding with their captors. So disenchanted were they, Tom Wolfe wrote, with "the endless exfoliations of American power," that he observed: "It is astonishing how often hostages come away from their ordeal describing the Hostage Taker as 'nice,' 'considerate,' even 'likeable.'" (The term "Stockholm syndrome" was coined in 1973, the year the bad guys won. The year we realized the game was rigged and it was better to be hostage-taker than a hostage.

When he wasn't watching Watergate, Polanski entertained. He invited cast and crew to the house most Friday nights for themed parties (Mexican, Italian, Chinese) with fitting musical accompaniment (mariachis, etc.), dinner, and dancing. Polanski loved to dance. Dancing helped him forget.

It was not Polanski's custom to host regular Friday night parties at the end of a week of filming; he was mostly exhausted, and unlike Nicholson and Evans Polanski couldn't count on cocaine for a boost. But the particular intimacy of this group and his lingering antipathy for the city below made Sierra Mar, for those months, a secure retaliation against the past. "He decided he was going to survive," Anthea said. "And the way he was going to survive [was] through his talent and having fun." He had both in his friends: "To me," he said, "this is the most important thing in life. Friends, and loyalty to them, which is almost synonymous. It *is* this most important thing in my life. I have a few friends who are more important to me than my family ever was." If any one of them couldn't make Friday night, Polanski would play offended, and demand attendance. What excuse did they have? Koch always wrapped them on time. Bring your families, bring your friends. Jack was always game, of course. "Nicholson could stay up until six in the morning," Polanski said, "but he would be [on the set] at eight or nine knowing his lines like nobody else." (Towne was persona non grata here. He was often with Evans, who liked to stay at home, in his projection room, screening dailies, discussing future projects.) There was night swimming. There were girls. There was a pool table downstairs, more girls, Warren, a little blow, a little forgetting. And all the time Watergate on the radio.

"I was amazed sometimes," Polanski said, "listening to the news programs, by the parallels between what I was hearing and what I was shooting." The crew felt the same. "It was bizarre," Koch remembered. "We were making *Chinatown* the movie, and America was becoming *Chinatown* the country." Corruption was hardly a new concept; it was only that America, dreaming for centuries, Polanski believed, was late to the dark awakening. "You find these things in any country," he said, "where money and power matter," where good intentions, as Towne might put it, invariably surrender to futility. To powerlessness and defeat. Polanski was making *Chinatown* about the price of learning that particular truth, "whether about politics or the relationship between a man and a woman," or the moment when the wall went up around the ghetto, and the phone rang in London and he learned, for all he thought he knew, that he didn't know anything.

"Roman," Bill Tennant's voice had said, "there was a disaster in the house."

"Which house?"

"Your house. Sharon is dead."

And now Bill Tennant was missing.

Nandu Hinds, at Sierra Mar, stepped from the revelry to a quiet corner of the house and saw Polanski, alone, gazing down at a magazine, at a picture of a pregnant woman. He was touching it, rolling his fingers over the face in the magazine.

"When are you coming home?" Sharon had asked.

"Soon," he had said. "Soon."

On December 4 production returned to Paramount for the scene that had bedeviled Towne for years: the moment when Gittes discovers the truth about Evelyn and her daughter. Towne toyed with the idea of giving the scene to Evelyn's old doctor, a man in the position to know the truth, and, in one early iteration of the story, Evelyn's ex-lover, but it was soon apparent that disclosing such a crucial piece of her long-suppressed history would be anticlimactic if it didn't come from Evelyn herself. And yet no one, especially a woman of Evelyn's formality and stature, would simply volunteer a secret they considered so shameful. Were Towne to follow convention, he might have allowed Evelyn, after making love to Gittes, to let down her guard somewhat, but, as a personification of Chinatown, as an unknowable, such a reveal would contradict the film's central theme.

These were strange emotional waters for any man to wade, especially given that no one who read *Chinatown* could think of a Hollywood precedent for an incest story. Towne dutifully solicited scene ideas from Edward Taylor and, respecting the pathological context for the big twist, his psychologist, Dr. Martin Grotjahn, and there were, consciously or not, ties to the Chase ordeal ("Sister!" "Aunt!") Towne and Taylor had heard decades earlier. But it was Polanski who finally suggested that Gittes, at last broken by the mystery, the deflections, and the lies, had to lose his cool. "She wouldn't say it, she wouldn't tell, she wouldn't tell," Polanski explained. "Whatever angle you would take, the only way she would tell it is if you physically force her, beat it out of her."

Before the day of the shoot, she and Nicholson had privately discussed the beating she was about to take; Polanski, they knew, wanted his violence real, a point of craft to which Dunaway, a supreme actress, agreed.

"Jack," she prepared him, "you're going to have to hit me."

"You sure, Dread?"

She nodded.

They worked at it for hours. Between the two of them, they had tried separating the slaps—*whack!*, line, *whack!*, line—but found, as the intensity built, it made more sense to climax in a succession of slaps, *whack!*, *whack!*, *whack!*

Dunaway loved Nicholson. His solidarity, his creative intelligence. His charisma and sympatico. A true actor, she thought, and a friend. She would complain to him about her struggles with Polanski, his line readings, his sadistic prods. "You think you've got problems, Dread?" Nicholson drawled back. "You realize this is the first time I'm playing a leading man, and I'm spending three-quarters of the movie with a bandage covering half my face?" They hung together throughout *Chinatown*, whether in her trailer between setups or on Sunday nights at El Coyote, sardined into their booth with Anjelica and Carol Kane and Harry Dean, passing the margarita pitcher between them. Dunaway had a big crush, but resisted the urge.

Paramount's Stage 31 was uniquely fraught the day of Dunaway's most demanding scene. The set was tense with the promise of rehearsed violence and the still-seething silence between director and star actress, who had kept their communication to a minimum, passing words, when necessary, through third parties.

Nicholson was visibly unsettled, scuffing a corner of the rug. "I don't like hitting women," he said to the floor.

"This is the place, right here, guys," Polanski said, bouncing a creaking floorboard.

A carpenter swooped in with hammer and nails to address the repair.

By now no stranger to Dunaway's insecurities, Alonzo reviewed the particulars with her, explaining how Polanski, careful not to replay the romantic clichés of movies past, was refraining from diffused lighting. For her close-ups, Alonzo told Dunaway he was using a little Obie light with a faint blue gel. Fading down the glow almost imperceptibly, he would turn the light onto her eyes, giving them the slightest kick to reflect, he explained, "in the iris of the eye."

Halting once more to redress her makeup—murmurs of "Here we go again"—Dunaway extended an affectionate hand to actor James Hong, playing her butler. "I noticed there's no name for you in the script."

"No, just the butler."

"What do you think we should call you?"

He thought. "What about . . . Hahn?" A name near his own.

"Hahn." She tried it out. "Hahn. That's it."

Polanski had wisely kept his distance, allowing Dunaway to primp as long as he possibly could, until he couldn't wait anymore.

"*May* we, Roman?" Koch asked.

Roman gave the okay; the actors took their places, Jack before the camera, Faye behind the draped archway.

"Okay! Very quiet! We're rolling."

"Speed."

"Action."

There followed an exhilarating hush. Nicholson, awaiting Dunaway's entrance, adjusted his position.

These moments of preparation the crew gladly allowed Dunaway—to give her all the time, all the space she needed to well up the feelings in her, privately, behind the drapery. Until then Polanski would keep the camera rolling through the silence, waiting.

She lurched through the curtain, sobbing, and dropped to the sofa.

Nicholson followed her. "Who is she?" he demanded.

She looked up and—

"Cut!"

Polanski stood, interrogating the light. It wasn't what he had in mind. "It's all *different now*," he said to the crew. "I light it and everything and it's all different now."

The gaffers tended to the adjusments, Polanski crossed to Nicholson. "You walk in too fast. I think it should be more of a stroll." He turned over his shoulder to the crew. "Let me see it once more, fellows."

So intent was Dunaway on maintaining emotional momentum that between takes, when she had to use the restroom, she would bypass her trailer to stand by a houseplant in the kitchen, and closing the doors—a signal to the crew—cage her attention to Evelyn's world, rather than venture outside into 1973. She would emerge jittery and withdrawn—"I'm ready. No, wait"—seemingly skinless and prone, stalling again for more makeup. "It would take hours," Nandu Hinds said. "It was a nightmare"—as if by layering on the powder, eyeliner, lipstick, Blistex, rouge, she could erase herself.

That day a weirder mood than usual haunted the stage. Released from the past, something's ghost heavied the waiting with bad comings, wrongs, and the vertiginous air of summer thunder.

Nicholson really hit her.

Watching from a distance, James Hong was amazed by the work Dunaway turned out that day. "She prepared intensely before every take," he said, "mumbling to herself, fussing with her hair. Her concentration was so intense you wouldn't want to talk to her." Alone among the cast and crew, Hong was compassionate to her process; it seemed to him she was doing the work of a Method actress, immersing herself in unhappy emotion, the rageful awareness of one who would so deeply despise her father, even her director, a father figure, and perhaps more. "I used to love my father very much," she said in 1967. "But as the years went on and he and my mother grew apart, I guess we did too. Now they've both remarried, and I don't see my father anymore. But I still have this desperate desire to be loved, to excel in everything, to win admiration and respect, especially from men." Money and success had brought her little comfort. "Deep down," she said, "I'm always running hard because I'm running scared. The children of the poor, the children of the divorced are not the most secure people in the world."

Between takes she would look over to her director, "a wicked grin on his face." She thought, He's enjoying this moment far too much.

It was because he was short. The young girls, she thought, his sarcasm and needless cruelty, directing movies. It was about power for him. All of it.

Her face burned where Jack's slaps had landed. From the blows across her right check, her neck ached.

"Once more please, fellows," her director said, "Once more . . ."

Howard Koch stepped outside Stage 31 and had a look around him. The Mountain was teeming, and to Koch, the son of Howard Koch Sr., Paramount's production head before Evans, all of it was familiar—the jolly bustle of crew folk, secretaries strolling two-by-two, sound guys soaking in the sun for the first time in days, P.A.s, teamsters, harried writers fumbling for car keys, editors out for a quick smoke, costume trolleys, passing truckloads of set decor, lifelong Paramount police officer Fritz, A. C. Lyles, the studio's professional friendly face ("Hiya, Howie. How's the old man?"), the pilgrim tourists come to see with their own eyes the warehouse grandeur of Stage 31, where Astaire and Rogers danced *Top Hat* only forty years earlier—the signs of a happy home, which is what a studio was, not just real estate but a haven, a complete creative nation dignified, in the case of Paramount, by sixty years of achievement.

For many like Koch, who at ten rode a horse with Clark Gable, it was only a culture, a tradition, a way of life, as Hollywood son Darcy O'Brien wrote, like any other. Sure, it had its downsides. The studio was, like any institution, susceptible to pressures of bottom lines and the usual exploitations of power. "Universal made shit," Polanski rightly observed, Fox and Columbia stumbled under unimaginative leadership, and MGM's James Aubrey, failing to produce films of merit, resorted to auctioning off Metro's heirlooms to the highest bidder. But Warners had John Calley, and Paramount, in the hands of Robert Evans, kept climbing on the rungs of popular art. Outside Stage 31 Evans's influence was everywhere apparent to Koch. He was awed.: "We were shooting the my sister/my daughter scene," Koch said, "and next door on the next stage [John] Schlesinger was shooting the premiere scene from *Day of the Locust*. And right across the street, Coppola and Al [Pacino] were shooting the Senate hearing room for *Godfather II*, and we all broke for lunch at the same time. And I remember, you know, like in *Sunset Blvd.* where you see all the extras walking down the street. Well, it was Jack and Faye and Al and Schlesinger and Coppola and Polanski walking down the street to the old Paramount commissary. And I thought, wow, I'm in Hollywood."

5

Jack and Evans on the tennis court at Woodland, before the party starts . . .

"I'm gonna get your ass, Bobby!"

They are evenly matched. "Nicholson is the vulnerable attacker," Evans said. "He's like a three-legged dog, too crazy to win, but he does."

They play hard but funny, "gutter players," Evans said, betting a hundred dollars a corner, betting to get a rise out of the other guy, like street kids who had picked up more quarters than they could carry.

"Would you get me a sweater?" Evans calls to his drop-dead girl du jour.

She lifts his navy cashmere.

"Not that one. The button-down."

Tuxedoed in the kitchen, butler David Gilruth sets lemon crescents astride the caviar, honey-glazing carrots, sprinkling fresh thyme on the roast Long Island duckling. . . .

On the phone in the living room, Henry Kissinger, a frequent overnight guest, engages in apparently serious conversation: "Mm. Yes. Yes, undoubtedly. . . ."

Gilruth swoops in to light pine-scented candles and slip a coaster under Kissinger's drink. Kissinger nods his thanks. Gilruth nods back. They've done this before.

The music, a comely mingling of rock and jazz standards: *"You must remember this. . . ."*

The threads of golden sconce light pinging off the roses . . .

The china, gilded with a naked girl riding a centaur, waiting contentedly on a dining-room table. Printed linen walls. . . .

"A kiss is still a kiss. . . ."

Gilruth—handsomely grizzled, William Holden with a tan—whistles while he works. "A sigh is just a sigh. . . ."

"Yes," Kissinger says. "Yes, goodbye." Click.

"The *fun*-da-mental things . . . *apply*. . . ."

Kissinger stands. "As time"—he croaks on his way to the guest room to change—"goes . . . by. . . ."

The cream and ivory of the French chenille sofas . . . The welcoming tower of art books shelved beside the art. . . .

"He's imprinted everywhere," Ali MacGraw would observe. "His habits, the books, which flower, what color candle, which music."

The little fire in the hearth. . . .

Through the windows, the liquid caress of fountains trickling into the pool. . . .

In his black velvet bathroom, Evans perched on the lip of his black granite tub, dabbing his neck with cologne, his Tonight Girl dressing at the mirror. . . .

In Woodland's foyer, the entrance of Jack Valenti, head of the Motion Picture Association of America: Together he and Evans would tour the globe extolling, in Evans's words, "America's gift, its greatest cultural export to every country in the world, the Hollywood film."

The entrance of photographer Helmut Newton, two or three of his models, and Helmut's wife, June, whom he loved more than any of his models in their delectably fascist bustiers and black leather masks. . . .

"You know, Robert," Newton would say, "you have a regal decadency in your bone structure that I can't find anywhere else in the world."

"That's a good line, Helmut."

Evans, always on the watch for bad behavior, would banish even the powerful if he caught them in violation. After witnessing his attorney, Greg Bautzer, slapping an actress around a party, Evans expelled him from Woodland forever. This was typical: At Woodland, a comparatively concise palace of only a few thousand square feet, there was no hiding permitted. For that one had the Playboy Mansion or the Chateau Marmont. But for Woodland to serve its purpose, intimacy, conducive to deal making, was critical. "It was built for me for a very good reason," Evans said. "To do my homework." A general on a hill, he would operate best with the aid of clean sightlines and—scanning the faces for promise, of one kind or another—keep his mastery at a Godfatherly premium.

The parties at Woodland that season were nonpareil, lit by the stellar potential of Paramount's nine films in production and the collective sense of career promises fulfilled, the professional matriculation of Polanski, Nicholson, Towne, Beatty, Sue Mengers, Bogdanovich, and Evans, their host at work and play. They had come up together, and now here they were, honed and sanctioned, the champagne pops of the class of 1974. Who among them hadn't realized their dreams many times over? Who hadn't *lived*? Mostly unmarried and without children, freed from domestic obligations, and not sufficiently wealthy to slow their production, most—still pitched to undivided professional and personal cohabitation—still needed one another. And as long as the lion's share of power stayed centralized with the studio, it was Evans, authorized to green-light a picture and assemble its personnel, who would keep them together—the stated intention of everyone involved.

Nicholson, delighting in the commune, began to dream with Towne, and Towne with Evans, about two sequels to *Chinatown*.

"This was the big one, the opus," Payne said. "The work of their lives, Chandler meets Upton Sinclair." Together they floated a grand scheme, a trilogy of Los Angeles' creation, "a social history of the region," Nicholson explained. Broad ideas took shape: *Chinatown* was about water crimes, part two would fix on oil and real estate corruption during the forties, and a third and final installment, set in 1953, would somehow implicate the city's travel industry, trolleys, cars. and planes. It would be Los Angeles, true myths of water, land, sky. Nicholson said: "The first story began in 1937—which is the year of my birth—and [the sequel would follow] my character eleven years later after he's been through the war. That's 1948; and the third story finishes off at about the time Robert and I actually met. In other words, it's a literary contrivance; an eighteen-year project. We wanted to do a project whereby you waited the real amount of time that passed between the stories before going forward." To age Gittes in real time was a new and exciting idea: "It's a big piece of writing," said Nicholson. "RT is a dear friend and whenever the opportunity arises—as it did on *Chinatown* and *The Last Detail*—we're inspired to work together. And that's the fun of it; that's part of the fun of lasting."

At Woodland, in walked David Geffen, Anjelica Huston, maybe Dustin Hoffman, tennis shoes under his arm. "Did I miss the game?"

Alain Delon. . . .

Mengers and Evans at the pool, drinking a bottle of white wine cellar plucked for the occasion:

"Now really, Sue . . . Do you get white wine at Columbia?"

Giggling: "You and I have never agreed on any kind of material. And so far you've been right."

Now down to casting. "I think of De Niro. . . ."

"Also Richard Dreyfuss, who I think would be very interesting—"

"He's an excellent actor. He would be wonderful. Not a *client*, but an excellent actor."

Dick and Anthea Sylbert cracking wise in the New York Jewish style that so delighted Polanski. . . .

Peter Bart, bemused by Woodland's old-Hollywood anachronisms, chuckled at the contrast of Modiglianis and hippies in their jeans and beads, but he couldn't resist celebrating his good fortune: "The turnout of guests was dazzling," Bart wrote, "the dealmaking was incessant, and the undertone of sexual adventure was pervasive. Like the studio itself, it seemed a wonderland of limitless possibility."

Dick Sylbert, though, snickered. His good taste inviolate, he openly derided the pretension he gleaned from the sense of grand style Evans bought, not loved. But in private even he was induced to reverie by Woodland's opulence, and let himself dream of the glamour not yet gone from Beverly Hills.

"Roman," Evans said. "Do you have an ending?"

"Almost, Robert, almost. Okay?"

"We need it, Roman."

It was winter in Los Angeles, but in the houses off Benedict Canyon, fireplaces warmed big rooms of white orchids and, Joan Didion noted, improbably open windows. These evenings ended early, after a preview screening and a vigorous but polite discussion of its merits, with the tentative feeling that all present had been careful not to risk too much of their opinions, "since there are enough imponderables in the business of Hollywood," Didion wrote, and no one knew who would be working for whom next. A gambler's town—entirely opposed to New York's picture of Hollywood as Gomorrah—its people played it safe. They went to bed early. As Didion put it: "It is in this tropism toward survival that Hollywood sometimes presents the appearance of the last extant stable society."

"The action is everything," she wrote, "more consuming than

sex, more immediate than politics; more important always than the acquisition of money, which is never, for the gambler, the true point of the exercise." There was more money to be made on Wall Street, more sex to be had in the theater, more drugs in rock and roll. In 1973 in the last extant stable society, the lure was still pitched to the gamesmen, to the companionable thrill of putting together and making the deal, and where the casino was still too intimate for indiscretion, it was not yet big enough to score at anyone's expense. "It's a very small group of people," agent Sam Cohn said, "and we can't afford to euchre each other too badly." Relationships, once built, had to last. To keep a place at the table, it was smarter to play fair than knock elbows greedily raking in the chips.

For the moment.

Didion was at lunch in Beverly Hills eavesdropping on a director and agent at a neighboring table. Dissatisfied with the script in hand, the director wanted out of his deal, and the agent, who represented many involved in the project, naturally wanted to keep the director in. But he also represented the director.

"You pull out," the agent said, "it dies right here, not that I want to influence your decision." He picked up their bottle of Margaux and examined the label. "Nice little red."

"Very nice," the director said.

There would be other deals.

"February," Didion wrote, "in the last extant stable society."

In his Mercedes, Polanski curled down his own driveway at nearly fifty miles an hour, stopping short an inch before the slowly opening gate, gunning for it to spread, and racing through, eyes dug into the windshield. He was going to Chinatown.

It was late and it was cold and he had only a day before cobbled the ending together, typing it up in his trailer and walking it into Jack's. "Put it into your words," Polanski had said. Producing a pen,

Nicholson obliged, and in a matter of moments, crossed out and added back in a line Polanski had taken from Towne: "As little as possible," as in, what you're supposed to do in Chinatown. "As little as possible": The line appears earlier in the movie, as Gittes and Evelyn, drawing closer, circle their way to the love scene, resisted by Towne, that Polanski had insisted on:

Evelyn: Tell me, Mr. Gittes, does this often happen to you?

Gittes: What's that?

Evelyn: Well, I'm judging only on the basis of one afternoon and an evening, but if this is how you go about your work, I'd say that you'd be lucky to get through a whole day.

Gittes: Actually, this hasn't happened to me for a long time.

Evelyn: When was the last time?

Gittes: Chinatown.

Evelyn: What were you doing there?

Gittes: Working for the district attorney.

Evelyn: Doing what?

Gittes: As little as possible.

Now, in the ending, set in Chinatown, the line would reappear, echoing a note of terrible irony.

Polanski met Sylbert at the location, a few blocks of actual Los Angeles Chinatown between North Spring and Ord Streets, hastily arranged, as the particulars of the scene were virtually a last-minute development, without the customary benefits of pre-production. Sylbert had already painted in mouthwatering rows of Packards, red-and-gold neon signs, David Yee Mee Loo's Cocktail Bar, the Fing Loy Café, a swarm of extras, the hot glare of movie lights.

Sylbert was tense himself. Tonight was about fate, a murder impossible to stop. He knew there would be gunshots, there would be shrieking. What had happened before would happen again. It was Polanski's story. "The point is the girl dies," Sylbert explained. "That's his whole life." Polanski wanted to end the film like an opera, in which the full company reappears in a burst of horrific communion.

Polanski congressed with Alonzo. The visual idea here was darkness, the darkness not of place but metaphor and mind; only enough visibility to follow the action, no more. "Okay, Earl," Alonzo had instructed his gaffer. "Just put a splash of light on that building over there and another splash on that other building, and be very subtle about it. Don't try to light the whole street." Earl Gilbert had gone to great pains to "reconfigure" the mercury streetlamps, which didn't exist in the thirties, illegally cutting the wire of every light. Additionally Alonzo directed Gilbert to hide lights under awnings and had Howard Koch Jr. station those extras, dressed in the lightest colors, in the deepest darkness; they would be their own illumination. The rest: black as empty space.

Polanski studied the atmosphere, Alonzo's work, Sylbert's work, the cold midnight sky. "I want a crane," he said.

"You want a crane?"

Roman Polanski knew what it was to be a detective, to fix all of one's purpose on a solution, studying friends' prescription glasses, stealing into their parked cars and dusting them for blood, finding something, maybe a clue, and holding its image under developing fluid, watching it lose its hoped-for meaning and turn to nothing.

"Yes. I've just figured out how to end this picture."

It appeared to Alonzo that indeed he had, and at just that moment, too.

"In the sequence, up to this point, Faye Dunaway has been shot," Polanski improvised. "You see the police officer fire a shot and you hear the car stop and, obviously, Faye Dunaway is dead, because you hear the horn blowing. Now, where do we go from there? Well, here's the idea: we go hand-held and all the actors come toward the camera and you do a news-documentary kind of thing. You whip-pan over to show Faye for just a brief moment. I want to see the destruction of her eye"—makeup artist Lee Harmon was somewhere close, using the inside membrane of an egg to simulate dripping flesh—"Then the police detective sits her up and you pan around onto him, then onto Nicholson, then back to the detective, then back to Nicholson as he's pulled away by his two friends. Then I want the camera to climb twenty-seven feet into the air—hand-held."

Alonzo hesitated. This flourish didn't fit. It contradicted the visual simplicity Polanski had maintained throughout. "Roman," Alonzo told him, "you're contriving a shot. You're contriving it because you don't know how to end the picture. You're performing cinematic gymnastics."

"No, no, no—it really fits. This is how it has to work."

Alonzo trailed Polanski to the old yellow Packard convertible, Evelyn's death car, and Polanski pitched over the windshield. "No, John, no," he said. "The blood on windshield is not right, blood on the bullet holes, must be much more, try again, spray more." He knew.

Every time Dunaway was killed, the crew snickered. Got what she deserved, they said. And every retake tried her patience until finally there was none left. "Roman was on one end of the street," one extra reported to actor James Hong, "and Faye was down the street where the car crashed, and they were literally shouting at each other as they approached, it was like a gun battle shooting match. None of Chinatown could sleep that night."

A day or two later Anjelica Huston turned up at the Chinatown location. As she writes in her book, she entered her father's trailer to find him with a half-empty bottle of Stoli.

"What took you so long?," he thundered at her. "What have you been up to?"

He was in character, she thought, though the line between Cross and Huston was always blurry.

Huston was called to set and out they went.

Drunk, he fumbled the first take. He fumbled the second.

"Now come on, John," Polanski encouraged, "we got it right yesterday, come, we try again!"

Lost in himself, Polanski drifted away from Huston, thinking.

Then he found what he needed. "Okay, now—this is important—Jack is to move only to this spot. I want it marked, where's the man with the chalk? Come on, I'm asking for a simple chalk mark, where's everyone? Aw shit!"

When chalk was futile, the crew would use a rubber disk, Polanski's own invention, that actors, without looking down, could find with their feet. The crew called it "Iksnalop," Polanski spelled backward.

"I want the mark now! Actors, you must prepare before the scene, maintain the internal rage we need here! I want you not wandering off telling stupid anecdotes, I don't tell you this again!"

This Polanski directed to the entire cast, but it was intended for Huston. When he wasn't drinking, Huston was, between takes, on the hood of a Packard holding court before a circle of fascinated grips, actors, and assistants too awed to speak, too exultant not to. An ace storyteller, Huston insisted he was no actor—his *father* was the actor—but he habitually ended up the arbiter of every audience, thrilled to the lure of a crowd.

His father, Walter Huston, dead for a quarter of a century, was vivid to him again. His loss hung over Huston's next film, *The Man Who Would Be King*, a picture he had always wanted for his father, and Huston's recent run of acting assignments (taken to recoup gambling debts), *Battle for the Planet of the Apes*, *Breakout*, Orson Welles's *The Other Side of the Wind*, and *Chinatown*—work he pretended not to take seriously—brought back the inevitable comparisons to Walter, long avoided, long denied. Ghosts gathered now in John Huston; they seethed past his decades of protest and evasions, picked up shards of his own biography, and, through the tarantular Noah Cross, pushed out the real actor. It would be the role of his life. "I liked myself in *Chinatown*," he would admit later. Still, he drank through it. Whenever he could. "He was very unhappy at the time," Anjelica said. "He was divorcing his last wife, and he was irascible, and it showed."

"Where is chair for Mr. Huston to sit?" Polanski called out. "Get one!"

A chair appeared, and Huston sat, falling over.

Polanski helped him up. "Where is Faye?"

In costume, she withdrew from her trailer and crossed to Evans. "Evans, you bastard," she laughed, an in-joke lost on the crew.

"Blood is still wrong!" declared Polanski from the driver's seat of the Packard. He smudged it a bit with his fingers and then tried again with a paintbrush. Then he reconsidered the whole thing. "No, wipe it off. It isn't real, try another color, this one looks like puke." He called for assistance and a blast of imitation gore sprayed the windshield. "Yes, *yes*, more! It looks like shot-out brains!"

The spectacular crane shot Polanski wanted would be exceptionally challenging for Alonzo. There would hardly be any room for the focus puller, surrounded in the bedlam of actors and extras (Alonzo, a handheld whiz, would operate it himself); in close up, it would be difficult to light the actors without casting camera shadows on their faces (Alonzo would mount a small night next to the lens, and, per Polanski's suggestion, disrupt the camera shadow with a hat over the light); Alonzo would have to whip between Dunaway, Huston, Perry Lopez as Escobar, Nicholson, back to Lopez, follow Nicholson as he's led away, and—in the same shot—backward-climb the platform of the Chapman crane, and head high into the air over Chinatown to watch Nicholson fade into the distant black.

Appearing as a coda, a sweeping flourish, as Alonzo rightly noted, a world apart from *Chinatown*'s stringent asceticism, Polanski's crane-up breaks powerfully from the subjectivity he carefully maintained throughout the picture, rising as it does from the ground level of Gittes's devastation to a more godly vantage point, from despair to a kind of cinema majesty. Though it offers no hope or resolution, ending *Chinatown* with a grand crane-up evokes a lost Hollywood—most famously the last shot of *Casablanca*—imbuing the wreckage with a shiver of romantic awe, not just in the movement itself, the feeling of sudden floating, but in a kind of longing for a tradition—dear to Polanski, Nicholson, Towne, and Evans—that might be called classical. At least that they could agree on.

They wrapped before sunrise.

"A film sums up the experiences of my life," Polanski had said. "You absorb the experience, you assimilate it and you make a decision. A film sums up everything—whom I see, what I drink, the amount of ice cream I eat. It is everything. Do you understand? Everything."

Racing home against the Hollywood Freeway, Polanski sneered at the concrete everywhere, a raised gutter strangling the city, its crime blurred in the low light of daybreak. "I don't know who designed this," he had muttered, "but they should be hung by the neck." And yet Polanski resolved to return. "This playing of endless children's games in an intellectual Sahara, a seductive place in which glorious child-toys called movies are made," as silly as it sometimes was, was Hollywood. Where would he rather be? "*Chinatown* was the first film where I had no struggle throughout the production because I was totally supported by the producer and had everything at my disposal," he concluded. "I was really like a racing driver with a bunch of people standing around you and just ready to respond to every gesture. So I know that it is maybe my greatest achievement because of that."

Returning home, the gates of Sierra Mar opened to a candy-colored hillside of banana leaves and birds of paradise and, farther in, the sunny blue splashings of waterfall into pool.

Years after fleeing the city in self-imposed exile, he considered selling his London flat and moving back, at least part-time. Maybe more.

It was Mr. Adolph Zukor's one-hundredth birthday. Zukor—who began as a furrier at two dollars a week; built his turn-of-the-century fascination with penny arcades and nickelodeons into Famous Players Company; merged his production and distribution business, in 1917, into Paramount Pictures, sixty years later oldest studio in Hollywood—.sailed into his birthday party at the Beverly Hilton that night dapper and peppy, a lean eminence, his eyesight failing, decrying the dangers of the small screen with emphatic whips of his cane. "Movies have competition from television," he opined. "They aren't a novelty anymore, so the material better be good." He lived in a modest apartment in Century City in the care of a housekeeper, but was still, to the evening's twelve hundred guests, their father-founder, the estimable Mr. Zukor. Some said he still kept tabs on every movie Hollywood made.

Robert Evans's natural glamour would surely steal him the official black-tie birthday gathering, with its triple-decker dais and fourteen-foot birthday cake, so it seemed only fair, at least to Frank Yablans, that he would assume the honor of giving a dinner party for Zukor at the Bistro, across from Paramount's offices on Canon Drive. Based in New York, Yablans had no claim to the Bistro, widely recognized as Evans's turf. "Yablans was very good at his job as a distributor," Peter Bart recognized. "But he was very greedy. There were fights between him and Evans between who would get a bigger piece of *Chinatown*, battles to the death about points. Every time they got together, instead of talking about the movie, they would talk about numbers. [Yablans] couldn't stand the idea that Evans might make a lot of money on this picture and he wouldn't." By his own admission, it was only about power for Yablans; it always had been. "I wanted to be president of a major company," he said. "I didn't care what kind of company it was as long as I was the number one guy." It was only by chance that he made it to Hollywood. "I didn't particularly like movies," he said.

From her place at the Beverly Hilton, Joan Didion observed the ceremony with something like admiration. On a formal occasion such as this, she saw Hollywood's worn but lasting rituals, despite their hyperbole and abstruseness to outsiders—those "gripped by the delusion that 'studios' have nothing to do with the making of pictures in modern times"—reaffirm its strength and survival.

6

When the lights came up John Calley didn't know what to say. *The Exorcist*, his movie at Warner Bros., violated just about every stronghold of good taste. "What in the fuck did we just see?"

He loved the movie, but—Satan, vomit, a little girl masturbating with a crucifix, "Your mother sucks cocks in hell!"—he was too afraid even to preview it. Would people see this thing?

There was a time, decades earlier, when the question almost didn't matter. The Hollywood practice of "block booking" (pioneered by Adolph Zukor, as it happened), forced theaters to take films *en masse*, good and bad, sight unseen. It was a boon for the studios, guaranteeing audiences for their product, curbing competition from independent producers and distributors, and minimizing advertising costs. But block booking ended with Hollywood's first golden age, as the major studios, felled by antitrust decision in *United States vs. Paramount Pictures, Inc.*, (1948) were divested of their theater chains and the lucrative, risk-averse distribution practice they had grown accustomed to.

In place of block booking, studios assumed the practice of "platform" distribution, in which a film is released gradually, over a period of months, beginning in urban first-run movie houses and disseminated outward to the suburban theaters, hopefully gaining interest along the way. With the modest aid of print ads, the free publicity of critics and the occasional ballyhoo, the advertising of motion pictures was thus a fairly sedate, even routine affair. The budgets of most Hollywood films weren't yet high enough to require exorbitant advertising campaigns to earn back their exorbitant price-tags (*Chinatown* came in ahead of schedule at just around three million dollars), providing the studios a supple climate of acceptable risk both for the artists and the executives. Said executive Alan Ladd Jr.:"What's a couple-million-dollar movie to a corporation?" In 1973 he could have been speaking for all of Hollywood.

That changed.

It was Tom Laughlin, director of the very-low-budget *Billy Jack* (eight hundred thousand dollars by one count), who had unintentionally dealt the first blow. Two years earlier, when Warners signed to distribute *Billy Jack*, Laughlin asked for and received approval of publicity and advertising, and was guaranteed a voice in the overall strategy for the film's release. But Warners broke their promise, Laughlin claimed, dropping the picture in twelve cities—no advertising. The film did no business. Incensed, Laughlin flew to a theater in Minneapolis and spent five thousand of his own dollars to "revise their method of selling it," and to his astonishment, it worked. Ticket sales for *Billy Jack* jumped and Laughlin reported his triumph to Warners vice resident of advertising, who vowed to reconsider the film's release strategy. But it didn't take. Laughlin sued Warner Bros. in February 1972, the studio settled in December, and, early in 1973, planned to rerelease *Billy Jack* with "a promotion campaign," according to Warners VP and general sales manager, Leo Greenfield, "that will be better than many first run features receive" based on "an entirely new advertising and exploitation campaign for the film."

The campaign, developed by Max Youngstein, president of Laughlin's distribution company, would change the course of Hollywood.

An industry veteran, Youngstein had observed the release strat-

egy of low-budget wildlife and exploitation films, "four-walling"—
oversaturating the market to generate quick returns before
potentially bad word-of-mouth cut them short—"and for years," he
recalled "I had been trying to get some company to follow their pattern with respect to a really top quality picture such as *Billy Jack* in
this way but I had gotten nowhere."

Then came *Billy Jack*. Youngstein continued: "We adapted every
proven principle of distribution and merchandizing from General
Motors to Coca-Cola, Revlon and the companies which had four-
walled the so-called nature pictures. We added quite a few innova-
tions of our own. . . . We booked it not into a single theater or two
theaters or even 20 theaters, but in our first week we booked the
picture into over 60 theaters." The results were extraordinary; in the
first week alone, *Billy Jack* grossed more than a million dollars. In
its first six days at sixty-one four-wall situations throughout L.A.,
Billy Jack grossed a phenomenal $887,460, approaching the record
held by *The Godfather*, which made just over a million at fifty-four
sites. "I have checked my personal experience," Youngstein wrote,
"and every possible company I could find and my conclusion is that
this is the highest gross for any picture, either new or old, ever to be
realized during a similar period for a single picture in that number
of theaters in Southern California."

All of Hollywood took note. The lesson, according to one executive, was that a "filmgoer should be able, after being completely
dunned relentlessly by the campaign, to fall out of bed and find a
theater where *Billy Jack* is playing."

"Completely dunned relentlessly."

"I don't claim that a terrible picture can be made into a winner,"
Youngstein had learned, "but I do say that, regardless of how bad it
is, with intelligent and imaginative distribution and promotion, it
will do a hell of a lot greater business than if you just let it go down
the drain because there are a few poor opening engagements."

"Regardless of how bad it is."

Billy Jack would make, by one estimate, $32.3 million.

Accordingly, Warners "four-walled" *The Exorcist*, "the biggest production," *Variety* wrote, "to be four-walled on a large scale by a major [studio]."

The movie came out in time for Christmas.

Leading critics Pauline Kael, Andrew Sarris, and Vincent Canby all hated it.

At three dollars a ticket, *The Exorcist* grossed, by one account, an estimated $160 million, a staggering sum for any picture, but for such an apparently niche offering, unprecedented. What was happening?

"Completely dunned relentlessly."

"Regardless of how bad it is."

When he heard about the gross, Warners executive Dick Lederer walked into executive Barry Beckerman's office and threw the *Exorcist* numbers down in front of him. "Kid, the fun is over," Lederer announced. "There are guys in New York looking at these figures, saying 'This is the kind of money you can make in the movie business?' We've been having a good time out here and been very successful, but it's gonna get real serious after this."

Nicholson and Polanski toasted the end of principal photography on January 18 with a glass of champagne upstairs at the the Rainbow, a dark rock and roll bar next to the Roxy nightclub, which had opened only months earlier. Coowner of both ventures, Jack's friend Lou Adler would provide Nicholson his own especially darkened corner of each, where he could inhale coke and cigarettes in semiseclusion, a one-man holdout against the next chapter in American youth culture, disco slick, silver and black, the sweaty crush of limbs and hard light and platform shoes stomping to dust the petals of revolution and love.

It rained in Los Angeles that weekend.

They finally found Bill Tennant, strung out on coke, living in a dugout somewhere, or sleeping in Griffith Park.

That January it rained for fifteen days, double the monthly average.

Polanski knew now he could abide the city when he was too busy working, but with the end of production upon him, and the dreaded first viewing of the rough cut still two weeks away, he would get out of town as soon as possible. On Saturday he would have dinner with Jack, Warren, Mike Nichols, and the British director Tony Richardson; On Monday he would appear at the Speakeasy on Santa Monica Boulevard for the wrap party; the next day he would leave. But he would come back. He would have to.

The *Erythroxylum coca* yields small star-shaped flowers, five wan-colored petals to every corolla, and thin oval leaves, which, when chewed, give one at first a feeling of warmth, according to neurologist and researcher Paolo Mantegazza, writing about coca in 1859: "Sometimes one experiences a very soft buzzing in the ears. At other times one needs space and would like to run forward as if searching for a wider horizon. Little by little, one starts to feel that the nervous powers are increasing; life is becoming more active and intense; and one feels stronger, more agile, and readier for any kind of work." Just over an ounce gave Mantegazza "pleasure by far superior to all other physical sensations known to me."

It had taken Europeans until the nineteenth century to discover coca. Only after cocaine, the principal alkaloid of the coca plant, was extracted from the leaf—a later development—could the substance be made to travel. But it wasn't until the 1880s that coca started turning up in syrups, pills and medical elixirs, the miracle cure of the new century. Coca-Cola was first poured in 1886: "The words *tonic* and *refreshment* had an inevitable appeal for a generation living in a culture of rapid economic, technological, and social change," writes the British cultural theorist Sadie Plant, "change that made Americans 'the most nervous people in the world,' as an early advertisement for the drink declared." The beauty of cocaine, at least for Freud, was in how gently the high enhanced being, as if independent of any drug at all. One felt magical *magically*.

As it soothed the strains of technological revolution Americans, coke suited the hardworking young—and suddenly very rich—Hollywood of the mid-seventies. " You can write, you can direct, you can act," Dick Sylbert said of coke. "A couple of toots, there's nothing you can't do." And in a town that traded, as Didion observed, on action, it gave the sparkle of success.

Jack Nicholson surmised that coke made its way to Hollywood from the music scene around 1972. It was about that time, Peter Bart sensed, that Evans met coke, his marriage to Ali MacGraw in collapse and the stresses of *The Godfather* mounting exponentially. But coke was then only an open secret, a game played among friends. In the white-hot blaze of *The Exorcist*, the game became a race to the top. "That was it," the producer Harry Ufland would reflect. "Addiction to box office and addiction to coke. Everything changed after that." When Bart saw Ted Ashley, family man and Warner Bros CEO, begin to show up at parties brazenly coked out, bimbos in tow, he sensed "a new, almost defiant openness" about coke in Hollywood. It portended ill.

It was around then that Evans and Bart's drives from Woodland to Canon ended, and so did Bart's trust in Robert Evans's ability to function reliably. "I was surprised Evans suddenly discovered [cocaine]," Bart reflected, "since he was not a druggie." But he was now changed, brittle, loopy, remote, on his own schedule. The shift was quiet but steady. There was no acrimony, no outbursts, but under the surface the marriage cracked, and the first tremors of total erosion quivered the studio floor.

After some time away, Polanski returned to Paramount to see Sam O'Steen's rough cut.

"What does it look like?" Polanski asked, leaning on O'Steen's shoulder.

"Great. You won't recognize it."

Funny, but not. Encountering his rough cuts always depressed Polanski. He knew that. But anticipating the depression didn't curb the unavoidable terror of facing, for the first time, the brutal facts of a film no longer dreamed but real, slogging, holed, unwieldy, the magic of the dailies gone. Were they deluded ever to have had confidence? Did it even make sense? Among all his rough cuts, Polanski's encounter with *Chinatown*'s was particularly distressing for him; none of his previous films relied on the thrill of plot concealed and revealed as a mystery does. But knowing in advance the surprise turns of the story would make it difficult for Polanski to gauge whether the surprises were working, whether the imagined audience was ahead of the picture, behind it, or precisely where he needed them to be. How to forget all he knew about *Chinatown* and watch it with *their* eyes?

This was why he had stayed away, O'Steen reminded him. This was why Ralph Dawson, O'Steen's mentor, had told him a film, after its cut, needed time to heal. It had been cut, after all. Let it recover. He said: "If you pick at a sore it'll never heal, but if you put it aside for a couple of weeks, you'd be surprised how objective you'll be."

Having O'Steen at his proverbial bedside was a comfort to Polanski. He would never forget how deftly O'Steen had rescued *Rosemary's Baby*, at the last minute, from an editor Polanski deemed incompetent, slimming a four-plus-hour rough cut down to two; it earned O'Steen Polanski's lifelong trust. "[Polanski's] film tells me where to cut, really speaks loud to me," O'Steen explained, "whereas with the others, it whispers to me."

They had a knack for eachother. O'Steen would sit with Polanski at the Moviola, helping him lose, with argumentative good cheer, those pieces of *Chinatown* Polanski loved but, for good reason, hurt the picture. "Sam taught me to sacrifice," Polanski said. O'Steen was strong, smart, and funny enough to debate Polanski, frame by frame, and patient when necessary, able to unfasten Polanski's grip with a joke—a good editor can tell a joke, O'Steen said, because "the timing is right and he tells just enough"—or compassionate nod and wait for his director to run out of explanations, excuses, denials, whatever stood between O'Steen and the inevitable killing of a darling.

In a "sunless, Paramount editing room," in the words of journalist Tom Burke, Polanski directed O'Steen. "We play that shot on Curly, for the line."

"Can't do it, Roman, Jack overlaps him every take."

"I bet you there is room, Sam, listen to me once!"

"I already know what you're going to say."

"No, no, no, we do *not* understand each other, do it exactly as you did it this morning, expect you use—"

"Can't."

"Lemme finish!"

Sometimes Polanski would have to go home and sleep it off before realizing that O'Steen was right.

Polanski only rarely used master shots,—takes of an entire scene with all the actors in the frame—a strategy he cultivated early on to keep the studio, restricted by a dearth of alternatives, from recutting the picture, but one that also favored the more claustrophobic proximity of medium shots and close-ups—some of them almost too close. When Polanski did shoot a master, O'Steen noticed, he would generally move the actors in the frame or move the frame itself,

making it difficult, for reasons of continuity, to cut into and out of
the shot, but Polanski learned to give O'Steen alternatives—not just
many takes of a particular shot, but variations in each performance.
It was especially useful to have as many takes as possible of Dunaway, whose performance, astonishing in a way, was also, it became
clear, clogged with self-conscious mannerisms, nervous stutterings,
and "the weirdest line readings," according to O'Steen. Leveling out
her work, he and Polanski found themselves digging through an
overabundance of unprinted outtakes "to find where she said 'father' in a normal voice" and append the good audio to the good
picture. They laughed at this—Dunaway might have been furious
with Polanski for all those line readings he forced on her, but in the
cutting room O'Steen could see quite clearly that those variations
brought her work to the next level.

Cooped up too long in the cutting room, Polanski would have to
blow off steam. He took O'Steen joyriding through the lot, racing
around soundstages, sending *Day of the Locust* extras and alarmed
studio personnel leaping to the walls. "God," O'Steen told him,
"we're going to kill somebody." But behind the wheel of his Mercedes, Polanski was in control. On the road O'Steen saw a man living
wholly in the present. If danger was an argument with death, then
Polanski kept returning, it seemed, to make his point and win. He
had won, so far, every time.

O'Steen could remember, when cutting *Rosemary's Baby*, how
Sharon would call just to check in.

Evans wouldn't enter the cutting room, but he would offer unso-
licited suggestions, none of which Polanski took seriously, doing
instead his best impression of a team player. But his political self
could only survive so long; under pressure, Polanski was not long
on patience. "Stop talking!" he would snap at Evans. Overruled by
Polanski's powers of argument, even a little intimidated, Evans would

invariably retreat, taking his opinions with him back to Woodland. But somewhere between ego and inspiration, he *did* feel there was something—he couldn't explain it—he would speak of "texture" and "grit" and "tone"—something missing from *Chinatown*. Flat on his back, he would watch and rewatch the dailies at Woodland, collecting opinions to help shape his concerns. But he knew it would be hard to really know what they had until they had the score.

"I'm a music freak," Evans insisted. "I'm rather fanatical. I put people's noses out of joint many times and hold up the picture to get the right score. On *Love Story* I threw out Jimmy Webb's score, and I went to Europe and spent the entire summer with Francis Lai working on a new score. And if it weren't for his theme, the picture wouldn't have worked. Francis Coppola and I had terrible fights on *The Godfather*. He wanted to use Nino Rota's music in many places where I wanted to use American music."

Scores were crucial to Evans, politically, commercially, artistically. They sold soundtrack albums; they were the yearning heart of any picture and, coming late in the production, the last chance to get it right. Or tilt it to his specifications. Or make the movie his to "rescue." In 1970, high on the success of *Love Story*, he met *The Godfather* and Coppola with the same sense of knowing, battling the director throughout the picture, not just on the score but as early as the casting of Pacino and Brando and as late as the editing. "He was so full of it," Polanski said, "always going on about [his contributions to] *The Godfather, The Godfather.*" Saving Paramount from the grave, didn't he already have enough to crow about? Couldn't he, like Calley, keep quiet and, even if he did contribute, discreetly cede glory to the filmmaker? "Evans felt that he was a filmmaker," Calley said. "His fantasy was him on a hospital bed in a projection room running reels of *The Godfather*, repairing the chaos that Francis had dropped on the world. It was his fantasies of what [Irving] Thalberg was like." Thalberg—the part Evans played in *Man of a Thousand*

Faces—was the dream of the august producer he intended to actualize fully with *Chinatown.*

They didn't have the time they needed to get the score right. The preview, scheduled for San Francisco was already set for May 3rd and the release date, June 20th, and though Polanski had brought the picture in a few days ahead of schedule, O'Steen had started late, and with the date of Polanski's next project—directing an opera at Italy's Spoleto Festival—fast approaching, they couldn't push the schedule, nor could O'Steen persuade Polanski to delay his next ski vacation.

"Why don't you wait until after we mix?" O'Steen asked.

"You mix the movie. I'm going skiing. Tomorrow I may be dead."

On a break from editing, Polanski met composer Phillip Lambro at Lucy's El Adobe, the Mexican restaurant across from Paramount. As Lambro writes in his book, they hadn't worked together before; Polanski's musical right hand, Krzysztof Komeda, composer of *Rosemary's Baby* (and three other Polanski films) was dead, drunkenly pushed by a mutual friend off an escarpment in Los Angeles. For his part, Lambro hadn't had a great deal of experience composing for film, but his *Structures for String Orchestra*, unsettling enough to serve as *The Exorcist*'s temp track, suggested to Polanski a bold composer, unafraid to renounce clichés, for as *Chinatown* sidestepped the visual vocabulary of the detective genre, Polanski intended the film's score to do the same.

His girlfriend was nervous about his meeting Polanski. A student of Zen macrobiotics, she suspected that Polanski had Yang Sanpaku—the white part of the eye, normally concealed by the lid, showed above his iris—a condition tied, according to certain teachings, to the heavy consumption of meat and highly spiced foods. Yang Sanpaku was thought by some to bring harm to those around the afflicted.

"Phillip," his girlfriend had said, "I'm worried. Look what

happened to those around him; look what happened to his last composer."

"I won't die," he assured her.

Lambro was more concerned about working for a Hollywood studio. A great admirer of Polanski's, he wanted Polanski's assurance that he, as the director, was in complete and rightful control of the picture. "On this one Bob Evans and I have complete approval of final cut," Polanski would explain. "The public thinks of him simply as [the] good-looking former husband of Ali McGraw and so on, but there would have been no *Rosemary's Baby* without him. Look, when you are making a picture, you are continually under *attack*—from your stars, crew, and studio with its financial statements. . . . There is one reason why you do a film at all: to make happen in cinema a vision, a concept, which is totally yours, only in your mind, no one else's, it is [a] cinema of one human being . . . the moneymen do not comprehend this. And here you need a man like Evans, who does."

Back at Paramount, Polanski set up a screening for Lambro, waiting an hour for Frank Yablans to arrive before finally deciding to run the picture without him. Several scenes, Lambro saw, Polanski had mixed with some of his music, and for those scenes, the combination worked. That wasn't the problem.

"It's the story, Roman," Lambro protested on their way out of the theater. "The story's weak; but maybe with more editing . . ."

"You think this piece of shit story is bad now? I'll show you the original script. Do you want to see it? It was the biggest pile of crap you ever saw."

"Who wrote it?"

"Robert Towne; but what you see here today on the screen, I actually wrote, but I'm not taking any credit for it. What do you say?" He smiled. "Do you have any musical ideas?"

In fact he did; music, he said, should work contrapuntally with the images. Why reiterate what's already on screen? Perhaps they should try a sound layered with Chinese flavor. It would bolster the title, whose literal influence seemed conspicuously absent from the film.

They began the process of spotting *Chinatown*—deciding where in the film to place the score—for four days, a long time, but Polanski was deliberate, wanting to analyze, as he had with Towne, every idea for its creative contingencies. At last, Lambro decided on ten first violins, eight second violins, eight violas, six cellos, two basses, and a battery of percussion, and midway into March set about the actual work of composition. He produced a score squirming with atonalities, fearsome percussive walls, lazy midnight horns, and trembling pianos—a jazz-classical atmosphere evocative of Kurt Weill, soaked in exotic mystery and menace—Polanski loved it. "That was wonderful," he told Lambro after a recording session. "Really great. It's just what I want.".

The phone rang in Lambro's apartment. It was night, late.

"Hi, Phillip, this is Bob Evans. How are you?"

"Fine. How are you?"

"Phillip, you'll be receiving a $1,000 bonus check for doing such a good job on the score. Everybody's very high on your work, and I want to show our appreciation by giving you this extra bonus; it's never been done before at Paramount."

There was something remote in Evans's voice, a vacancy Lambro couldn't quite place. "Thank you very much."

"I want you to promise me one thing, Phillip. Can you keep a secret?"

He didn't respond.

"I want you to promise me that you won't tell Roman that I telephoned you. Everything now is just between you and me, all right?"

Lambro hedged. All right.

"*Chinatown* needs more of your music, Phillip"—he kept saying his name—"Phillip, this picture just needs more of your music. Give me ten more minutes of music and I'll get you an Academy Award. Would you like an Academy Award?"

Evans was, in effect, asking for them to respot the picture. Adding ten minutes of music would prompt more than ten minutes of music: It would effect changes to the entire score. And they already had a completed score. Lambro resisted.

The love story, Evans persisted. It needed a more romantic melody.

There *was* no love story, Lambro countered, so why have a love theme?

"Phillip, I've made a hundred and ninety-seven pictures. Do you know what a hundred and ninety-seven pictures are, Phillip?"

Lambro heard a neurasthenic lethargy behind his voice, a blur of seduction and disarray, but even that didn't account for *what* he was saying.

"Phillip, I want you to tell Roman—do not, under any circumstances, tell him I told you—that you want to write more music for *Chinatown*."

"Okay, I'll see what I can do."

"Is there anything else I can get you, Phillip? Is there anything else you need?"

Stalling, Lambro said nothing to Polanski, but Evans persisted, checking in about the ten additional minutes of score, calling for Lambro, it seemed, just at the right moment, whenever Polanski disappeared from the soundstage or the cutting room, to remind Lambro of their deadline, which was to be the San Francisco test screening of *Chinatown* in May. How Evans knew exactly when Polanski left Lambro's side—that is, when to call—baffled Lambro to such an extent that he began to suspect he and Polanski were under some kind of surveillance.

Finally, Lambro burst. In the dubbing theater he told Polanski everything.

"Listen, you leave Evans to me," Polanski advised. "I'll handle him. You just be polite and pretend you're taking his suggestions seriously."

Evans's maneuvers were unseemly, but his concerns were founded: *Chinatown* would benefit from a stronger love story. It was what Evans originally wanted from Towne and, in his early drafts, what Towne had written. But to keep the water mystery moving, Polanski had reduced Gittes and Evelyn's courtship—originally a protracted dance of suspicion, attraction, and jealousy—to a few meaningful glances and a brief bedroom scene.

And there was a more mercenary factor:

"If you give me ten more minutes of music," Evans whispered to Lambro in April, three weeks before the preview screening, "I can get an album out of the score. There was an hour of music in *Love Story* and we won the Oscar for that."

Prestige.

Evans would remember, thirty years earlier, his father riding the elevator down from rich Uncle Abe's apartment: "The wealthy will get wealthier and the young will die." His father, the piano-playing dentist.

"*I'll live.*"

[SPACE BREAK

A week before the big preview, a small screening of the uncorrected print was set for Woodland. On the day, Evans was detained from welcoming his guests by a bullying call from Frank Yablans—they were becoming more frequent-but those who had already arrived—Nicholson, Polanski, Dick Sylbert and Susanna Moore, and Sam O'Steen and a handful of others—needed no hosting. Only Lambro could have used an introduction. New to Woodland, he stepped into the projection room somewhat unsettled. All this Hollywood—they weren't his people.

Evans's circle gathered in the cutting room and took their seats and Robert Towne and Julie Payne dashed in just as the lights were dimming.

They watched the movie.

The story tottered. The score was harsh.

When the lights came up two hours later, all were discreet. Standard praise was handed to Lambro for his score, which he accepted credulously.

Attuned to the timbre of lies, the sound of kid-gloves slipping over fingers, Evans knew to approach his guests individually before they sat down to dinner, the classic hot dogs *à la maison*, and get the truth.

The score wasn't bad, Sylbert whispered to Evans; it was just the wrong idea.

Susanna Moore, the youngest of the group, was not one to comfortably volunteer her opinions to Bob Evans (though Sylbert, chortling, had told her Evans needed others' opinions to formulate his own), but when pressed, she humbly suggested more period music. Jazz standards. She loved, for instance, Bunny Berigan's version of "I Can't Get Started."

The score was an abomination, Towne thought. But that was nothing compared to what he thought of the film itself. He hated the movie. It was cold and cynical, just like Polanski and his hopelessly despairing finale.

Payne agreed about the score. "The score assaulted my senses," she would say. She asked Towne if it would be appropriate to tell Evans. Towne told her it was, moreover, he told her she *should*; there was only a short time for the lab to finish the film and a release date had been set, but it was not too late to be changed.

Polanski, keeping his physical distance from Towne, remained somewhat in Lambro's corner.

Payne, meanwhile, found the right moment to approach her host. "Evans," she said. "The score is a piece of shit."

"The composer is right behind me."

She whispered, "It's no good, Bob."

"We're in trouble."

A moment later, Towne and Polanski collided, tussled, and grumbled off to opposite ends of Woodland. Dinner was eaten, smiles forced, guests cleared. Finally, Evans asked Lambro to join him and Nicholson in the living room. It was time to talk.

"Listen," Jack began. "You don't have to defend Roman to us. We know what he is, and we know what you are. So you just don't worry about Roman. I'm telling you that *Chinatown* needs more of your music."

"Okay, I'll do whatever you people decide."

"Wouldn't you like an Oscar, Phillip?" Evans asked.

The phone rang in the cutting room, and Lambro picked it up.

It was a girl's voice.

"You have the wrong extension," Lambro told her. "There's no Paul here."

"That's for me," Polanski said, reaching for the phone.

Lambro had earlier browsed an adult newspaper left in the cutting room, glancing a personal ad, circled, fifteen-year-old girl, "confidential, likes relationship with European man in forties."

The first audience preview of *Chinatown*, scheduled for May 3 1974 in San Francisco, was changed, at the last moment, when it was decided that news of a recent Bay Area murder, feared to be the return of the Zodiac Killer, would disincline the local mood to the film. In haste the screening was moved south to a theater in San Luis Obispo. Towne, Sylbert, Evans, O'Steen, and Polanski attended; Lambro remained at Paramount, composing—now with Polanski's approval—additional music for the picture to be recorded as soon as Polanski returned to Los Angeles.

The screening was a disaster.

Many audience response cards blamed the music—shrill, clamorous, brazenly strange—and Polanski's crew, which included his guest, legendary film composer Bronislau Kaper, was in complete agreement. The story was challenging enough without the added trouble of an avant-garde score.

"I'm going to fight," Polanski told Lambro by phone, "but I think it's no use. . . . I'm so tired. I don't know what I'll do."

Polanski *was* tired. Contracted to direct his opera in Spoleto, he wouldn't be in town to oversee *Chinatown's* final mix, let alone the future of its score.

"Aren't you in control anymore?" Lambro asked.

"I've lost all judgment. I'm so tired, Phillip. What can I say? They've canceled your recording sessions. Look, I'm going to try and fight them and I'll let you know what I can do."

"Who's them?"

"The Paramount executives."

"Which executives?"

"What the fuck difference does it make?"

Early one morning, Jerry Goldsmith answered a knock on his front door.

It was Evans. "I need you to save my life."

Goldsmith was one of the most esteemed film composers of Evans's generation. He had already been Oscar nominated six times, most recently for *Papillon*. Evans barely knew him. But he knew where he lived.

"Jerry, you've gotta help me. I need your music."

Goldsmith was born in 1929, in Los Angeles, and vaguely re-membered the music of the thirties, similar sound Evans still felt from the Harlem nightclubs around his father's practice. Lambro had written too modern a score, Evans told Goldsmith. He wanted now to go back—back to the period.

"Bob," Goldsmith replied. "I don't think so. You see that on the screen. Why should I do that in the underscore?"

Evans paused. He didn't have the language to bring his musical inclinations to reason or justify a creative impulse. He spoke only in moods and feeling and gut instincts about the dreams of women and men. Since Susanna Moore had mentioned to him "I Can't Get Started," which Bunny Berigan made a hit in 1937, the year in which *Chinatown* was set, Sylbert had endorsed the recording to Evans. It had been on jukebox rotation at Dominick's—where Evans and Towne first discussed *Chinatown*—and Sylbert, a restaurant regular, played it often. Evans didn't hesitate. He pounced on the song, playing it over and over. "Sylbert was more than a great art director," he would say. "He was man of great, great taste. [He had] the heart of a true artist." They were swells of New York, born two years apart.

The sweet lonely sound of Berigan's trumpet clung to Evans's ear, and he suggested in his only note to Goldsmith that he have a listen to the recording and riff from there.

"What do you hear in the orchestra?" Evans asked Goldsmith.

"What do I hear?" he laughed. "I don't hear anything. I've got to sit down and—" He didn't know why he said it: "I hear four pianos, four harps, strings, solo trumpet and two percussion."

"Oh, I like that!"

"I'm glad you do. I haven't the foggiest idea what it's going to sound like."

He only had ten days.

Evans ran the picture for Goldsmith. Its evocation of lost Los Angeles simply amazed him, the aridity, the empty silences of the city before traffic, a soundscape so still and void you could hear, as Goldsmith heard again on screen, even the buzzing of a fly. He remembered a golden age. "In the 1940s," he recalled, "L.A. was a haven for all the European intellectuals who came here to escape the war." Max Steiner, Erich Korngold, Franz Waxman, Miklós Rózsa—the greatest film composers of their day, all émigrés, complaining under the sun about the crass commercialism of the Hollywood studios, and by extension, the city that housed it. But not fellow émigré, twelve-tone composer Arnold Schoenberg: "I have come to a country where I am allowed to go on my feet," he lectured a gathering of UCLA students, "where my head can be erect, where kindness and cheerfulness dominate and where to live is a joy, where to be an expatriate of another country is the grace of God." They were as much a part of Goldsmith's aural education—literally in the case of Miklós Rózsa, his professor at USC—as the city itself. That fly for instance: Goldsmith would score around it. It was, he knew, a player in the urban orchestra.

Early in June, Goldsmith and his musicians, crowned by Uan Rasey and his King Silver Flair trumpet, took over Paramount's Scoring Stage M, and recorded the score to *Chinatown* in two days. Evans, Nicholson, and Towne (Polanski had already left for Spoleto) listened from the booth, floored by Goldsmith's title theme, "a period piece," Goldsmith called it, "with more updated harmonies," but the jazziness was all Rasey's. Universally regarded the best trumpeter in Hollywood, Rasey was sixteen when he came to Los Angeles in1937. By then he was already a horn player. Polio brought him to it. "There was a limit to what I could do," he said. "I couldn't run out and play football, so I played trumpet." For the price of an instrument, mouthpiece, mute, and a self-teaching book he bought from Montgomery Ward—nine dollars total—he practiced his way to a steady gig, in a wheelchair, on crutches, out in the L.A. suburb of Monterey Park for five much-needed 1937 dollars a night. "We could live on that," he said. "Our furnished house was twelve dollars a month. Both my sisters slept in my mom's bedroom; I slept on the davenport. We had a refrigerator and a stove, so we were home free." A year later he was playing with trumpeter Frankie Zinzer and Larry Sullivan, the first trumpeter at Warner Bros. ("I could play higher than he could, and read just as fast"). They'd get together in Bronson Canyon and improvise Saturday mornings—a bunch of old-timers and one kid, hitting impossible high Cs over the quiet of the park. At twenty-eight, Rasey became MGM's first-chair trumpeter; at thirty, he played the blowsy wail of *An American in Paris*; *Chinatown* was easy. "It was nothing to play, really," he said.

The sound stunned Evans. The ache, the longing, dying but sweetly pleading, like a happy memory drowning in truth. It was what he had been searching for, not just for *Chinatown*, his love story in need of love, but for those long Woodland nights he waited out alone in bed, flipping through old photograph albums, the pictures of Ali, whom he had let go, pictures of Ali and his son. Josh, the family he had faded, one night at a time, for *The Godfather*. He knew he had fucked up. Goldsmith's music was scant consolation, only magic, but where love and real life failed his foolish cravings, the music ennobled them in brass and piano and harp. Their glissandos were running water, growing in him the feeling, easy to forget, of why he was right, despite all the shit, to love Hollywood in the first place. The feeling was that word he lost so much trying to find and hold on to—now he had it—a word, in the time of Nixon, almost embarrassing to speak—"romance." For Evans it was more than moonlight and ocean winds and Gatsby's green flare across the bay; it was not fantasy but palpable evidence of a dream becoming true, the rare and shivery threshold of immeasurable pleasure, the promise imagination grants the mundane, and the mountain stream through which beauty and goodness, against all probability and reason, flow down into the world as art.

It was, out of the darkness, a faith. Like Polanski's crane, a lift, redemption, grace. True or false, it didn't matter; as long as it was felt once, it could be felt again.

Hearing that music for the first time, thinking of his father, he cried.

On the night of *Chinatown*'s New York premiere, Bluhdorn called his warring sons, Evans and Yablans, to Pietro's for a steak dinner intended to heal the family wounds. By then, May 1974, there were too many: Yablans's jealousy of Evans's celebrity; Evans's distaste for Yablans's brashness; Evans's continuing retreat from the studio, the result of the "back pains" Yablans put in quotation marks; Yablans's contention that *Chinatown* presented a conflict of interest for Evans;

Bluhdorn's discovery that Evans, exercising his right as producer, had taken points in *Chinatown*, further supporting Yablans's argument against him ; and most recently, the contentious end to Paramount's richest *beau geste*, the Directors Company. Originally the deal entitled each director (Bogdanovich, Friedkin, Coppola) to a financial interest in the others' films, a happy arrangement when the pictures hit, like Bogdanovich's *Paper Moon*, which paid all nicely, but Bogdanovich's second Directors Company offering, *Daisy Miller*, had bombed prominently in May, spurring a crossfire of blame, beginning with Friedkin, who had always thought it a vanity project to begin with. But Friedkin, Bogdanovich argued, had no leg to stand on; he had made a grand total of zero films for the Directors Company (Coppola made one, *The Conversation*) and the dream exploded in rancor. Yablans said I told ya so—another excuse to dump on Evans.

Coursing with bad blood, Paramount, Bluhdorn knew, needed a thorough cleaning if it was to return to the good old days of commerce, art, and camaraderie. The latter was an element of great consequence for Bluhdorn. Joined with his failure to install his own son, Paul, in the line of studio power, Bluhdorn's "almost dynastic need for a surrogate son," according to Bernard F. Dick, had informed the chairman's impulsive hirings as far back as Evans. "Charlie was a father to me," Evans said, and the feeling was returned. Of his two "sons" Bluhdorn favored Evans, his way with women, his glamour and élan. Yablans knew it.

At Pietro's, Bluhdorn raised a glass and toasted the partnership.

"Charlie, we're not a partnership!" Yablans screamed. "I'm an employee and Evans is an employee, even though Evans won't open his mouth 'cause he ain't got the balls to open his mouth."

There was little talk that night about *Chinatown*.

A screening of the final release print was held at Paramount. Sylbert, Alonzo, Nicholson, O'Steen, Towne, Evans, and certain select others would have their last looks at the finished picture complete with Jerry Goldsmith's new score.

As expected, the music thrilled them. But what they saw on screen horrified them.

For one thing the print was brighter than anyone had remembered, far too bright.

With Polanski out of the picture—he hadn't much communication with Goldsmith and left the supervision of the score to Evans—suspicion turned to the producer. Had Evans pressured Alonzo into submission, the way he had Lambro, or had Alonzo willingly agreed to the change?

The lights came up.

"Is there anything anyone would like to say?" Evans asked the gathering.

Nicholson rose. "I'll disown this movie if this print is used."

Sylbert smelled a fight; he could see Nicholson holding in rage as he explained how he had tried hard to "stay in the shadows as an actor," no easy feat when he also had to *act*. Turning to Evans, Jack demanded he restore the print to the darker, more mysterious incarnation Polanski had had in the dailies.

As he always did, Evans consented, but so close to the release, there was no telling if he would, in the final hour, hedge and hold them off until it was too late.

The first public screening of *Chinatown* in Los Angeles was held at the Director's Guild Theater on June 17, 1974.

"Evans is nervous," Robert Towne warned Julie, "and he doesn't want you at the screening."

"He doesn't?"

"He doesn't know what you're going to say." At Woodland, she had told him, quite plainly, what she thought of the score.

"I'll stay home."

The theater that night was packed with critics, industry professionals, and members of the *Chinatown* cast and crew. "Evans was
a great marketer," Hawk Koch explained. "He knew how to fill a
house." ABC executive Barry Diller sat with Towne; they had grown
up together in Brentwood. But the presence of a familiar face did
not lessen Towne's worry. The last time he saw *Chinatown* it was too
bright, and of course, there were Roman's changes, the love scene,
the ending he still vehemently opposed. . . . Surrounded by discerning peers and the covert jealousies consequent to any industry
screening, he could foresee public humiliation of the worst sort, pity
plus gloating par excellence.

He was also personally vulnerable. For *Chinatown*, the first big
studio picture to bear his name and only his name as writer, represented a thing more formidable than an original screenplay produced; it was the agonized flowering of a mission, a vocational piece
of himself that, for all Roman had done to it, contained, in seedling,
his long friendship with Jack, with the city, and his enmity toward
environmental destruction—the very best of his good intentions.
There simply was nowhere to hide.

But when the lights went down and the picture came up, Towne
found he no longer entirely hated what he saw. Of course he still
hated Polanski's nihilistic ending, but the new music somewhat soft-
ened the blow, and the old shadows—returned, courtesy of Jack–
helped.

Well, Towne thought, maybe we'll get away with it.

"This is a fucking great movie," Diller whispered in his ear.

Was Diller full of shit?

Elsewhere the mood was mixed. About forty-five minutes into
the picture, Koch overheard one high-ranking executive gleefully
remark to another: "Evans has a bomb."

The picture ended.

An eerie quiet filled the theater, and Evans interrogated the silence for a tell: Were they asleep? That not a body moved could have

indicated either dumbstruck awe or paralytic revulsion. Which was it? Defensively he had premised a marketing scheme on concealment. No prepublicity, no softcover novelization, no glamorous tie-ins with the movie's costumes or music as he had done on *Gatsby*. Jack would get his footprints in Grauman's cement, which had already been arranged, but as best he could, Evans would keep *Chinatown* a mystery, like a secret worth keeping—or, would they say, a product not worth selling?

In the lobby Sue Mengers rushed toward him: "What kind of dreck is this shit?"

Gossip columnist Rona Barrett: "How could you make this picture?"

Freddie Fields didn't try to contain his delight: "Sorry, kid."

Dressed for victory in suede vest and open-necked shirt, Evans, smiling anyway, lit a cigar and headed to Chasen's—catered Chinese instead of chili—kissing and backslapping Jack and Anjelica, talent agent Irving 'Swifty' Lazar, Kris Kristofferson, Dunaway, Sue and her husband, Jean-Claude Tramont, well past midnight. It was another night of work.

What could he do now? The picture was done. It was done.

His fate no longer his to control. Perhaps his opponents were right: Running the studio and producing was too high a gamble. He had already earned Beatty's and director Alan Pakula's wrath for setting the release of *The Parallax View* for June 14, potentially burying it a mere week before he opened *Chinatown*. And his wars with Yablans were taking their toll. "After *Chinatown*," Evans confessed that year, "I think I'll concentrate on running the studio for a while." He might even leave Hollywood: "The movie industry outgrows everybody." They were coming for him.

7

Charles Champlin of the *L.A. Times* loved *Chinatown*. He named it the best of the year, and Roger Ebert plainly hailed it a tour de force. Most critics followed suit, praising every facet of the production, the uncompromising intelligence of the screenplay, the design, Nicholson and Polanski, the very idea of using an "old-fashioned" genre, like a detective movie, to touch audiences with unsuspected grandeur, a tragedy of the modern world. *Chinatown*, it was almost universally agreed, was that rare, if not unprecedented, private-eye movie that was really *about* something. The voice of (qualified) dissent came from Pauline Kael: "The film holds you, in a suffocating way," she wrote. "Polanski never lets the story tell itself. It's all over-deliberate, mauve, nightmarish; everyone is yellow-lacquered, and evil runs rampant. You don't care who is hurt, since everything is blighted. And yet the nastiness has a look, and a fascination."

Drawn by the reviews, people came.

On June 20 the line outside Grauman's Chinese swelled with L.A. adults hip to the movies. They had read Champlin, his praise of *Chinatown*'s "vision of a time, a place, and a life-style," its "total recapturing of a past, in its plot, its vivid characterizations, its carefully calculated and accelerating pace, is whole demonstration of a medium mastered," a film, he wrote, that "reminds you again—and thrillingly—that motion pictures are larger, not smaller than life; they are not processed at drugstores and they are not television."

Not television, no. The adults of Los Angeles would have to go out to see *Chinatown* (kids, angling for something more dangerous than television, would have to sneak in); they would have to set aside an entire evening; to see *Chinatown* they would have to spend time and money (tickets, nanny, parking, popcorn, dinner)—an investment that, rather than diminish the experience, actually dignified the film, the filmmakers, and the entire moviegoing enterprise with value and anticipation, the romance and high talk and longing for something important almost about to happen. Even standing on line was an event. As *Chinatown* only opened in three theaters in L.A. (the Chinese, Westwood's National, and a drive-in in Van Nuys), none of them multiplexes, the the city's adult filmgoers were all funneled to one of only a handful common points. Waiting on line, they were their own society, greeting like-minded strangers, trading movie gossip, flirting, passing joints, debating *The Parallax View, Blazing Saddles, Thieves Like Us, The Conversation, The Sugarland Express*, citing Pauline by her first name, Canby by his second, gauging the faces of the preceding audience as they flooded from the theater: Would we wear those expressions in two hours time? Would what happened to them happen to us?

America's morale fell further that summer, but the sidewalk filmgoers kept a sturdier faith. They were adults, they were well informed by informed critics, and they went to the movies because the movies were still good.

"Longing on a large scale makes history," Don DeLillo.

Hollywood had answered their call.

Evans was elated. He had been in the business long enough to know that these were the kinds of reviews that predicted Oscar nominations, and while he didn't expect *Chinatown* to do titanic business, having decided—unlike Paramount's *Godfather* strategy—to open the picture slowly, hoping for the kind of word of mouth *Chinatown* was now getting, it would not be long before he knew for certain he had a modest hit on his hands. But even more than that, he had, at last, what he had been angling for since he first stepped into his big office at the studio, if not before, since he first learned the meaning of the word "producer": respect. Not power—as an executive he had already had that—but the patina of awe and good fortune that comes to one intimately affiliated with a stately work of art. He had not produced *The Godfather*; he had not produced *Love Story*. He had produced *Chinatown*. "We had something," he said, "that had something. We had a little magic."

It wouldn't last. What he had felt coming finally came.

In September 1974 Charlie Bluhdorn had given up on trying to smooth the way between Yablans and Evans: "[They] hated each other too much," explained Peter Bart. "Both wanted more money and more fame." Yablans would exit. And Evans, at the peak of his power and success, would find himself demoted, withdrawn as head of the studio, and given a production deal. He would be only a producer now.

It would be, surprisingly, something of a relief to Evans to step from the throne, shed the politics and headaches, and join his friends, the artists, in doing exclusively what he had set out to do in the first place: make movies.

At the top of Paramount, Bluhdorn installed a new president, Barry Diller. Evans would report to him, effective in six months' time.

On one level Evans's demotion made no sense. With more than twenty films released and nearly three hundred million dollars in after-tax profits,1974 had been a banner year for Paramount: the studio's best ever. Emotional turmoil aside, Evans had done an extraordinary job. But of Paramount's incredible 1974 only $103 million were attributable to Evans's motion picture releases, a marked decline from 1973's $120 million, 1972's $142 million, and 1971's $139 million. The difference was television; the big screen was down, the small was up. And Barry Diller would be coming from ABC.

If Evans had followed the box-office trend—one that forecast Hollywood's out-and-out supplication to escapist entertainment—that had begun with Universal's *Airport* in 1970, and given Paramount a disaster picture to match the monster returns of Fox's *Poseidon Adventure* (1972's highest grosser after *The Godfather*) or Fox's *Towering Inferno* (1974's top grosser) or Universal's *Earthquake* (1974's third-highest), his position might have been different. But Evans distained disaster movies. He had made a concerted policy of avoiding the pack for what he deemed "man-woman" stories:. "I've always been a proponent of people pictures," he said.

But the people, it seemed, no longer wanted people. In 1974 critic Stephen Farber warned of "Hollywood's New Sensationalism," a post-*Exorcist* trend toward "gaudier and more lurid" pictures predicated on sensation and visceral shock, a regression that historian Tom Gunning compared to film's earliest, primitive period (1895–1906), a "cinema of attractions" that preceded the advent of narrative.

"One thing," Evans told Bluhdorn "If you're going to fire me, I want you to do one thing."

"What?"

"Hire Dick Sylbert as my replacement."

No production designer had ever headed production at a major movie studio.

"He has taste, Charlie. He has elegance, taste, and glamour. And he'll bring the best the best to the Mountain, Charlie, because he *is* the best. If you don't hire Dick Sylbert, I'm not leaving!"

Bluhdorn agreed.

Of his own accord, Peter Bart left the studio. He had no intention of working for Diller, a thirty-three-year-old television executive, creator of *Movie of the Week*, who admitted to Bart he "didn't really know the movies."

"We're gonna do great work together," Evans gamely enthused to Diller. "Michael Douglas has a great project, *One Flew Over the Cuckoo's Nest*. We should get in."

"No one wants to see those movies."

"Five million."

"Bob—"

"Jack's interested. Ashby's interested."

"Bob," Diller said: "You work for me."

Julie Payne felt the change. Something was happening at Hutton Drive. It was the one-two-three punch of *Last Detail*, *Chinatown*, and early in 1975, *Shampoo*. Their phone now rang incessantly with calls from Robert's associates, old and new, genuine and obsequious, with invitations to dinner, to parties, to tennis at Woodland, offers to write or rewrite. Dino De Laurentiis would pay Towne a hundred thousand dollars and unlimited Cuban cigars to write a single voiceover; Calley would give Towne more—money and an office at Warners and a title—just to read and report on scripts. Sue Mengers called, offering Towne a permanent seat at her dining-room table. Evans wanted to know what was next for Mr. Shakespeare. *White Dog*, an adaptation of a Romain Gary novel? The sequel to *Chinatown*? What else?

Pauline Kael came to Los Angeles, lavishing Towne with adoration. Julie picked her up at the Beverly Wilshire and took her to lunch and dinner. "She was allergic to the sun," Payne said. "She always looked like a beekeeper." She talked, talked, talked that trip, but she didn't want to talk *Chinatown*; she was crazy for *Shampoo*. *Shampoo*, she wrote, got Los Angeles better than *Chinatown*: "Los Angeles itself, the sprawl-city, opens the movie up, and the L.A. sense of freedom makes its own comment on the scrambling characters." Towne, Beatty, and Ashby nailed "the emotional climate of the time [the presidential election of 1968] and place. Los Angeles has become what it is because of the bright heat, which turns people into narcissists and sensuous provcateurs." Her review was a singular rave for Robert Towne, a reinterpreter of old forms, "a great new screenwriter in a structured tradition—a flaky classicist." He had at last shed the shackles of credited and uncredited script doctor and come into his own, a writer with a point of view, distinctly late-sixties American, boiled soft, not Watergate-hard: "Towne's heroes," Kael wrote, "if we can take Gittes, of *Chinatown*, and [*Shampoo's*] George, here, as fair examples, are hip to conventional society, and they assume that they reject its dreams. But in some corner of their heads they think that maybe the old romantic dream can be made to work." She had little crush, Payne thought, on Robert.

That year, all of Hollywood did. The phone at Hutton Drive once rang seventeen times in twenty minutes. But between rings their little house on the hill, formerly hushed with writer's intention, took on strange new silences, edgy and absent of purpose. Payne filled them with concerns. She wavered over the big parties she didn't want to host or attend, the coming hazards of fame and temptation, her own memories of neglect, the silences of her childhood on Beverly Drive. An old chord struck. She was scared.

Towne didn't seem to notice. His spectacular momentum powered him through awards season. So richly nominated, and a veritable shoo-in, he didn't worry. He blazed. For the BAFTAs in London, Anthea made him a magnificent three-piece tuxedo, paid for by Evans, and Evans installed him and Julie in the resplendent Cecil Beaton Suite of the Connaught Hotel, arranging for a Rolls-Royce to ferry them to and from the ceremony, where he would be not once but twice nominated, for *Chinatown* and *The Last Detail*, which had opened in London only that year.

At the BAFTAs Towne was not seated with Polanski: "I said I wouldn't work with him," he laughed to Julie. "I didn't say I wouldn't have *dinner* with him!"

Spotting Towne across the room, Polanski bounded over and,

putting their war in the past, joined in the laughter. It was that kind of night for *Chinatown* was fast becoming that kind of movie; Towne won Best Screenplay honors, as writer of the year, for both *The Last Detail* and *Chinatown*, as Nicholson won Best Actor for both, and Polanski, for *Chinatown*, won Best Director.

They were on a rol. That year Polanski and Towne would win Golden Globes as would the film itself for Best Picture of 1974. At the New York Film Critics Circle Awards, held at Elaine's—New York's legendary literary hangout—Towne and Nicholson would win again, and celebrate back at the Carlyle in beyond-belief suites once again provided by Evans, their benefactor. "He would just give his friends everything," Payne said. Back in Los Angeles, Towne would claim the Writers Guild Award for Best Drama Written Directly for the Screen.

Thus it was no surprise when *Chinatown* received eleven Oscar nominations. The surprise was just how many nominations Paramount had received—an astonishing forty-three. No one could remember the last time a single studio so dominated the nominations, nor had all five nominations in a single category—in this case, Best Costume Design—ever gone to a single studio, Paramount again. That year three of the five Best Picture nominees—*The Godfather Part II*, *Chinatown*, and *The Conversation*—were Paramount's. It was by any estimation Hollywood's greatest showing of the decade; in 1974 box office had reached a record $1.9 billion, and the films themselves, as evidenced by nominees—*Lenny*, *A Woman Under the Influence*, *Alice Doesn't Live Here Anymore*, *Harry and Tonto*, *Young Frankenstein*, *Hearts and Minds*, *Phantom of the Paradise*, *Murder on the Orient Express*—were, in their way, winners all. Even the unnominated of 1974—among them *Bring Me the Head of Alfredo Garcia*, *California Split*, *The Gambler*, *Parallax View*, *The Sugarland Express*, *Thieves Like Us*, *The Taking of Pelham One Two Three*— showed what a great year it was for Hollywood.

In retrospect 1974 represents the final flowering of a film garden passionately tended by liberated studio executives and an unspoken agreement between audiences and filmmakers. As Towne had once observed. the American films of World War II benefited from shared beliefs; now, "there was a common assumption that something was wrong," he said, "in the wake of Vietnam and Watergate and assassinations and riots," that gave rise to "a hunger on both sides for something new" and produced a movie year as powerful as 1974. But the poison was in the perfume: These films, Towne said, "did their jobs too well. There was"—presently—"nothing left to expose."

Could anything be more despairing than the pervasive corruption of *Chinatown*? Hollywood had presented visions of mass iniquity with equal force—there is *Kiss Me Deadly*, with its nuclear finale—and there were films to come, *Nashville* and *Network*, *Taxi Driver* and *The Deer Hunter*, that would hold up a black mirror to fallen America, but the wreckage of *Chinatown*, transmitted metaphorically, transcends its story and characters. Chinatown is a condition. The condition is the terrible awareness of one's helplessness, what Towne had always called "the futility of good intentions." If its resonance surpasses the literal, it is due not only to Towne's overall concept, the thematic rigor and omnipresence of power and abuse in the script, but to Polanski's cinematic rendering of Chinatown itself. He insisted it must be in the film as a literal location, but he filmed it metaphorically, amid the vacant black limbo of nightmare. It's hard to see and it's too quiet. It doesn't seem real. The events themselves land with the perfect timing of melodrama. Everything goes wrong precisely at once, and some of it isn't entirely logical—Evelyn *not* killing her father at such close range, the police *killing* Evelyn in the dark at such long range—it moves too fast for comprehension, evoking, in pace, sound, and color, the figurative, a state of mind, *Gittes's* state of mind, his Chinatown past, now his Chinatown present, creating a temporal Sisyphean circle that implies the fruitless persistence of return, emotional incarceration, the failure to mitigate incomprehensible trauma.

What makes Chinatown so uniquely disturbing as an American metaphor is that it is so unlike the whiteness of Ahab's whale or the greenness of Gatsby's light. However illusory, these are totems of aspiration, of possibility. Futility and fate, by contrast, are concepts that defy the capitalist's dream of agency and advancement, the (graying) Protestant work ethic that assured pre-Watergate Americans that life was linear, not cyclical, and the game wasn't rigged against them. It is no wonder, then, that Towne's metaphor should borrow its desolation from Polanski, a European. "The American has not yet assimilated psychologically the disappearance of his own geographical frontier," wrote the philosopher William Barrett in 1962. "His spiritual horizon is still the limitless play of human possibilities, and as yet he has not lived through the crucial experience of human finitude." A decade after this writing, that spiritual horizon reached its finitude in Vietnam and Watergate, and symbolically in Los Angeles, the geographic end of America.

As Towne foresaw, the only place left to go was up—up to *The Sting*, to "Happy Days," Bogdanovich's *At Long Last Love*, to "a mix of nostalgia and parody," Kael wrote, the mass denial of the terrible truths Gittes was powerless to undo.

As President Ford pardoned Nixon, so would Hollywood pardon the difficulties of the recent past. A tilt, backward and downward, had begun; it was pandering, the need to please. And not filmmakers but audiences. "Perhaps no work of art is possible without belief in the audience," Kael wrote: "The kind of belief that has nothing to do with facts and figures about what people actually buy or enjoy but comes out of the individual artist's absolute conviction that only the best he can do is fit to be offered to others. . . . An artist's sense of honor is founded on the honor due to others. Honor in the arts—and in show business, too—is giving of one's utmost, even if the audience does not appear to know the difference, even if the audience shows every sign of preferring something easy, cheap, and synthetic. The audience one must believe in is the great audience: the audience one was part of as a child, when one first began to respond to great work—the audience one is still a part of."

The bittersweet sense of having reached the summit, beginning the decline, was felt powerfully Oscar night, April 8, 1975, by none more than Robert Evans, who could rightfully claim authorship of Paramount's annus mirabilis just as he bowed from his post as head of production. Evans's date for the evening was his brother Charles.

It rained that Oscar night.

Polanski stayed away. "I didn't think we would get any words," he explained, and went to Japan for *Chinatown*'s opening in Japan.

Towne and Payne took a limo to the Dorothy Chandler Pavilion with Jack (tuxedo, sunglasses, beret) and Anjelica (Halston gown, transparent sequins over painted silk) and Robert and Charles Evans. Nicholson viewed the whole thing—black tie, red carpet, winning and losing, the after parties—with hearty amusement. The Oscars was a feat of public relations, and he was more than happy to do his job. "It's good for who it's good for and bad for nobody," he said. "And it's a great night out, seeing everybody down there. Who doesn't like seeing movie stars? That's why I started working in the business." Since his stardom, he had taken pains never to appear on television; he despised the artlessness of the small screen and felt talk shows and interviews hindered the public's ability to accept the illusion that he could become, on movie screens, someone else. Knowing that Nicholson made an exception for the Oscars, the Academy made sure to reserve him and Angelica front-row seats. "I've only heard two opinions on the subject of Academy Awards that stick in my mind," Nicholson said. "Lao-tze, the great Chinese philosopher, once said, 'All tribute is false.' And then there's what my old and good friend John Huston used to say about it. He said he supported the Awards out of respect for 'all others who have gone before us.'" A movie fan above all else, Nicholson had been following the Academy

Awards his whole life, handicapping the winners and losers since he was a kid, a practice that continued into adulthood, through his own nominations. Nicholson felt going in, whether he deserved the win or not, this wasn't going to be his year. This year, in the friendly company of Evans, Towne, and Lou Adler and Adler's date, model and actress Lauren Hutton, he would simply *enjoy*; he would applaud his friends, his favorite filmmakers from around the world (Fellini was nominated for *Amarcord,* Louis Malle for *Lacombe, Lucien*), and, like a fan, cheer on all that was golden of Hollywood, his favorite team sport. Jack knew that sort of stance wasn't fashionable, especially now, with a nation in the economic, social, and political dregs, but wasn't it, in some way, why Americans watched? Didn't Fred and Ginger dance through the Depression? Silly, unjust, occasionally crass—granted—but what business wasn't? At least this one also made movies. . . .

It was still drizzling as they pulled up to the Dorothy Chandler, and stepping from the limousine, all were asked to mind their long gowns and trouser cuffs and step carefully—the drains weren't working—along the soggy red carpet. Inside, the squeak and squish of watery footfalls was the source of shared amusement, a great leveling of pretensions and worry that culminated, semihilariously, in power players in their stocking feet and some slippery bits of slapstick.

"It's your night," Coppola said to Evans behind the theater.

"No, Francis. It's yours."

Coppola, twice nominated that year for Best Picture, was convinced that the Academy would split its vote, losing him the win for either *Godfather II* or *The Conversation.* But Evans knew that the Academy, having previously awarded *Cabaret* Best Picture over *The Godfather,* would give Coppola his due this year.

Towne and Payne took their seats with the writers, in the back, behind Bert Schneider, nominated for his documentary *Hearts and Minds*; Jack and Anjelica found their spots in row one, between Faye

Dunaway and Fred Astaire, and in front of Howard Koch Jr., whose father was producing the show.

"Hiya, Bullhorn," Jack greeted Koch.

The show opened with some welcoming remarks from Academy president Walter Mirisch, who turned the house over to host Bob Hope.

"Yes, ladies and gentlemen, we're here at the Music Center, and we'll soon know if it has any significance holding these ceremonies so close to Chinatown."

A rumble of nervous applause.

The first Oscar, for Best Supporting Actor, went to Robert De Niro for *Godfather Part II,* an early indication that the night was not headed *Chinatown*'s way. Soon thereafter, the Oscar for Best Adapted Screenplay, presented by novelist James Michener, was awarded to Coppola and Mario Puzo for *Godfather Part II* and confirmed—Evans was right—the likelihood of a sweep.

When the applause died down, Michener took the podium once again. "Why don't the authors of original books write original screenplays?" he teleprompted to the auditorium. "The sad fact is that most of us do not have that talent for the concise and demanding art form, and tonight we honor those that do have talent. For the Best Original Screenplay, the nominees are . . ."

When he opened the envelope: "And the winner is Robert Towne for *Chinatown.*"

The audience yelped, seemingly as relieved as Towne, who pushed up from his chair and calmly walked down the aisle. Accepting the trophy from Michener, he bent forward to the microphone, a very tall deer in the bright lights, disbelieving the glare: "Um . . . If, uh. . . ."

He shook out the implausibility from his head. It *was* happening.

He spoke clinically, like a surgeon in a hurry. "If you've ever been on a film that didn't quite work out you know how much you owe to the people on a film that did, and so I can only reiterate my gratitude toward everybody who worked on the film, toward Faye and Roman and especially to Robert Evans who put us all together, and to Jack, who's really magic." Then, almost inaudibly, "Thank you," and coolly disappeared.

(Edward Taylor was at home, watching with his family. "He was very excited," said his daughter, Sarah Naia Stier.)

From there the night raced ahead. To shorten the show's running time, the producers had eliminated much of the customary banter, compressing the lags between *Godfather II*'s wins and enhancing the feel of a sweep. That Paramount kept winning via Coppola was cold comfort to Evans; the Mountain was not his anymore; he was exclusively a producer now, and, after Towne's win, the swift bleeding out of *Chinatown* predicted he would go home a loser.

Julie Payne, still waiting for Towne to return to his seat with his statue, came to wonder if something had happened to him. Looking around her for signs, she could see Towne's wasn't the only empty seat in the auditorium. Other winners were missing. But the show went on. At an opportune moment she made for the aisle doors and started banging quietly. The man who came for her was—a total shock—her ex-husband, actor Skip Ward.

"Julie—"

"What are you *doing* here?"

"I'm producing the show."

"You never told anybody that the winners aren't coming back to their seats!"

"He's here. He's here. We're keeping them for the final bows."

"Jesus, guys. I was sitting there *alone*!"

Towne's was the only Oscar win for *Chinatown*.

Best Picture went to *Godfather Part II*. It was Coppola's third Oscar of the night. In none of his acceptance speeches did he acknowledge Evans. He was crestfallen.

Nicholson was philosophical. That's how the game was played. Next year he could foresee a win for *One Flew Over the Cuckoo's Nest*.

After the show they climbed into the limo, Jack and Anjelica; Jack's agent, Sandy Bressler; Robert and Julie. Evans and Charlie, his brother, who rode up front in the passenger seat. They were losers that night, save for Towne. Semiashamed, he hid his Oscar, Anjelica saw, in the cushion wedge between seats. There followed some embarrassed joking, but if she ever won, Anjelica reflected: "I did not want to do that. I was going to enjoy it."

They drove onward to the Governors Ball.

The rain slowed.

Rolling down the window to let out his cigarette smoke, Nicholson was blithely tabulating the evening's effects on *Chinatown*'s potential box office. Losing Best Picture would surely cost them in the long run, but he wasn't too worried; he had a piece of the movie.

It got quiet.

"It's not like that, Jack," Bressler said.

"Whaddya *talkin'* about, Sandy?"

There must be some confusion, Bressler corrected him. He didn't have points in *Chinatown*.

Nicholson, bristling, turned to face the window and exhaled into the rain.

Nicholson was philosophical. That's how the game was played. Next year he could foresee a win for One Flew Over the Cuckoo's Nest.

Richard Sylbert took over production at Paramount in April 1975.

He and Susanna Moore moved into a sumptuous house on Outpost Drive up in the Hollywood Hills, a sprawling Spanish built, of course, in 1937—MGM art director Cedric Gibbons had designed it for his then-wife, Mexican actress Dolores Del Rio—that Sylbert thought would have been a perfect location for *Chinatown*. It even had a pond. On just about an acre of hillside green, he planted thirty camellias, rows of fruit trees, and a vegetable garden. Susanna was pregnant.

The high-water mark of Sylbert's intellect, evident in his designs, open erudition, and smart and fancy friends, branded his administration and conferred on Paramount the pleasant aroma of culture and sophistication. Sylbert's detractors suspected he was, in fact, too refined for the job, a professor in a whorehouse, but Barry Diller would function as Sylbert's corrective and vice versa; together they were the balance of counterstrengths: film and TV, art and commerce. "Frankly," Sylbert said, "most people haven't the experience to think a picture through—they have never been on a picture from one end to the other"—that is, as a designer, one whose eye guided production from beginning to end, Sylbert was uniquely oriented to the overall aesthetic life of a film: "They have never dealt with those day-to-day problems you deal with when you make a picture. When you read a property from the vantage point of fifteen years of making motion pictures, you see it from a very different point of view than when you read it as an ex-agent."

Every morning, Sylbert would confer with Evans, his predecessor, by phone, sometimes for hours, deepening an association that would benefit both parties, Sylbert gaining from Evans's decade of experience, Evans keeping close ties with the power. Though Sylbert's taste was more literary than Evans's—Evans, famously didn't read; Sylbert read, and wrote beautifully—Sylbert advanced Evans's policy of people pictures, not event pictures, as early as his first days on the job: "There is still an audience for pictures that have an original idea in them," Sylbert told the *Hollywood Reporter*, "that are terribly well-performed, that are based on relationships with people . . . reactions of people." Soon after he took office he optioned the challenging *Looking for Mr. Goodbar* and picked up Robert Altman's *Nashville* and Bernardo Bertolucci's *1900* for distribution. He fell in love with and optioned John Cheever's *Falconer*; it was, he decided, worth every risk: "With all the difficulties this book presents," he wrote to his team, "and with all the areas never dealt with in films before I firmly believe that it is a remarkable a powerful idea for a film. There is more humanity and heart in this piece than I have seen in a long time. More of the truth of our lives and the desire to live—of the essential nobility, and the humor and despair of our collective existence in this story of Farragut and his life both in and out of prison than I expect to find in a small novel." (He sent the book to Mike Nichols.) Further literary motions followed: Sylbert took *A Piece of My Heart*, by Richard Ford, and Norman Maclean's *A River Runs Through It*, the latter a lasting dream for Sylbert, a fly-fisherman. In time he wrote his own screenplay, an adaptation of Virginia Woolf's *Jacob's Room*.

Sylbert showed common sense. Capable of adjusting his taste to the box office, he green-lit (reluctantly) *The Bad News Bears*, and pushed for a film of Anne Rice's *Interview with the Vampire*. But he would not pander to the brazenly commercial: "Science-Fiction is an escalating area that will offer serious competition," he wrote, but he was "personally sick of this kind of pistol-pussy contrivance." But Sylbert was no snob either: "It is the longest 125 pages I have ever read," he wrote of Terrence Malick's script, *Days of Heaven*. "Actually I don't know if it is a screenplay; it often seems like a late Victorian novel out of its time, forced to be a screenplay almost against its will."

Included in these discussions was Sylbert's chosen executive assistant, formerly an out-of-work tennis hustler, Don Simpson. "When he'd lose," said Simpson's courtmate, actor Peter Cannon, "he'd rush up to the net, drop his pants and piss on the net. He'd say, 'I can't take this shit,' and he'd piss on the net." Simpson's fury dated back to his father, who would make his son, at seven years old, hunt wild animals and slaughter them with bare hands. In the Simpson household, there were consequences for failure. "He used to pick me up and throw me against the wall," Simpson said, "and as I hit the ground, he'd kick me." His mother was no better.

Simpson had worked his way up from the advertising end of Warners and came to Sylbert via businessman-producer Steve Tisch. "He's the brightest, most interesting guy I've met here," Tisch enthused to Sylbert, "and he knows everything about Hollywood. You have to meet him." Simpson was so green and so hot, he moved up the ranks quicker than he could find a new wardrobe. It was his pal Jerry Bruckheimer who lent him a sport coat for his interview with Sylbert, a meeting that proceeded beautifully; they found they shared a love of fly-fishing, Sylbert's instinct told him to go for it and they got down to work.

It turned out fly-fishing was the only thing they had in common. Reading the script for the *Love Story* sequel, *Oliver's Story*, Simpson suggested they leave the ending open—for a third *Love Story* film. Sylbert was appalled at the suggestion of one, let alone two more of these movies. He was more interested in Ingmar Bergman's proposed remake of *The Merry Widow* to which Simpson crassly protested: "Even the best Bergman is never strong at the box office."

Attuned to the encroaching cinema of sensation, Simpson consistently sought the easy pleasures of so-called character likablity and visceral intensity ("a picture like this should scare the shit out of an audience"). He and Sylbert clashed again over *Moontrap*, a Western Jack Nicholson wanted to direct. Predictably, Simpson didn't think the project was "strong enough to make this a commercial movie." Sylbert, guided by head and heart, was all in: "It is to the West what James Fenimore Cooper's work is to the East," he argued. And Jack was a friend.

"Dick knew he made a mistake hiring the odious Don Simpson," Susanna Moore said. "Simpson spent the entire time that he worked for Dick undermining him and doing bad things to try get rid of him. It was absolutely a deliberate sabotage." According to Simpson himself, "Dick never played the game you've got to play to be a successful studio executive. His attitude was, 'I'm the best art director alive. If it doesn't work out, so what?'"

Described by Bruckheimer as "someone who likes to be the center of attention," Simpson didn't believe in the auteur theory; he believed in cocaine.

Sylbert and Simpson were working for two different Paramounts, past and future. And the Paramount Barry Diller favored belonged to Simpson. To Sylbert's great discomfort, Diller would bring on Michael Eisner, his former colleague at ABC, to serve as president. It was TV time. "When Eisner came in," Sylbert said, "the atmosphere at Paramount changed completely. It was a group of people sitting down at a table, doing what they did for ABC. It was very difficult for me to get with what they made enormously successful, which is manufactured product aiming at your knees."

But the writing was on the wall for Sylbert's tenure only three months in, on June 20, 1975—a year to the day after *Chinatown* opened—when *Jaws* hit America.

In a dramatic break from the customs of movie promotion, Universal had spent more than seven hundred thousand dollars, an enormous sum, to advertise *Jaws* on television, and opened the picture wide, incredibly wide, in more than four hundred theaters. À la *The Exorcist*, the combination—which carried *Jaws* to record grosses—furnished Hollywood with an infinitely repeatable, money-magical formula of more is more: giant advertising campaigns and wide releases to storm the public with high-intensity, thrill-packed entertainment, the cinema of sensation.

Hollywood had always been a gambling business, but *Jaws* demonstrated it could be a *big* business *less* gamble. An executive no longer needed a great, or even good, script; he no longer needed an actual story (was *Jaws* really about anything?), only the requisite thrills—"set pieces" in executive-speak—and the advance approval of the marketing department to assure the bosses he was choosing wisely. The tail would wag the dog: As promotional costs ascended, budgets increased, decreasing the funds once available for script development and preproduction—components "fundamental," Howard Koch Jr. said, to the aesthetic mastery of *Chinatown*.

Equally dispiriting was *Jaws*'s—forgive the expression—political toothlessness. "The picture's only villain, outside of the shark, is the mayor," author Peter Biskind astutely observed. "An elected official, a politician. But *Jaws* was a film of the political center: of the three men who take on the shark, Quint, the macho man of the right is killed, while Hooper, the intellectual Jew of the left, is marginalized, leaving Brody, the everyman cop, the Jerry Ford . . . to dispatch the shark." For all its many virtues, *Jaws* ratified the growing trend in disaster pictures and the end of the Hollywood counterculture. "Vietnam is like cancer—people don't want to be reminded of it," said Robert Evans of the new audience. "They want catharsis, escape."

Heretofore an outspoken adversary of the disaster picture, Evans himself tried *Black Sunday*, a thriller about a terrorist plot to blow up the Super Bowl. He labored to make the film as apolitical as possible: "Paramount thought it was going to be their *Jaws*," he confessed, "and so did I." It wasn't. But still, he stayed on the band-wagon, developing yet another disaster movie, *Blizzard*.

Evans did, however, go one more round with the old Paramount. He produced *Marathon Man*, a picture born of the old Palm Springs decree—hip director, genre-based material—the revolutionary artistic-commercial strategy that gave rise to *Rosemary's Baby, Chinatown,* and *The Godfather*.

"Try this," Evans said to Howard Koch Jr. on the set.

Until then, Koch had always thought of coke as elite, "but [by then] the fucking craft service guy had it," he said, "the prop guy had it. It was everywhere."

A year into the job, Sylbert's projects were regularly denied for the sort of "high-concept" ideas—Don Simpson's term for an easily simplified, obviously commercial story—Simpson-Eisner-Diller could fit into a promotional tagline or *TV Guide* blurb. The double onslaught of *Jaws* and Eisner brought in "the television mentality," Sylbert said, endless meetings, "and manufacturing stories and manufacturing movies." "Until then, Sylbert said, "We worked with writers on material we believed in." Eisner's orientation was not covert. In a memo Eisner would circulate through Paramount, he wrote: "We have no obligation to make history. We have no obligation to make art. We have no obligation to make a statement. To make money is our only objective."

"One thing must be very clear to everyone," observed Charles A. Pratt, president of Bing Crosby Productions: "There's more money to be made in the movie business today than ever before. Never has there been such a succession of multi-million-dollar grossers in such a short space of time. I don't mean pictures that gross five, 10 or 15 million dollars, but those in the 20, 30, 50 and even more millions of dollars."

Sylbert retreated.

"These people," He confided to executive David Picker. "What can I do? I can't get anything done."

As little as possible . . .

In a corner of his attic Sylbert would fashion fly rods and flies and dream disconsolately of setting out from the San Pedro Harbor in a rowboat.

The year 1975, when Sylbert took over Paramount and *Jaws* opened, was the year Michael Ovitz, Ron Meyer, and three other agents defected from William Morris and founded Creative Artists Agency. "These five nothing TV agents from William Morris think they can start a new agency," scoffed Sue Mengers at a meeting with her boss, Freddie Fields, not knowing that that very same year, Fields was to sell their agency to Marvin Josephson, and merge into International Creative Management, ICM. As sharks CAA and ICM swallowed up talent, monopolizing a marketplace once diversified by small agencies like Ziegler-Ross, they recouped power. But their job was not to make movies. Where Zieg thought in careers, the new agents thought in packages—not how to make the best movie for their client but how to get the most clients in it.

With so many clients at hand, power shifted: the behemoth agencies, not the studios, would call the shots. It was an industry-wide holdup, and a rich one to boot. ICM represented the producer, the director, the screenwriter, and the author of *Jaws*, earning them, according to the *New York Times*, a staggering "ten percent of 53¾ percent of the profits." Backed by the tremendous power of ICM, Mengers could negotiate a fee of one million dollars for Gene Hackman to appear in *Lucky Lady*. "As long as they're dumb enough to pay these prices," she maintained, "I'm willing to let them." Fees skyrocketed, budgets skyrocketed, and the attention paid to a film project zeroed in on the deal, and, to defend the enormous upfront investment, the marketing—the beginning and the end of a project—leaving the middle, the actual film itself, almost an afterthought.

"Studios now have an enormous amount of various executives who need to justify their existence by meddling into the creative process," Polanski said. "The problem with it is that it becomes more and more of a committee," he said. "Before, you dealt with the studio." That was Robert Evans. That was John Calley. "What used to be quick can now take months," Towne said. "It can vitiate your momentum, bleed your enthusiasm of interest. By the time you finish the dealmaking, you sometimes feel that you've already made the movie. That and because the cost of making films nowadays is so expensive that the executives are less venturesome, tends to take some of the joy out." He said, "Just the damn fact of the in-house lawyers, endless tin cans tied to your tail. It takes months and years to get a contract done. Used to be, somebody just did it on the phone. Never had a damn deal. Now, the deal is everything."

As Hollywood's energy shifted from filmmaking to deal making, its people and culture shifted from old hippies to young yuppies. Right on time—just before Annie Hall broke up with Alvy Singer at the Source, by then cliché enough to inflame his allergy to L.A.—the Souce and the Aware Inn surrendered, in 1975, to Ma Maison. The arrival of chef Wolfgang Puck ended the informality of organic cuisine, the small-town ease of fresh juice and salads, for the hierarchically Continental milieu of Ma Maison's French bistro, its Poulet à la Moutarde, its unlisted phone number, its roll of Rollses valet-parked out front, its vaunted maître d' Patrick Terrail, scion of Paris's La Tour d'Argent with an emphasis on the *argent*. "There were practical reasons for everything we did," Terrail claims, "but it was taken as snob appeal." Terrail had his favorites. "People hated Patrick," Puck said. "Some of the famous ones liked him. But the others didn't feel welcome. When the head of Fox came in, he made a huge fuss; his wife came, he let her wait 45 minutes. So then the wife would end up saying: 'You know, I'm not going back there. He treats me like shit.' One thing I learned from that: You have to be nice to everyone."

In the preceding years, wrote Jim Harwood in *Variety*: "Hollywood has swelled its executive suites with more and more outsiders with no experience in the entertainment industry. One high-salaried second-level exec, for example, was recently recruited from the pharmaceutical industry for his expertise in taxation and the ways of Capitol Hill, both handy talents in finding profits not directly involved in the sale of the product." Enter the so-called Baby Moguls—isolated from the world outside Hollywood, their life was the deal. People outside the movie business, they called "civilians." Agent Michael Black, who once attended SDS (Students for a Democratic Society) meetings at SUNY Buffalo and sheltered protesters in his apartment, confessed, "If I ever talk about politics, it's to see if there's a screenplay in it." They were workaholics, never home. "None of us cooks," said Paula Weinstein. "I barely know anyone who owns a dining room table." "What we learned in the sixties," Tom Mount said, "is that trying to build an alternative structure outside the system, given the power of the system, is never going to work." They were amenable to the corporate superstructure. They called the Polo Lounge the Polio Lounge. "Bob Evans," John Landis said, "is the classic example of everything that does not interest me."

The new breed no longer feigned taste and knowledge of movies, but touted knowledge, hardly feigned, of box-office trends. When Sylbert said "art" they heard "risk." Nor did Outpost become another Woodland.

At one dinner party chez Diller, Susanna Moore felt, from across the table, whispers she sensed were intended for her ears.

"Who's *that*?" asked Diane von Furstenberg loudly.

"That's Dick Sylbert's wife."

Moore refused to have dinner there again.

By the end of 1976, Sylbert and Moore had split, and he had vacated his post at Paramount: "When I saw the new movie people

from the television world coming into the studio, I was happy that
I had a day job as a production designer to fall back on and I left."

Barry Diller took over, and Don Simpson moved up.

Sylbert sold the house on Outpost Drive.

Respecting the sanctity of the writer's closed door, how as a girl she
was made to tiptoe by her stepfather Charlie Lederer's office, Payne
knew to contain herself until Towne emerged; then she would speak
with him. On one urgent occasion, however, he evaded her. She
would wait, she would try to speak with him, he would ignore.

Payne continued to wait outside Towne's office door. For weeks
she attempted to approach, asking him when, now or later, would
be the moment to have their conversation, and each time he had
answered, gruffly, "Not now."

At night she heard screams and then gunshots echoing through
the canyon below Hutton Drive. She ran to the window and out on
the street saw bloodied young people, their clothes torn, wandering
outside a neighbor's house. They were filming, she saw—*Helter Skelter* for television.

"Robert," she finally said to the closed office door, "I need to speak
with you about something very important." She got no answer.

She threw open the door, heaved one of two Selectric II typewriters off his desk, and, knowing there was a backup, smashed it to the
ground.

He punched her in the eye.

She fled to a girlfriend's house.

She would go back to him; he told her he was sorry. He told her
it would never happen again.

In Italy, Polanski directed Alban Berg's opera *Lulu*. He partied in
great style at his estate on the via Appia Antica in Rome, before

moving, at last, to Paris, where he took an apartment on the avenue Montaigne.

He decided he was through with Robert Evans. Once again, Evans had done his savior thing with *Chinatown*, bragging to one particular journalist (Polanski read) that he had single-handedly rescued the picture, hiring a new composer at the last minute, and that Polanski, a brilliant tyrant, had been properly managed. That was the last straw for Polanski; their talks of another collaboration ended. "It was the memory of that interview that made me say no," Polanski said. "I'd considered Bob Evans more than a producer; he was a friend."

Polanski agreed to meet Barry Diller in London.

Polanski's new project, *Pirates*, a cheeky but ambitious romp in the spirit of *Vampire Killers*, was tailor-made for Nicholson, who had agreed to a star for the price of one million dollars. The fee stunned Polanski. But he knew the studios, eager for a Nicholson-Polanski reteaming, would pay, and with Diller's interest, decided to move forward at Paramount.

Upon his arrival in Los Angeles, Polanski discerned an unwelcome change in the studio. The people Polanski knew had left. Sylbert was still somewhere upstairs, but a wholly different breed walked the lot. Where Evans would simply write a check at the starting gate, the new regime required Polanski to sign a promissory note for every preproduction dollar Paramount advanced him. It was a kind of blackmail: Now that Paramount had agreed to *Pirates* and Polanski had gone to the trouble to move his production to Los Angeles, he wasn't liable to refuse Paramount their new conditions. Nor was he likely to refuse Nicholson his new asking price, despite their original agreement, which now climbed beyond his cool million to $1.5 million. "The minute they paid that money," Sue Mengers said, "Jack Nicholson said, 'Wait a minute. If Gene Hackman gets that much money, I should get X.' And Warren Beatty says, 'Well, if Nicholson gets that, I should get X.'"

Negotiating at this level would slow down the deal-making process, bringing many worthy projects to an early death and severely decreasing the productivity of Hollywood as a whole. Those films that did survive the deal would, in many cases, suffer the pressures of ballooned budgets, their artistry cautiously curtailed. The 1975 production of *The Missouri Breaks*, which tantalizingly paired Nicholson and Brando, came after such a protracted bout of deal making—Brando would take a million for five weeks' work plus gross points, Nicholson would take $1.25 million plus points—that contracts were not signed until six weeks before the scheduled start date, cramping rewrites, preproduction time, and of course production itself, squeezed into a corner to accommodate the stars. On the first day of photography, Brando still found problems in his contract, and Nicholson still took issue with the script. (Towne was called in.)

Accepting his Academy Award for 1975's *One Flew Over the Cuckoo's Nest*, Nicholson made telling reference to Mary Pickford, who earlier that evening had won an honorary Oscar, and "who, incidentally, I believe, was the first actor to get a percentage of her pictures." Henceforth Jack would want both—up front and back end.

Orson Welles approached Jack to star in *The Big Brass Ring*, to be written and directed by Welles. But Welles couldn't meet Jack's fee, and their talks collapsed. Welles never made the film.

Polanski, however, persisted. Negotiating for Nicholson's participation in *Pirates*, Andy Braunsberg, Polanski's deputy in arms, asked Jack to level with him. Didn't he realize his financial demands would sink the project? Didn't he want to make this happen? Raising his fee, exactly what was it he was after? To Braunsberg, Jack answered, "I want *more*."

The future, Mr. Gittes. The future. . . .

PART FOUR

Gittes vs. Gittes

PART FOUR

Gittes vs. Gittes

1

Anjelica would travel the earth for Jack. She would follow him to a basketball game in Oregon. She hated to fly, she hated basketball, and after the game, which they lost, he turned on the television in a foul mood. It was *The Newlywed Game.*

"Oh, little marriage," he grumbled to the screen. "Little tiny marriage game."

"If you had any balls," she said, "you'd marry me."

"Marry you? Are you kidding?"

Love, like the ground, like the past, can be dug up, put aside, but never removed. Bring in the shovels, the Caterpillar D9s, the analysts, the exorcists, the art—they can all only move the dirt. In piles beside the ditch, it will wait to be moved again.

She was in Jack's trailer on the set of *The Fortune* , Mike Nichols's film "about a time in America when everybody thought everything was possible," Nichols said, "as opposed to now," when the telephone rang. A reporter from *Time*, Jack was told, was researching a cover story on Jack, and had pursued the facts of his parentage. It seemed his sister June was not in fact his sister but his mother. The woman he thought was his mother, Ethel May, was actually his grandmother.

The man who Nicholson believed to be his father, John Joseph Nicholson, husband of Ethel May, father of Lorraine and June, was dead. June and Ethel May were dead. The only call he could make next was to his sister, Lorraine.

Her husband, Shorty Smith, picked up the phone.

"Shorty," Jack is quoted to have said in Patrick McGilligan's biography of Nicholson. "This is the most fucked thing I've ever heard. A guy calls me on the phone, and says that my father is still alive, and that Ethel May wasn't really my mother, that *June* was my mother, and—"

"I'd better give you to Lorraine."

He passed the phone to his wife.

"Yes," Lorraine began. "June is your mother. And as far as this man is concerned, I don't know. June dated him, but she dated a lot of people."

He didn't want to know the details. But the new facts were unavoidable: Ethel May was Lorraine's mother and, suddenly, Nicholson's grandmother. June, Ethel May's daughter, whom Nicholson had always thought was his sister, was, suddenly, Nicholson's mother.

Lorraine would explain to *Vanity Fair*: "My mother [Ethel May]'s intimate friends, her card group, knew June was pregnant. One of them told me that they did that thing where they all put their hands on top of each other and swear to secrecy. When Mud [Ethel May] turned up with Jack, they simply called him a change-of-life baby." When Jack was two months old, June brought him home to New Jersey, got a job, and left. "Mud just grabbed that baby and made him hers," Lorraine would say. When Jack reached his teenage years, Lorraine proposed to Ethel May and June that they tell him the truth. "But they were both so afraid of losing him," she said. "They didn't trust what his reaction would be."

Thirty-seven years of conspiracy, a secret kept from him—but to protect whom?

Nicholson would never find out.

If family itself had been a conspiracy, what, going forward, *wouldn't* be? Could it be love if it was lies? "After Jack found out the truth," observed Julie Payne, "it changed his relationships with women."

On *The Missouri Breaks*, Anjelica found love notes from a girl saying how much she missed Jack, missed their lovemaking.

She left him for Ryan O'Neal. She came back.

Her father wanted Jack for his daughter, infidelities and all: "I think we should marry this man," he told her.

In March 1977 she went to Jack's to pack up some boxes of clothes she was taking to Ryan O'Neal's and noticed, on a banquette in the kitchen, cameras and a denim jacket Polanski had worn to the movies the night before—she and Roman had gone out, just the two of them, to see *Seven Beauties* and have a bite at Nate n' Al's. Jack was in Aspen.

"Is anyone here?" Anjelica called into the house. There was no answer.

She made her way downstairs.

"We'll be right out!" came Roman's voice. A moment later he appeared with a girl, quite tall, Anjelica noted, in platform heels. They had been taking pictures, Polanski explained, and swimming. Hastily, he collected his things from the kitchen, and they all left, Anjelica with her boxes, Polanski with the girl.

The girl's name was Samantha Gailey. She was thirteen.

She had no memory of her biological father, and her mother, a striving actress (dinner theater, car dealership commercial), was so frequently absent that when she finally did realize her dream of moving out of their little town of York, Pennsylvania, for New York City, leaving Samantha at home with her stepfather, Samantha didn't notice much of a change at home.

Mother and daughter reconnected in New York and moved to L.A. in 1975. "Many little girls fantasize about becoming actresses," Samantha Gailey, now Geimer, would write. "In the early years, I didn't—but then again, I think my mother dreamed that dream for me. . . . She tried to get my sister an agent when she was seventeen, and she got me my first modeling job—for those Astroturf daisy doormats—when I was ten." Despite Samantha's ambivalence about show business, her mother kept her auditioning in Los Angeles. The girl had a Tatum O'Neal look.

On February 13 1977, Roman Polanski, a friend of Samantha's sister's boyfriend, appeared at their home in the San Fernando Valley. He was doing a photo shoot for *Vogue Hommes*, he explained, and was interested in taking some test shots with Samantha.

Samantha had heard of him. She knew he was the director of *Chinatown*, a movie she didn't really like, but she surely loved the idea of being in a magazine, of being photographed like Polanski's previous model, the stunning Nastassja Kinski—and Samantha's mother and her mother's latest boyfriend, encouraging her, "knew [Polanski] was powerful and famous and could do things for all us."

On the day of the test shoot, Gailey's mother suggested she should accompany Samantha and Polanski on the test shoot, but Polanski discouraged her—the mother's presence, he explained, might make her daughter self-conscious in front of the camera—her mother conceded, and off they went.

Leaving the house, Polanski would recall, "[Samantha] was a different girl—lively, chattering incessantly." She told him she had a boyfriend with a black belt in karate.

At their shoot, on a hillside near Samantha's house, Polanski, snapping pictures—"Things like, you know, 'Sit this way,' and, you know, 'Put on this shirt and don't smile,' you know,'" she would tell the court; he would remember asking her about a love bite on her neck, which she explained was from her boyfriend ("but it wasn't karate")—before asking Samantha to take her top off, and she did, uncomfortably. That must be the way this works, she told herself. (Polanski remembers asking Samantha to change into a new outfit. She removed her blouse, he recalls, and wasn't wearing a bra. Polanski took pictures throughout.)

In March, Polanski decided he wanted Samantha for the magazine. Receiving the offer, Samantha was of two minds; excited to be in a fashion magazine, but at the same time uncomfortable about what had transpired during the test. Gailey's mother sensed her daughter's discomfort. And yet her mother was eased, apparently, when Samantha's best friend, Terri, agreed to accompany Samantha and Polanski on the photo shoot. But at the last minute, Terri realized she couldn't stay out so late and changed her mind, leaving Samantha and Polanski alone to their work.

This is how she remembered it:

The sun was going down as they left Samantha's house the evening of March 10th, 1977. Polanski, racing against sunset, was in a rush.

To better catch more light, Polanski drove them up to Jacqueline Bisset's house on Mulholland, but when they arrived, he saw the shadows were stretching and the available light was still too dim. "I'm going to call up Jack Nicholson and see if we can go down to his house," Polanski said. At that hour, the light on the southwest side of Mulholland, Jack's side, would still be good.

He made a phone call to Nicholson's house and they got back in the car.

It was then, she remembers, he asked about a boyfriend. "Do you have a boyfriend?" he inquired.

"Yes."

"Have you ever had sex?"

She said yes.

"How many times?"

Once, but she said twice. He was a professional, famous, and she wanted to seem grown-up.

At Nicholson's, Polanski greeted Jack's friend Helena Kallianiotes and helped himself to a bottle of champagne. "Should I open it?"

"I don't care," she said.

They drank and he pointed Samantha the patio where they took pictures, then returned inside, to the living room, where he instructed her to pose with the champagne beside a Tiffany lamp, and take off her top, which she did. He took pictures of her around the house; she drank the champagne; he kept refilling her glass. She got tipsy. Jack was in Aspen.

She changed into a blue dress and posed for more pictures in the kitchen.

"Let's take some photos in the Jacuzzi," he said. He offered for her to call her mother so she wouldn't worry.

On the phone Samantha's mother asked her if she was all right. Samantha assured her mother she was fine.

"Do you want me to come pick you up?"

"No."

Polanski got on the line and explained to Samantha's mother that they were at Jack Nicholson's and that he would be bringing her home "kind of late," Samantha would tell the court, "because it had already gotten dark out." He told her they were taking pictures in the Jacuzzi. ("I thought, 'Why a Jacuzzi?'" her mother would later tell a grand jury. "But I didn't say anything. I just didn't.")

"We went into the bathroom before," Samantha would tell the court, "and he took this little yellow thing. It don't know what it was. It was some kind of container. And he had—he walked in before me. When I walked in he had the container. And he had a pill broken into three parts." She took off her dress.

"Is this a Quaalude?" he asked her.

"Yes," she answered. She had seen Quaaludes before. She'd even taken a piece of one once.

"Oh, do you think I will be able to drive if I take it?" he asked.

"I don't know."

"Well, I guess I will." He swallowed a piece. "Do you want part?"

"No," she said. Then changed her mind. "Okay." She swallowed a piece.

Outside, nearing the Jacuzzi, he asked her to take off her underwear. She did.

Naked, holding a glass of champagne, she stepped into the bubbling water.

Polanski took a few shots of Samantha in the Jacuzzi before giving up—it was too dark, he said—removing his clothes and getting in too.

"Come here," she remembers he said.

"No. No, I got to get out."

"No, come down here."

Lying, she told him she had asthma and that she had to get out.

"Just come down here a second," she remembered him saying.

Later that night, when Anjelica Huston, returning for her things, found them back inside the house, Polanski had performed cunnilingus on Gailey, had sex with her and sodomized her.

Anjelica was back at Jack's the following night. Startled by what seemed like flashlight beams lashing through the garden below, she looked down from a high window and got a clearer look at the fracas—a group of men, Roman among them, approaching the downstairs porch.

"What is it?" she asked, opening the door.

"It's nothing," Roman said. "Just some confusion about last night—these gentlemen"—three or four plainclothes detectives—"want to have a look around, if that's okay."

She held the door for them, and without explanation, they pushed around her and spread through the house.

The police, Polanski scrambled to reassure her, had a warrant, though he didn't say what for. "It's okay," he whispered. "It's not about drugs or anything."

But a detective soon shone his light on a pack of rolling papers left in an ashtray. "You better show me the drugs," he commanded Anjelica. "Otherwise we'll take this place apart."

She led him upstairs. It didn't occur to her to ask what they were doing there, what Roman was, once again, doing there, who the girl from last night was or what had happened between them or if Jack was in any way involved. Anjelica was too scared to do anything but cooperate. She took them to the grass she kept in a drawer in a bedroom and turned over her handbag for their inspection. They found in it a gram of cocaine.

She rushed downstairs. "They've got it," she whispered to Polanski.

"What?"

She didn't have time to explain. Neither, for that matter, did he. Both were placed under arrest, read their Miranda rights and led to separate police vehicles.

Hours later, on a bench in the West L.A. Precinct on Purdue Avenue, Anjelica lifted her head as Polanski, escorted, was walked passed her.

"I'm sorry for this, Anjelica," he said.

Polanski was indicted on six counts: unlawful sexual intercourse; furnishing a controlled substance to a minor; raping a child he had allegedly drugged; committing a "lewd and lascivious act upon and with the body and certain parts and members thereof [of] a 13-year-old girl"; perversion; and sodomy. A plea bargain was reached: Polanski pled guilty to a single count of statutory rape. Acting on behalf of the victim, the prosecution held that a single-felony plea and a conviction would protect her from having to go to trial and testify in court. This Samantha did not want. She did not want further publicity. She wanted it over.

Polanski and his team complied. In their classified report on the case, the prosecution cited: "The fact that the family believes that Roman Raymond Polanski's admission of guilt is a satisfactory solution and [other] points indicated that the offered plea constitutes a fair resolution of the case of *The People v. Polanski* and gives appropriate public protection." An understanding was reached. "We all understood that avoiding a trial meant Polanski would get off with a minor punishment for his major crime but we were clear where our priorities were," Samantha Geimer would write. Because the crime was unlawful sexual intercourse, she and her family knew there would be probation, but no jail time. All parties agreed.

The deal as presented to the court on August 6, 1977, called for court-appointed psychiatrists to examine Polanski to determine if he was a mentally disturbed sex offender but did "not in any way involve a sentence commitment."

The following day, two days before the eighth anniversary of Sharon Tate's murder, Polanski knelt at her grave at Holy Cross Cemetery to place flowers beside her name when man leaped out from behind the bushes, snapping pictures of Polanski in grief. "Fucking Nazi!" he screamed to the bushes. "Fucking Nazis! Fuck off! All of you!"

A day later Polanski, in court, formally made his plea: "I had sexual intercourse with a female person not my wife, under the age of eighteen."

In September, Judge Laurence J. Rittenband ordered Polanski to undergo further evaluation at the California Institute for Men at Chino; it would be a ninety-day diagnostic study. In addition Rittenband granted Polanski's request to delay his Chino probation for three months so that he could complete preproduction work in Polynesia for his next film, *The Hurricane*. Once again, all parties agreed, and Polanski left town.

On his way to the Hillcrest Country Club for the annual Columbus Day Ball, Judge Rittenband glimpsed a photograph of Polanski printed in the *Santa Monica Evening Outlook*—a shot of the director clearly not engaged in preproduction work, but seemingly enjoying himself, in Munich in fact, not Polynesia, puffing on a cigar in the company of a young-looking girl. They were at Oktoberfest. Rittenband was humiliated. Publicly criticized for going soft on Polanski, the judge ordered him to return to Santa Monica immediately for a hearing on the exact nature of his preproduction practice and set his Chino evaluation date for December 19.

As ordered, Polanski returned to Los Angeles.

Jack Nicholson presided over a farewell dinner for Polanski the night before he was to begin his sentence at Chino. Nicholson, by now cleared of any involvement in the scandal, would remain unfailingly committed to Polanski without arguing for his innocence. Nicholson's loyalty to Polanski was briefly complicated by Anjelica's interests; it was said in the press that she was prepared to testify, "against" Polanski—of, in effect, offering damning evidence to buy her way clear of charges of cocaine possession, which had been dropped. Ever the peacekeeper, Jack would clear the air: "She's been very wronged," he said. "The district attorney sent Anjelica a letter saying they'd been unethical, because in reality, Anjelica could not say anything because she didn't know that much about it."

As ordered, Polanski submitted to Chino. His ninety days, reduced to half, ended on January 29, 1978; the following day Judge Rittenband convened the lawyers, prosecution and defense, in his chambers.

"Forty-two days is not enough time in custody," Rittenband announced.

"If it's forty-eight more days you want," prosecuting attorney Roger Gunson replied, "why don't you just give him forty-eight days in the county jail? Then you will have accomplished him serving the full ninety days in jail."

Rittenband explained his concerns quite clearly and without shame: He was getting too much negative press to let Polanski off so easily, Rittenband said. But he had a plan, a way of saving face, and for it to work, it required the collusion of all involved. "I want people to think I'm a tough sentencer," Samantha Gailey's lawyer, Larry Silver, remembered Rittenband explaining. "So we'll do this, and then when the attention is off the case, you"—meaning Douglas Dalton, Polanski's lawyer—"petition for a change of sentence and I will sentence him to time served." In the meeting Rittenband proposed that he would, for the benefit of the press, send Polanski back to Chino and then on to jail for an indeterminate period, but once the sentence had been actuated, he would recall Polanski and covertly release him from prison. It was a ruse, a public relations ploy. "He was flatly admitting," recalled Silver, "[that] he was weighing public opinion and press opinion in his sentencing decision." Following Polanski's release, Dalton was then instructed to argue for probation, Rittenband said, and Gunson, true to his role as prosecuting attorney, was to argue for more time in custody. Then the Judge would rule as discussed. That was the plan.

Leaving Rittenband's chambers that afternoon, Dalton and Gunson reviewed what they had just heard. Comparing notes, sharing their shock at the unabashed corruptibility of the judge, they drew together, no longer a prosecuting lawyer and the defense, but allied witnesses to "a sham," as Gunson later described it. In solidarity, Gunson vowed to Dalton that he would be "available to disclose this information to anyone at any place at anytime." But Dalton, considering his next move, was utterly paralyzed: He had to advise Polanski the very next morning. If he were to trust Rittenband, Polanski would, theoretically, be released in time, but at an unspecified date subject to the judge's (obviously highly variable) whim. But were Dalton to resist Rittenband, who had clearly stated his intention to make an example of Polanski ("He gave as his reason that he was getting too much criticism," Dalton said), it could lead to a far worse sentence. How bad, there was no telling. Dalton said, "I didn't know what I was going to do the following day."

As little as possible . . .

The next day, January 31, a riot of freak thunderstorms dumped rain on Los Angeles.

Dalton told Polanski everything: "It was my opinion that the sentence would be illegal," he would explain, "that we could probably obtain relief on appeal but that would involve a long procedure and Polanski would be incarcerated during that period of time. I said that the judge had said that if Roman agreed to waive any deportation hearing and be deported that he would then be released if he also had by then served forty-eight days."

"Can we trust him?" Polanski asked Dalton.

"No. We can't trust him. We have no idea what he may do. We've all agreed that he can no longer be trusted and what he represents to us is worthless."

"*Shove off*," his father whispered.

Polanski stood. "I'll see you guys later."

He walked out into the rain, and the next day he boarded a plane for London. He would never return to America.

Writing had never come easily to Robert Towne, but the hat trick of *The Last Detail*, *Chinatown*, and *Shampoo* would be a difficult run for any writer to best. Instead he rewrote crucial scenes of *Marathon Man* (Evans gifted him a BMW 3.0CS) and bits and pieces of miscellaneous others (adding, per John Frankenheimer's request, a line to *Black Sunday*), and in his credited work careened from false starts and stops to voluminous and thwarted outlines and exploratory outpourings of *Greystoke*, his cherished Tarzan story, swelling it to hundreds of pages, and, throughout, producing thickets of notes for the *Chinatown* sequel, originally called *The Iron Jew*, then renamed *The Two Jakes*. In 1975 his professional status and friendly association with John Calley earned him a special consultant position at Warner Bros. It didn't require writing, but reading and talking.

Towne and Payne moved into a house out on Malibu Road. For property-tax reasons, they decided to marry in November

1977—incognito. "I was extremely private," Payne explained. Towne's lawyer, Wally Wolf, and his wife, Carolyn, held a short secret ceremony at their house in the Pacific Palisades.

Payne got pregnant. It was a girl.

"Robert," she said, "you're the writer, the giver of names. What should we name her?"

"A classic name. Katherine. Katherine with a *K*. It's stronger."

"No *e*—*a*. Katharine."

Katharine Payne Towne was born on July 17, 1978. Anthea Sylbert, who had let her childbearing window close, was made child's Godmother.

Costume designing *F.I.S.T.*, a picture about the labor movement, a subject close to Anthea Sylbert's heart, she recognized, as Dick Sylbert had, an unwelcome change in the culture of Hollywood filmmaking. On set, she watched Sylvester Stallone, in the middle of a big strike scene, "walking out with this jacket thrown over his shoulder like he's walking on the Via Veneto." Annoyed, she approached director Norman Jewison.

"Norman, you have to tell him he can't do that. He has to put it on or not wear it at all."

He said, "I don't want you to interfere with my actors."

"Then tell somebody to get me a ticket out of here," she told Jewison.

It was time, she decided. "I didn't want to be a designer anymore if this was how it was going to be," Sylbert decided. Under Calley she began a new career as a Warner Bros. vice president. She would never design another film.

Perhaps two years after Katharine's birth, Payne was reminded of *Chinatown*, that the name of Evelyn's daughter, born of incest, was Katharine, not with an *a* maybe, but a Katharine nonetheless. She was disgusted.

"What is *wrong* with you?" she shouted at Towne. He had picked the name.

"Roman did that!"

"Roman didn't do that. *Robert* did that!"

In October 1978, the year Katharine was born, Towne coolly announced to Payne he was going to start using cocaine. "It was deliberate," she said. "He was going to write. He was going to do it like Freud, and he was going to do it on cocaine." If he controlled the amount he took, he assured her, it wouldn't control him. To level out, he drank vodka.

He disappeared emotionally.

"That was it," Payne said. "That was the end of Robert as I knew him."

It was the year Betty Ford revealed her dependency on alcohol and painkillers, prompting an inundation of similar announcements from public and private figures—Barry Diller would found a twelve-step program at Paramount—demonstrations of the malaise, long submerged, that had been growing under the American ground, some said, for a decade.

Something—a faith—had been lost. Christopher Lasch, in his 1979 *The Culture of Narcissism: American Life in an Age of Diminishing Expectations*, observed: "Since the society has no future, it makes sense to live only for the moment . . . to become connoisseurs of our own decadence, to cultivate 'transcendental self-attention,'" to become, in short, narcissists, who, bereft of faith, live by a survivalist mentality, "expressed in its crudest form in disaster movies," seeking escape in fame, sex, power, drugs—any delusion to resist the growing awareness of failure and futility. Drugs; addictions to wealth, celebrity, quick pleasure, and omnipotence—harbingers of Reagan America and eighties Hollywood, were the narcissists' response to emotional abandonment on the national scale—and, as the ordeal of Evelyn Mulwray attests, took their toll on yet another institutional faith: The family. The children.

By 1979 Towne had so transformed, Payne remembered, Katharine didn't recognize him. Once, she mistook Edward Taylor for her father.

Meanwhile, as ever, people came to Hollywood seeking glory. If acting was a billion-to-one shot and directing required specialized access to film equipment, screenwriting was most of America's best way in. All you needed was paper, pen, and a copy of Syd Field's bestselling 1979 *Screenplay*, a book that ably separated the art of screenwriting from the very teachable craft. In his classic, Field presented the dos and don'ts of traditional story structure with arresting simplicity, and if, in the wake of his insights, Hollywood screenwriters, in greater numbers than ever before, willfully eschewed the innovative for the formulaic, they weren't entirely to blame; writers had to sell, and Field, unintentionally, had written a buying manual for nervous executives looking to cover their asses.

Field wrote that Robert Towne's *Chinatown* was the "best American screenplay written during the 1970s." He successfully argued that the script was a work of exemplary craftsmanship, systematically checking the boxes beside his paradigmatic talking points; though why—when any number of great screenplays of the seventies check as many boxes—Field deemed *Chinatown* the single best he never fully clarified. "What makes it so good," he wrote, unsatisfactorily, "is that it works on *all* levels—story, structure, characterization, visuals—yet everything we need to know is set up within the first ten pages."

Field's preference for the script caught on. His acolytes, growing in number with each reprint, with each new film school, spread the good word, and Field's assertion of the *Chinatown* script's primacy—much like those about *Citizen Kane* or Hollywood's "best" year, 1939—became so widely accepted it was (and still is) practically taken for fact. The guru of screenwriting had deemed it so.

Money, formerly peripheral to Towne, became central. He began complaining that his agent, Evarts Ziegler, who had once loaned him MONEY TK to support him through the writing of *Chinatown*, was unable to secure him a million-dollar payday for *Greystoke*. In December 1978 Towne fired Ziegler and signed with Michael Ovitz of CAA.

Payne and Towne separated.

He moved into a hotel in Westwood. She started drinking herself to sleep.

She would check herself into the CDC at St. John's Hospital for alcohol dependence. When she gave her name to Roxie at the front desk, she asked Payne if she was related to Lou Towne.

"Yes," Payne said.

"He was the worst patient we ever had."

Edward Taylor's stepdaughter Katherine Andrusco drove Kate to the CDC every afternoon to have Jell-O with her mother in the cafeteria. "Robert," Andrusco wrote, "was completely unsupportive of any effort to have Skip visit and refused to take her to the hospital himself." He had become, since working on *Personal Best*, "unspeakably cruel and mean-hearted," Andrusco wrote, telling his daughter, the day Julie was released from the hospital, that her mother was crazy and drunk. In front of Kate, he called her—the child—a cunt.

"Don't call her that!" Andrusco shouted. "What are you saying, Robert!"

"She has to get used to it, you know, because she'll hear it."

After Payne was discharged, at a July 4 celebration in Malibu, Kate, playing in the water, was knocked over by a gentle wave, "at which point," recalled a family friend, "Bob Towne scooped her up in a blanket, charged into the house, and in front of about fifty people berated Julie, calling her unfit to be a mother, etc. His behavior was extremely erratic and bizarre, ranting and raving from subject to subject, none of which was in any way related."

In January 1983, Payne served Towne divorce papers. In June

custody proceedings began. Dr. Rocco Motto was appointed as the psychiatrist tasked with recommending custody arrangements.

Towne's long-term cocaine abuse, Payne alleged, rendered him unfit for custody of any kind. In court documents, Towne called her allegations "slanderous. If allowed to continue they will impair not only my employment but my ability to negotiate successfully with the producers and/or studios for whom I write scripts."

"Mommy says you take cocaine," Kate said to Towne one night.

"This remark greatly disturbed me," he would report in his Declaration of August 2, 1983, "not only because it came from my five year old daughter, but also because it can adversely affect my professional reputation."

Payne implored Motto to interview any number of witnesses who could testify to Towne's alleged drug abuse, but Motto, Payne would say, "flagrantly ignored them," one after the next. "Warren Beatty called me several weeks ago regarding Julie, Skip and Robert," wrote psychologist Barbara Phillips Wright to Motto, "In fact, he telephoned four or five times in one day. His concern is for Skip. At that time he said, 'Well, Julie is sober and Robert is not.' I could not agree more." Towne, in sworn statement, claimed this an outright lie.

"He was gaslighting me," Payne would say later.

"In the 7 sessions with Robert," Motto observed in his evaluation, "he admitted to his periodic use of cocaine, but he denied that he was or had ever used it excessively. He offered as proof or as a refutation, a number of individuals who have known his work over a 5-10 year period or longer. When I interviewed all of them, I was consistently told, 'Robert is producing more work and of a higher quality than before. We see no evidence of a fall off in quantity or quality.' All his comments re his daughter revealed an intense concern and wish to be in contact and involved in her growth and development."

In Motto's report, Payne was described as "non-attentive" mother as well as "over-solicitous," "harsh and bitter." It cited her period of "very bad" alcohol abuse. Towne, by contrast, was characterized as a "very loving and very gentle" father, "very tolerant and very, very patient with [Kate]," and "extremely devoted." Glancing at Motto's letterhead, Payne noticed Motto's address—440 South Bristol Drive—he was her father-and mother-in-law Lou and Helen Towne's next-door neighbor in Brentwood. "They were covering for an abusive drug addict," she said. "And they were going to make sure to take my daughter away from me."

Edward Taylor was deposed:

"What is your present occupation?"

"I'm a writer, an editor, and I do some producing-type work," he replied.

"By whom are you employed at the present time?"

"Robert Towne."

"And how many hours a day or week do you work for him?"

"It varies on the nature of the project, but usually it's full time."

"And what is your salary with him?"

"It is set at the moment at $1200 a week."

Taylor was asked, "Did you tell Dr. Motto that Robert used coke regularly?"

"I did not say he used coke regularly," he replied.

David Geffen, producer of Towne's *Personal Best*, was deposed.

"Going back to the period of time when [*Personal Best*] was shut down, which was somewhere around February of '81, I believe, did you know a man by the name of Peter Peyton at or about that time."

"Yes," Geffen replied, "he was a close friend of Robert's and was the associate producer, I believe, on the movie."

"Did you know him to be a supplier of coke?"

"I was told that he was a supplier. I didn't know it from personal experience."

"Did you ever discuss Peter Peyton with Robert Towne?"

Towne, Geffen reported, denied any involvement with cocaine.

Katherine Andrusco, Taylor's stepdaughter and an employee of the Townes, was deposed.

"Did you know about an account at City National Bank here in Westwood?"

"Yes. There were several accounts there."

"Okay. You're right. Sorry about that. I'm talking about one account with Robert [Towne], Peter [Peyton] and Edward [Taylor] only on it."

"Yes."

"And do you know what that account was used for?"

"It was used for paying monies out that Robert didn't want Julie to know about."

Patti Dennis, assistant to the Townes financial manager, was deposed.

"Did you talk with [Towne] about the fact that there was a lot of cash going out?"

"Yes, I did."

"And that therefore—"

"And that I suspected that the cash was going for drugs."

"You told that to Robert?"

"Uh-huh."

In her deposition, Andrusco would clarify: "Peter [Peyton] came to me in April or March of '82, to tell me there was money that I didn't know about from 1981. And I would have to know about this income for tax purposes. And I said, 'How much money?' And he said, 'Oh, around $90,000.' And I said, 'Well, I want to know where the money came from and where the money went. I need a full accounting in order for the taxes to be done.' He eventually after several months provided me with an accounting only of between 20 or $30,000 worth of this $90,000. There was a $62,000 check that was a *Chinatown* residual. There was a $6,000 and something check that was a *Shampoo* residual. . . . There was a $12,000 to [Towne's allergist], which was a personal loan. . . . And I said, 'Well, I need to have an accounting of all the money, Peter, because it's a lot of money and you have to—if it's a business expense then you have to show that to the government.' And he said, 'Well, the money went to drug dealers because we're writing this *Tequila Sunrise* [a film about a drug dealer].' So that was the only explanation I got."

Towne's allergist, whose personal loan, eventually forgiven by Towne, would reach $17,000, would swear in his statement: "I have been [Towne's] personal physician and allergist for many years. In examining his nasal mucous membranes I can tell you he is not addicted to cocaine. He does snort chromalin [sic] sodium, but that is not cocaine."

A contemporary source remembers a story meeting with Towne, where he openly snorted from a supply of Merck medicinal cocaine he kept by his typewriter.

Psychologist Barbara Phillips Wright would remember a one-hour session wherein Towne went to the bathroom six times, each time returning more agitated than before.

In later notes left by a subsequent evaluator, Towne would admit to taking anywhere from an average of a quarter of a gram to half a gram of cocaine at his greatest period of use, which he estimated to between 1980 and '81 when his daugther was two and three years old.

Towne would be awarded joint custody of Kate.

"Dr. Motto," Payne pleaded after the decision. "Are you listening to Lou Towne?"

Motto was silent.

Dr. Wright would come to believe there had been collusion against Payne. "She has no power," Wright said,

It was Lou Towne, Payne felt. Allied with Motto, his next-door neighbor, she sensed he was letting a "drug addict parent his own granddaughter," Payne said. "Just to keep Robert looking employable. It was all for money and reputation and I couldn't stop it. I couldn't help my daughter. It was like the ending to *Chinatown*".

2

In the summer of 1984, Robert Towne, Robert Evans, and Jack Nicholson gathered at the mahogany table in the projection room at Woodland to discuss the terms of their next association, TEN Productions—named for the initials of its participants. Roman Polanski was unavailable, of course.

By that meeting, each of the TEN trio had stalled. They needed *The Two Jakes*, each in his own way.

Robert Evans was at an all-time career low. Plagued by the persistent stigma of a 1980 conviction for cocaine possession and a run of unsuccessful pictures (*Players, Popeye*), he was roundly considered a liability, a loser at the box office and to the new generation of baby moguls an *alte kocker* before his time. He fell still further with *The Cotton Club*, whose production, a Chinatown of its own, was beset by bad money, coke dealers, and a murder—investor Roy Radin, found dead, shot through the head, sixty-five miles north of Los Angeles. Unable to make *Cotton Club* payroll and, without a studio, on the hook for the picture, Evans was advised to declare bankruptcy. His chance at the *Two Jakes* was a godsend.

Robert Towne was determined to direct *The Two Jakes*. It would be his resurrection too. In the ten years since *Chinatown*, he had acquired no distinguished credits.

And *The Two Jakes* would be Nicholson's artistic resurrection as an actor. After his 1975 Oscar win for *One Flew Over the Cuckoo's Nest*, his productivity had declined and the films he chose were largely those that offered him opportunities for flamboyant self-parody (*The Shining*) and amenable fluff (*The Witches of Eastwick*). Gone was the impotent outrage he showed in the six years between *Easy Rider* and *Cuckoo's Nest*, when at the peak of his artistry and productivity, Nicholson had made an astonishing fourteen films, most of them astonishing in their own right.

The Two Jakes, then, would attempt to turn back the clocks for all, not just by revisiting old story turf, continuing the saga of Jake Gittes, but by returning to a purer ethic of Hollywood film production, more seventies than eighties.

"Let's not have any agents or lawyers in the room," Evans requested in advance—they killed the romance. "By the time you start a film, you're tired out." At Woodland, glamour restored, "we all put our hands together," Nicholson said, "and swore no agents or lawyers were going to screw us up." All were in agreement that TEN Productions, to ensure its independence, would take no money up front, split a percentage of the gross, and share creative control. Waiving his actor's salary, the old Nicholson reemerged.

Chinatown was set in 1937. Towne was setting *The Two Jakes* eleven years later—it had been eleven years since they shot *Chinatown*—in 1948, after World War II. Towne said: "[Gittes] came back much more relaxed, having felt we actually had done something to make the world a safer place to live." But the crimes of land and oil, the corruption Gittes encounters in *The Two Jakes* would unbury the old wounds, Cross and Mulwray, and what happened to him, twice, in Chinatown. It would happen again.

Around that mahogany table in the projection room, Towne revealed that he had modeled the second Jake in his script, Jake Berman, a developer, a salesman, a most romantic Jew, on Robert Evans. Towne wanted Evans to play the part. And Nicholson, savoring the thought of playing opposite one of his best friends, fully endorsed the idea. As Berman, Evans would be playing himself.

"Both of ya," Evans laughed, "go fuck yourself!"

"Trust the Irishman, Kid," Nicholson said.

Evans, as amused by the notion as he was fearful, gamely consented. But he hadn't acted in a movie in thirty years. Nor had he ever been any good.

Evans had offered to host Towne's wedding to Luisa Selvaggio. Finish writing *The Two Jakes*, Evans negotiated—the script was late, naturally—and I'll throw her the wedding of her dreams, two hundred guests and three hundred of Woodland roses under the old sycamore, and bottomless crates of imported champagne. Deal.

But on the day of the wedding, October 17, 1984, Towne delivered a script Evans felt was only 80 percent complete.

It was the drugs; he was in chaos. One assistant, it was reported, left Towne and went immediately into therapy. Another stayed and got high with him. Towne and this assistant, one aide said, "spent long periods in the bathroom together. I thought they were doing it to get away from the phones." The call he was trying to get away from was Nicholson's. He wanted the script. When Jack finally got a copy, it disappointed. What had happened to Gittes? In *Chinatown* Gittes was cool. In *Two Jakes* he was flummoxed—by not just one but two women. "The changes reflected the change in Towne himself," an associate theorized. "When he wrote *Chinatown* he was a stable guy. By the time he wrote *The Two Jakes*, he was caught in a war with his ex-wife"—avoiding a settlement hearing—"while he was falling over backward to accommodate his volatile new wife." Jack kept calling.

The script was still in a state of flux as production drew near, as a cast—Kelly McGillis, Cathy Moriarty, Dennis Hopper, Joe Pesci, and director Budd Boetticher (an echo of director John Huston) as the oil tycoon—was assembled, as Dick Sylbert built Gittes's office at the Laird Studios in Culver City, as locations were scouted up the coast to Ventura County, as Towne, between revisions, coached Evans, every night, through his actor's anxiety. The script was still in a state of flux as Towne began to shoot hair and makeup tests.

On the day of his tests, Evans stayed locked in his trailer for hours, worrying, apparently, about his hair. There was concern that the wrong haircut would expose, some speculated, Evans's thinning hairline. Or was it just nerves, Faye Dunaway all over again? "When [Evans] did show," one crewmember said, "he was tense and nervous and stiff." By the time Towne finally massaged Evans to a place in front of the cameras, the issue of the hair had been superseded. On camera, Evans's plastic surgery was showing. Wrapping the tests, Towne had his doubts—about casting Evans, about the whole thing.

As the first day of photography approached—at the Bel Air Bay Club—the crew looked on as Towne and finally Evans lost their control. Producer Harold Schneider believed that Towne, his brains fried on coke, knew he wasn't up to directing—"He was in a fetal position under the couch," Schneider said, "screaming, 'I can't go on. They're out there, and they're gonna kill me.'" Evans went around approaching—by some accounts, begging—people on set to tell Towne to give him another chance, pleading that the humiliation of getting fired, on the heels of the *Cotton Club* fiasco, would destroy his chances of ever working in Hollywood again, not to mention Towne's. "There was terror and fear," one observed, "on the part of both of them."

Towne decided it had to end. "Bob," he told Evans at Woodland, "you should drop out of the cast. I haven't had enough time to rehearse you."

"Robert," he said, "the picture starts in four days. Are you crazy? Forget Evans the actor. Evans the producer won't accept it."

But Towne had made up his mind.

"What about Nicholson?" Evans asked. "Did you tell him?"

"I just left him."

"What did he say?"

He looked down. "It's okay with him."

Unbelieving, Evans took off for Jack's. Nicholson, beset with hemorrhoids, opened the door.

"Why ya backin' out?" Jack asked.

"Backin' out? Towne tells me he doesn't want me in it and that you said fine."

"You're making my head hurt as much as my ass!"

Nicholson got on the phone with Towne and told him, point-blank, no Evans, no Jack. No Jack, no movie. "Loyalty," Evans would say of Nicholson. "That he's given to me like no one else."

But Towne wasn't about to let a long friendship kill his movie. Thirty-six hours before filming was set to begin, an emergency meeting was called at Woodland. Towne and Nicholson, who was too pained to sit, lie, or stand, fought openly and bitterly over Evans's role in *The Two Jakes* until the phone rang with a call for Ned Tanen, a Paramount executive attending the meeting. The news was horrendous: His ex-wife had committed suicide, and his children found her. Tanen, trembling, fled Woodland, and it was suggested that they reconvene the next day, but Towne, raging, would not cease. "Listen, Beener"—A Nicholson nickname for Towne—"With Evans, I take nothin'. Without him, I want my six mil against fifteen percent of the gross. Is that clear?" Nicholson then reached for a piece of paper and a Magic Marker, wrote a big red 2 on the blank page followed by the world "million" and slipped the paper to Towne. "From me to you," he said, "for your cockamamie script," but he also insisted that Evans stayed. Towne—not willing to cede control, as he had on *Chinatown*—rejected the offer.

The Two Jakes was off.

TEN was flooded with numberless lawsuits for nonpayment. Nicholson left town for New York, where he was already meeting on another (Nicholson fluff) project, *Heartburn*, for Mike Nichols. Sets—worth four million dollars, according to Dick Sylbert, five months of "impeccable" work—were struck. Soundstages at Laird Studios were bulldozed—there were no funds to have them assiduously disassembled and removed—to accommodate its next production,

SpaceCamp. And Kelly McGillis moved on to *Top Gun*, Don Simpson's next production for Paramount.

In January 1985 Evans called Julie Payne.

"I know the fix you're in," he said.

Payne, running out of money—"I could hardly afford to eat," she said—footing the bills for her daughter's countless therapists and her own lawyers and doctors, was quickly losing the means to get Towne back into court, a court, she believed, that was enchanted by Towne's celebrity. "I was so scared," she said.

On the phone, Evans told Payne he could have Towne put in jail for not making his court-mandated payments. He had "people" in the D.A.'s office, he assured her.

She could hear men's voices murmuring in the background.

Payne declined Evans's "generous offer," knowing that when Towne was released, he would tell Katharine it was her mother who sent him away.

Evans had a message, Payne recalled, he asked her to give to Towne's lawyer: "The money men wanted [*The Two Jakes*]," she said, "and they would hurt him if he didn't sell."

Fearing for her daughter's safety, she called the court psychiatrist, Dr. Gary Chase, "who didn't care." Chase—who would serve as court psychiatrist in a trial that awarded custody to Dr. Khalid Parwez, later tried and acquitted for the killing and dismemberment of his eleven-year-old son, and who would be put on probation in 1993 for gross negligence and sexual violations with a patient and named as defendant in a 2014 wrongful death suit—was still waiting for his visit to the set of *Two Jakes*.

In 1986 Paramount had a dream year, an eighties dream. *Top Gun* was the year's number-one movie. *Crocodile Dundee* was third. *Star*

Trek IV was fourth. That year Paramount's entire marketing team, formerly housed away from production executives in New York, was relocated to Los Angeles, a more than symbolic reconfiguration. "I've never separated production, distribution and marketing . . . ," Chairman and COO Frank Mancuso said. "For me it's one continuous process designed to get your film before as large a public as possible." Stanley Jaffe, a former Evans-era executive at Paramount, felt it was a mistake: "The head of distribution shouldn't be reading scripts and telling people to make movies. . . . I don't get that, truthfully. I just don't get it. I will never get it."

John Huston died in August 1987. At the funeral, a private gathering of twenty at Hollywood Memorial Park, a sprawling sixty acres of Los Angeles abutting Paramount, Maricela Hernándes, John Huston's last romance, watched as Nicholson, holding on to Anjelica, "wept and wept and wept like a little boy."

Polanski took pains not to reason with his unconscious; he staunchly refused to study his dreams, but he dreamed. He dreamed regularly of flying over the English Channel in an old man-powered airplane, pedaling, hard against gravity, to keep the machine aloft. It is either dawn or dusk and he is trapped in the cockpit and the plane is falling and he pedals harder, pedaling for his life, knowing that if he slows down, even a bit, he will crash into the sea. He falls, and when he wakes, his legs ache.

It never goes away. It only hides.

In 1987 Towne flew to Paris to help Polanski with the script of *Frantic*, a film about a man whose wife vanishes.

Polanski dreamed once of a strange cinema somewhere, a precarious structure on pillars, like a house perched off the Hollywood Hills. Someone was telling him it was the largest cinema in Warsaw, and beside it was a building in ruins, missing its front half, seemingly blown apart by war. Moving into the ruins, he dreamed its watery wallpaper, blue with swimming silver fish, or silverfish, took him to Beverly Hills, and from the building's second story, walled all in gray, he could look out on the endangered cinema next door.

"No one at Paramount wants to do business with you," head of business affairs, Richard Zimbert, told Evans. It was his commercial failures, the lingering stench of the *Cotton Club* murder, and, some whispered, his playboy reputation, formerly an asset, now adverse to the new family image of Mancuso's Paramount.

"Been expecting it," Evans conceded. "When it's over, it's over."

Drive across America, Nicholson said.

"Our country is becoming corrupted little by little by conglomeration and conglomerative thinking," he said in 1986. "And, baby, you or I ain't going to change it."

Drive down to Kansas City, he said, and question all those elevated light boxes along the highway, the signs for Radio Shack, Chicken-Bicken, Roller Skate World, sky stains of the fast-food epidemic, "blockbuster city," Jack called it, the future.

"When I started," he said, "if a movie made 8 or 10 million dollars it was considered an enormous success. Today, that sort of money doesn't mean much."

Nicholson turned fifty in 1987. Filthy rich, as popular as ever, approaching legendary status, and a king of California enthroned on dreams come true, he had no need for nostalgia, and yet: "I was always attracted to older people [who] were already [in Hollywood], like Sam Spiegel and Billy Wilder. I just got there in time to know them and have a chat or two with them. And they talked about class a lot. This was an important thing to them and you don't hear it so much anymore."

"The world," Nicholson predicted, "is going to miss the movie-going experience."

There was still a pull, John Huston's voice cannoning through his memory: "The one thing you must not do," it said, "is lose interest."

And then his own voice: "Dream on, dream on. I can't do nothing about it."

Back and forth. Round and round. "A few years from now," he said, "if you can still portray a human being, you'll be quite a valuable commodity. I intend to be there. It's where my hopes as a director lie."

Back and forth. "I still make the movies I want to make. I'm just talking about—where's the soil for them? Where's the informed intelligence?" He had signed to play the Joker in *Batman*, "the Trump Tower of movies," per producer Julia Phillips, but he still lived in the same house on Mulholland with the same view of L.A.; he still had the same friends, the same allegiance to Evans, Bob Rafelson, Mike Nichols, and others. They all had new movies for Jack.

But Robert Evans was in the dumps.

Bob Rafelson had directed two features in the last ten years.

Mike Nichols had gone to fluff.

He had to do something. But to think about making art in what had become of Hollywood was contemplating a Chinatown "so huge," he said, "that you begin to dysfunction. But I have to whip up a foam in my spirit, or I'll stop seeing where it's at, too." To believe in the viability of the dream, a little bit of forgetting was required. Maybe that's what a dream was.

He would strike out against all those elevated light boxes along the highway and take another shot at *The Two Jakes*. After *Jakes*, there was still *Gittes vs. Gittes*, part three of three, set in 1959, when no-fault divorce becomes California law and Gittes—"a detective,"

Towne explained, "who's spent his whole life in matrimonial cases getting sued by his wife"—loses almost all of his business. *Gittes vs. Gittes* was only just a dream—a few notes, a paragraph synopsis in Towne's drawer—but, since Towne's divorce and custody entanglements, it was gurgling hotter underground, lava on a low flame. The trilogy, once completed, would be the most ambitious work of their lives. For Nicholson, who had achieved everything else, it was a last paradise.

In September 1988, before heading off to shoot *Batman*, Nicholson drove, once again, through the old gates of Paramount and reintroduced the subject of *The Two Jakes* to Frank Mancuso. Nicholson had rescued *Heartburn* at the last minute, and it was Mancuso's chance to return the favor. This time, though, they would do *Jakes* the old-fashioned way, the secure and plentiful way, the way they did *Chinatown*—with Paramount's support. Towne would finally sell his script to the studio—grandiose spending had drained his cash flow—and with it the right to control the project; Nicholson would take his usual actor's fee but direct the picture himself—for scale—a necessary concession to bring *The Two Jakes* home to Paramount. Robert Evans would produce.

The script was still unfinished; wisely Nicholson refused to sign his contract until he had a completed draft in his hands. It came in to Nicholson, in London for *Batman*, toward the end of 1988, a jumble of ideas, good, bad, confusing, poetic.

Returning to Los Angeles in January 1989, Jack began to work with Towne on the revisions. As ever, it was a question of simplifying Towne's ideas. But whereas Polanski was an ace editor, fearlessly logical and determined to wrestle Towne to simplicity, Jack, a weaver in his own right, was a maximalist and struggled to rein him in.

With an April start date set, Towne, with Edward Taylor at hand, kept revising. Jack split his duties between giving Towne notes and prepping the picture, which Nicholson loaded with as many friends and old colleagues as he could collect. Nicholson's emotional presence, meanwhile, was suddenly required by Evans; he was desperately low on money, shattered, isolated, and full of nightmares, the paranoid conviction that Woodland itself was going to turn against him and see to it that he died there.

In February, Evans sold Woodland. He sold it, he felt, for half of what it was worth, the house and everything in it. He would rent it from its new owner, as long as he could, until the money ran out. That was it.

This was, Nicholson could see, a living suicide. To salvage what he could of Evans's life and mind, he paired him with Harvey Keitel, cast as the second "Jake," Jake Berman, and asked Evans to coach Keitel, to imbue him with whatever he could of his manner and mystique. Nicholson compassionately absolved Evans of any further producer's responsibilities, though *The Two Jakes* would still bear his name, and to keep Evans's head above the grave, told him to look forward to *Jakes* dailies every night at Woodland. "Strange," Evans said, "here's a guy directing and starring, knowing that showing the dailies at my home would cost him a much needed two hours' sleep. But it mattered little. He knew by doing that it gave me a much needed legitimacy."

Still recovering from *Batman*—he hadn't done back-to-back pictures since *The Passenger* and *Chinatown* fifteen years earlier— Nicholson allowed for two weeks of private rehearsals, as much as he could, to fill in character backstories, "deep roots," Nicholson called them, like telling his secretary, played by Rebecca Broussard, that her fiancé had been lost in the war, and bringing actors up to his house on Mulholland, to talk them about what Los Angeles used to look like: "When I came here, you used to see these mountains all along the way [down Sunset]. See how it goes? If those buildings weren't there—which they weren't—it's a totally different landscape. You'd just have the line of palms and mountains."

Nicholson brought script supervisor, Joanie Blum, up to the house to time out the picture—to read aloud the script and approximate how long it will run—the weekend before they were to start filming. "I've never done that with another director," Blum said, but Nicholson, dedicated to calculating the most accurate time estimation as possible, hung in there with Blum, starting in the evening, breaking for dinner, and resuming work late into the night.

Confused by the script, Blum pressed Nicholson for clarity, but he held fast to notions of subtext, aiming to honor the audience's intelligence by implication and subtlety, the "fabric" woven under the dialogue.

"But the audience has to understand at least sixty to sixty five percent of the mystery clues," Blum insisted. "If they don't understand at least half, you'll lose them, because they have to be able to develop their suppositions based on what they already know. You've got to give them something to chew on."

Jack laughed. "You sound like a kindergarten teacher."

He doted on the costumes, the tailoring, the color palette. He wanted the early scenes evocative of Charles Sheeler, painter of the modern technological landscape; he wanted the later scenes likes Maynard Dixon, desert painter. "Jack cared about the clock on the nightstand," Blum said. He pictured a visual correlate to the theme of doubling, foreground-background layering the film's images, bleeding them in cross-dissolves, devising ways to state, in screen terms, the feeling of return.

But nearing the first day of production, the script still wasn't ready, and Towne's revisions were slow to come. Why wasn't clear. Some contended the writer, cast aside as director, had turned against the project. "Let's just say that maybe sometimes it's like he didn't want to succeed," said someone close to the film.

Towne was on set in Pasadena, but three weeks into production, he disappeared. No one could find him. He and Luisa took off—a much-needed vacation, he claimed—for Bora-Bora. "He simply left every time someone was trying to get ahold of him," said Payne. "He was getting back at Jack for not supporting him against Evans."

Nicholson was abandoned, without Evans, without Towne, making a picture he had undertaken to repair friendships that now seemed beyond repair.

He and Towne stopped speaking.

"Jack was one of the most important people in my life," Towne said, looking back. "We grew up together. He taught me how to write by watching him act. I swore he would become a movie star, and I would write for him, and one day that happened. He was the closest friend I had."

The eleventh-hour defection of Towne put Nicholson under terrible pressure, forcing him to rewrite at night, after the day's shooting, sometimes down to the very minute before they went before the cameras, compromising his attention, as director, as actor, draining his creative reserve, patience, enthusiasm, but Nicholson, aware of the effect his mood had on the set, the downward spiral his stress could set off, largely protected the cast and crew from his trials, or tried to. To his closest, he conveyed his disappointment, hurt, and worry. Against the clock he called in a favor from James L. Brooks to rewrite where possible.

One morning in downtown L.A, as Nicholson, not a morning person, checked out the shot, dozens of screaming kids surrounded a *Jakes* location chanting, "Joker! Joker! Joker!".

It was hot that summer. And Jack was a sweater.

Blending with cinematographer Vilmos Zsigmond was a challenge; Nicholson knew what he wanted, but he wasn't the clearest communicator, speaking as he did in notional abstractions difficult for anyone to translate, let alone a harried Hungarian late to English.

"Is Gittes eight feet tall?" Nicholson shouted at Zsigmond's proposed POV shot. "I'm sick to my fucking cock of this!"

Arriving on set drained from the night's rewriting, Nicholson was visibly tired; it caused problems for Zsigmond—"I had to cover up all that weight and use tricks to hid the red in his eyes," he said—necessitating further adjustments to the shot. While the crew worked out the changes, Nicholson would repair to his trailer for a twenty-or thirty-minute nap—anything he could get. For the sake of the picture, cast, and crew, Jack resolved to stop yelling.

"Look," his gaffer said to him. "You've got to start yelling again."

"What do you mean?"

"You're so quiet, it's making the crew uptight! We're walking around on eggshells, you've got to get back to just hurling yourself about."

Every night after the shoot, Nicholson would race back to his house for a shower before meeting Evans at Woodland for dailies. The Robert Evans he met there could hardly function. Thinking suicide, he had been in and out of Scripps Memorial Hospital—as "Mr. Lombardo," too paranoid to use his own name—where he was plied with antipsychotics and closed in a claustrophobic cell. At Woodland, Nicholson took him in his arms. "Jack saw me shrivel in front of him," Evans said. "We cried together, we actually cried together, because I didn't have my house." Nor did he have his butler. Woodland, in his absence, had turned into an empty hotel lobby. Heeding the call, Nicholson ordered in pizza for dailies and tried to keep the spirit up with jokes pointed at his waistline. "I look like Mike Tyson!" he yelled at the screen, throwing a pillow at Joanie Blum in the row ahead of him. "Why the fuck did you let me look like this?"

Evans, medicated, would wander in and out of the projection room in slippers, murmuring.

Nicholson rewrote the end of *The Two Jakes*, as Polanski had *Chinatown*, replacing the bittersweet poetry of Towne's intended ending, set in an L.A. snowstorm, with a decisive downbeat. He assembled a cut, added a voiceover in a desperate bit for coherence, screened the picture for Billy Wilder ("Two good lines of narration can save you a half-hour of a boring picture"), and asked Anjelica to dinner. His invitation, she thought, was oddly formal.

They had changed. She had moved into her own place. She no longer obsessed over the girly perfumes she found by his bathroom sink, choosing instead not to ask, to stay away from the truth and Mulholland and Jack. Out of habit, they would still appear together in public, but when the bulbs flashed, they now turned from each other's smiles to face the cameras. She was making movies herself now.

"I have something to tell you," he declared over dessert. "Someone is gonna have a baby."

She thought of her father: The day he summoned Anjelica and her brother Tony to Rome to tell them they had another brother, Danny.

"Is it Rebecca Broussard?" she asked.

Gittes's secretary. Anjelica had seen her in *The Two Jakes*, a rose between her teeth, and had a bad old feeling.

"Yes, she's going to have the baby. But I don't want nothin' to change."

It was over for her. It had to be.

It wouldn't end, but it was over.

By phone or in person, Towne would consult with Edward Taylor until Taylor's death on February 12 2013.

Seeing *Mission Impossible: II*, for which Towne received sole screenplay credit, Taylor's daughter, Sarah Naia, would note the female lead's name, Nyah, and giggle to herself.

Towne arrived late to Taylor's funeral. "Robert refused to say anything good or gracious about Ed . . . ," Virginia Kennerley, Edward's widow, observed.

This, she recalled, is all he said: "Much has been shared. Some of which should not be shared."

A quarter century after her divorce, Payne was still in court, and almost out of money.

"My opinion," she would write to herself in notes she kept on the case, "is that the California divorce and child custody laws treat women and children as chattel . . . as long as the man pays his lawyers to retard procedures or have gaslighting letters written that force my legal fees up . . ."

Towne would appeal for sole custody. "When I think of the people who are with and around Kate in her mother's home," he would alert the court, "I can only add that my thoughts disquiet me. There is [Payne's] background—her own acknowledged chemical dependency. There is Marie, the maid, newly divorced. There [are Payne's friends] Marlene, divorced and not remarried. There is Cheryl, divorced, and never remarried. There is Patti, never divorced, never married, and very angry."

An evaluator would note, "The phrases [Payne] uses to describe [her daughter's] alleged abuse by [Towne] are sim [sic] to her descrip [sic] of her own childhood."

Our parents, they thought their pasts were behind them; they never were. Our children, we think they're new, without pasts; they aren't. They're old with our memories. They're born old.

Memories we don't know we have.

"I have flashbacks every day," she said.

The day after he finished shooting *The Two Jakes*, Nicholson flew to Monte Carlo, to the Hotel de Paris, where he found Tony Murray, the new owner of Woodland, in his room, in his bathrobe, shaving.

"Will you please sell Evans back his house?" Nicholson pleaded.

Murray had denied his repeated entreaties; now Jack Nicholson was standing in his bathroom.

"Are you crazy?" Murray answered. "I just bought it."

"To you it's a piece of real estate. To us, it's . . . the center of our creativity. We don't want to lose that. Please sell it back."

"It's my home."

Nicholson got on his knees. "Will you *please* . . ."

It worked. Evans got his house back.

The Two Jakes fizzled upon its release in October 1990. The picture is everything *Chinatown* might have been without Roman Polanski: slack, overcomplicated, confusing. Nicholson, the actor, seems tired. None of the film's echoes sound with the menace or majesty of the original. What's worthwhile in it is what's worthwhile in a memory.

Jack Nicholson announced: "This is the end of J. J." There would be no *Gittes vs. Gittes*.

Polanski was pleasantly surprised by much of Nicholson's work on *The Two Jakes*. He admired many of the performances and the look of the film, but found it, like most everyone else, impossible to follow, a critical lapse that Polanski, though he knew that Towne never completed the script, laid at Nicholson's feet. "Even if he was aware of the fact that he had [script] problems, this does not excuse him," Polanski said. "So it was Jack's fault that he shot it as it was, knowing there might be serious problems with the story. But the execution— it's quite remarkable for an actor who only directed two films before to pull this off."

In his exile, Polanski would rarely see his friends Nicholson and Evans. "They travel a lot, these people," he said, "so I see them in Paris or at Cannes or wherever." But with the years, Nicholson's and Evans's trips to Paris grew even less frequent, though not for any lack of feeling. Of course Polanski would not be coming back to Los Angeles to visit them; he was—and probably always will be—a fugitive from justice. "I would say I'm a fugitive from injustice," he said in 1993. "Don't forget that whatever happened I went to prison for it." From France he will not be extradited to the United States.

Where once he protested the seriousness of his crimes on grounds that "it was all done with innocence" and "because I don't think that anybody was hurt," he would, in time, darken his public view of his own guilt, though still not allowing himself (or being unable) to accept, in part or in full, the monstrosity of his violation. "I know now," he told Diane Sawyer, rather benignly, in 1994, "it was not [the] right thing to do, but there was no premeditation. It was something that just happened . . . [she was] certainly too young."

"There was something considered generally positive about erotic experience then," his victim, Samantha Geimer, would reflect, "even in the absence of anything beyond the sex itself. The idea was that emotional growth came about through an expanded sexuality—for both the person in power *and* the relatively powerless. This is important to consider, because this is the cultural paradigm Roman Polanski was sopping up in 1977. As wrong as he was to do what he did, I know beyond a doubt that he didn't look at me as one of his victims. Not everyone will understand this, but I never thought he wanted to hurt me; he wanted me to enjoy it. He was arrogant and horny. But I feel certain he was not looking to take pleasure in my pain.

But I was in pain."

Polanski married the actress Emmanuelle Seigner and they had two children, a girl and a boy, Morgane and Elvis.

At night, before bed, after he put Morgane to bed, she would ask him to tell her about his past. The stories of the war, how he lived. She could see her father straining, trying to guard her from certain terrible details, and perhaps to mitigate both of their suffering, she began to imagine him, like Oliver Twist, cheerily scavenging the ghetto streets. But truths crept in. "Even now, there are certain things that make him sad," she said. "When we have leftover food, even just bread, I can tell he feels weird about throwing it away."

She wanted to make movies. "I like psychological thrillers," she said. "I like to be challenged. I like to be shaken. When I leave a movie, I think, 'This is what I want to do to people. This is how I want to make people feel. This is what movies should do.'"

Meeting new people, she found herself hesitant to speak her full name.

"I'm Morgane."

"Morgane what?"

"Isn't Morgane enough?"

Her father was Roman Polanski. In 1977 he admitted to having unlawful sex with a minor and fled America never to return. He also made *Knife in the Water, Repulsion, Rosemary's Baby, Chinatown, The Tenant, Tess, Frantic, Death and the Maiden,* and *The Pianist.* He won Golden Globes, Césars, BAFTAs, the Golden Bear, the Palme d'Or, the Academy Award, the Zurich Film Festival's Golden Icon Award for Lifetime Achievement, and the Karlovy Vary International Film Festival's Crystal Globe for Outstanding Artistic Contribution to World Cinema.

Once, dining in a Paris restaurant, he looked up to find Jack Nicholson, in a Hawaiian shirt, arms outstretched, running toward him. The planned surprise for Polanski was enhanced when, moments later, from the other side of the restaurant, Robert Evans appeared on cue.

"Sharon," Polanski would say, "seems a very long, long way away."

In Woodland there are still roses, and the mercy of old colleagues helping each other from the crime scene. "Evans and I sit up at his house alone," Nicholson said, "wondering if we're the last ones left who feel [that] the main artery pumping blood into Hollywood is glamour, excitement and fun." Nostalgia blurs the edges of empires, and yet it did happen, didn't it? The movies are the proof. They were made. People made them.